THE CHANGING FACE OF
WORLD CITIES

THE CHANGING FACE OF WORLD CITIES

YOUNG ADULT CHILDREN OF IMMIGRANTS IN EUROPE AND THE UNITED STATES

MAURICE CRUL AND JOHN MOLLENKOPF, EDITORS

RUSSELL SAGE FOUNDATION • NEW YORK

The Russell Sage Foundation

Library of Congress Cataloging-in-Publication

The changing face of world cities : young adult children of immigrants in Europe and the United States/Maurice Crul and John Mollenkopf, editors.
    p. cm.
    Includes bibliographical references and index.
    ISBN 978-0-87154-633-3 (pbk. : alk. paper) 1. Immigrants—Cultural assimilation—United States. 2. Immigrants—Cultural assimilation—Europe, Western. 3. Children of immigrants—United States—Social conditions. 4. Children of immigrants—United States—Economic conditions. 5. Children of immigrants—Europe, Western—Social conditions. 6. Children of immigrants—Europe, Western—Economic conditions. 7. Group identity—United States. 8. Group identity—Europe, Western. I. Crul, Maurice. II. Mollenkopf, John H., 1946–
    JV6475.C42 2012
    305.9'06912094—dc23

                                                                                    2012013791

Text design by Suzanne Nichols.

RUSSELL SAGE FOUNDATION
112 East 64th Street, New York, New York 10065
10 9 8 7 6 5 4 3 2 1

Contents

Contributors

Maurice Crul is professor of sociology and organization sciences at the Free University of Amsterdam and Erasmus University Rotterdam.

John Mollenkopf is Distinguished Professor of Political Science and Sociology and director at the Center for Urban Research at the Graduate Center, City University of New York.

Richard Alba is Distinguished Professor of Sociology at the Graduate Center, City University of New York.

Susan K. Brown is associate professor of sociology at the University of California, Irvine.

Leo Chávez is professor of anthropology at the University of California, Irvine.

Louis DeSipio is associate professor of political science and Chicano/Latino studies at the University of California, Irvine.

Rosita Fibbi is sociologist and senior researcher at the Swiss Forum for Migration and Population Studies, University of Neuchâtel, and senior lecturer at the University of Lausanne, Switzerland.

Nancy Foner is Distinguished Professor of Sociology at Hunter College and the Graduate Center, City University of New York.

BARBARA HERZOG-PUNZENBERGER is head of the research program on multilingualism, interculturality, and mobility at the Federal Institute for Educational Research, Innovation, and Development in Salzburg, Austria.

PHILIP KASINITZ is professor of sociology at the Graduate Center, City University of New York.

ELIF KESKINER is postdoctoral fellow for the research group on Citizenship, Migration, and the City at Erasmus University.

JENNIFER LEE is professor of sociology at University of California, Irvine, and 2011 to 2012 visiting scholar at the Russell Sage Foundation.

LAURENCE LESSARD-PHILLIPS is research associate at the Institute for Social Change at the University of Manchester.

LEO LUCASSEN is professor of social history and director of the Institute for History, Leiden University.

LIZA REISEL is senior research fellow at the Institute for Social Research in Oslo, Norway.

JEFFREY G. REITZ is R. F. Harney Professor of Ethnic, Immigration, and Pluralism Studies and professor of sociology at the Munk School of Global Affairs, University of Toronto.

JENS SCHNEIDER is senior researcher at the Institute for Migration Research and Intercultural Studies (IMIS), Universität Osnabrück, Germany.

PHILIPP SCHNELL is researcher at Institut für Stadt- und Regionalforschung, Österreichische Akademie der Wissenschaften (Institute for Urban and Regional Research, Austrian Academy of Sciences), and Ph.D. candidate at the Institute for Migration and Ethnic Studies at the University of Amsterdam.

PATRICK SIMON is senior researcher at Institut National d'Études Démographiques.

THOMAS SOEHL is Ph.D. candidate in the Department of Sociology at the University of California, Los Angeles.

VAN C. TRAN is Robert Wood Johnson Foundation Health and Society Scholar at the University of Pennsylvania and assistant professor of sociology at Columbia University.

CONSTANZA VERA-LARRUCEA is Ph.D. candidate in the Department of Political Science at Stockholm University.

MARY WATERS is M. E. Zukerman Professor of Sociology at Harvard University.

MIN ZHOU is professor of sociology and Asian American studies as well as Walter and Shirley Wang Endowed Chair in U.S.–China Relations and Communications, at the University of California, Los Angeles. She is also visiting professor at Sun Yat-Sen University in Zhongshan, China.

PREFACE

This book has traveled a long way since its inception. It began, in a sense, in 1998 when the University of Amsterdam invited John Mollenkopf to spend a month as Wibaut Chair visiting professor. Seeking out colleagues then working on immigrant immigration issues in Amsterdam, he met Maurice Crul, a recently minted Ph.D., and Frans Lelie, his partner and also a sparkplug at the university's Institute for Migration and Ethnic Studies (IMES). A long and fruitful friendship and collegial partnership ensued, built partly around the conceptualization, development, fielding, and analysis of the studies described in this book.

Along the way, the editors and authors received strong support and helpful guidance from many sources that we are gratified to acknowledge here. First and foremost is the Russell Sage Foundation and its president, Eric Wanner, and program officer, Aixa Cintrón-Vélez. Scholars of immigrant integration owe a profound debt of gratitude to this remarkable institution and its leaders. The current and former members of the Foundation's Immigration Program advisory committee, especially original members Alejandro Portes and Mary Waters, have helped to shape the trajectory of this field and have offered us countless insights into our work. It is no understatement to say that the intellectual and scholarly prowess of the social sciences in the United States would be markedly less developed without the Russell Sage Foundation. In our case, this included the initial and propelling support for the Children of Immigrants Longitudinal Study (CILS), the Study of the Immigrant Second Generation in Metropolitan New York (ISGMNY), and the Immigration and Intergenerational Mobility in Metropolitan Los Angeles Study (IIMMLA). In addition, Russell Sage enabled Mollenkopf and his colleague Philip Kasinitz to spend a year as visiting scholars at the Foundation in 2000 to 2001 and Crul in 2009 to 2010. The Foundation made it possible for us to bring the authors together for intensive review of draft chapters during Crul's visiting scholarship. Claire Gabriel assisted with editing chapters, Galo Falchettore helped with data analysis, and Alexsa Rosa assisted with organizing the conference. Suzanne Nichols brilliantly facilitated our effort to translate our thoughts into this book, and April Rondeau has been a superb production editor.

The Rockefeller Foundation also provided critical support for two meetings at the Bellagio Conference Center. The first took place in June 2003 as data collection was ending on the ISGMNY and was designed to help coalesce a similar study in Europe. Partnering with Hans Vermeulen in the initial stage and with the sage advice of Rinus Penninx, the founding director of IMES, Crul then recruited and, with Jens Schneider, coordinated a team of researchers to study the children of immigrants and their native parentage peers in eight European countries—The Integration of the European Second Generation (TIES) survey. As IIMMLA data collection was also completed and TIES data collection nearly complete, the Rockefeller Foundation authorized a second meeting at Bellagio to enable the authors of the chapters in this book to clarify the issues facing cross-national comparison and launch into writing. (The Russell Sage Foundation provided travel support for both meetings as well.) As those who have had the privilege of spending time at Bellagio know, it is an ideal place to have concentrated and productive discussions free of outside distractions. We hope much of the spirit of the place remains in the following essays. We deeply thank both the Rockefeller Foundation and its Bellagio Conference Center Program staff. Two key participants in that meeting, Frank Bean and Jennifer Hochschild, shared many insights.

Our third debt is to the additional funders of ISGMNY, IIMMLA, and TIES; fellow members of our research teams; and the centers that hosted our work. Mary Waters and Philip Kasinitz served as coprincipal investigators for ISGMNY, which also received vital funding from the Ford Foundation, the Rockefeller Foundation, the Mellon Foundation, the UJA-Federation, and the National Institutes of Health. At the City University of New York (CUNY) Graduate Center, the Center for Urban Research anchored ISGMNY. Jennifer Holdaway led the in-depth interviewing effort for that study while Joseph Pereira, director of the CUNY data service, provided invaluable analysis of U.S. Census data sets. The IIMMLA project was conceptualized, fielded, and led by Rubén Rumbaut (also coprincipal investigator on CILS) and Frank Bean of the University of California, Irvine, along with a team that includes coauthors of the following chapters. Rubén and Frank have contributed to our thinking in numerous ways.

Public and academic interest in the fate of the children of immigrants developed later and more slowly in Europe. Nevertheless, by 2003 the Swiss Stiftung für Bevölkerung, Migration und Umwelt (BMU) was willing to award a planning grant to the research team at IMES for developing TIES. Subsequent funding from the Volkswagen Stiftung supported a study of the Turkish second generation in four countries. With tireless work from the national partner research teams in TIES and funding from the European Science Foundation, the European Union 6th framework research, and the Marie Curie training program, as well as many local and national funding agencies, it was possible to extend the study to eight additional countries and to collect additional samples of immigrant and native ancestry young people. The coauthors of the following chapters all belonged to the national research teams, but they express deep thanks to the other researchers who fielded these studies. We owe a particular debt to the Netherlands Interdisciplinary Demographic Institute (NIDI), where Liesbeth Heering and George Groenewold played crucial roles in housing and standardizing the data from the different national TIES studies. NIDI also hosted Laurence Lessard-Phillips as a postdoctoral researcher. Finally, the University of Amsterdam's Institute for Migration and Ethnic Studies also provided a stimulating and supportive home during the years when TIES was carried out.

ISGMNY, IIMMLA, and TIES were consciously modeled on one another in part to permit comparative analysis across their research sites. Although doing so may have been an obvious idea, given their similar format, it was far from easy, either conceptually or logistically, to realize our goal of transatlantic comparative analysis. We could not have done it without the support of these organizations, the willingness of their leaders to believe in this ambitious project, and the fact that they are not afraid to think big.

We also thank our partners. From the beginning, Frans Lelie has been involved in the TIES project as editor, webmaster, and conference organizer. She was indispensable in bringing together the transatlantic book conference and radiated a welcoming spirit to our American team members from the East and West Coasts. Both editors thank her for her thorough editorial assistance. Though Kathleen Gerson played a more indirect role, she has illuminated our thinking about the life course stage through which all our respondents have been passing. Frans and Kathleen also made it possible for both of us to spend many days away from home work-ing toward the day when this book would be finished.

Our final thanks go to the thousands of young people who shared their life stories with us. Not only are they truly changing the face of the world cities in which they are growing up, but they will also surely make them better places in the process.

Maurice Crul and John Mollenkopf

Editors

FOREWORD

Demographic change in Europe can be described accurately with three key terms: *fewer, older, more diverse.* According to Eurostat, the European Union's statistical office, the number of people aged fifteen to sixty-four in the European Union will decline by 50 million between now and 2050 and those sixty-five and older will increase by around 60 million (while the EU's overall population is estimated to fall to 450 million). Although immigration and family policies might mitigate this shift, it cannot be stopped. A response of defeatism, however, would be misplaced. Rather, it is important to acknowledge that this change has advantages as well as disadvantages and to learn how to deal with them most effectively. But that is precisely where we fall short.

In recent decades, Europe has become more "colorful" in terms of the ethnic origins, languages, religions, and cultural traditions of different population groups. In Germany alone, according to the Federal Statistical Office, one in five residents is a so-called person of migrant background, that is, according to the official definition, all those who have immigrated to the Federal Republic of Germany as well as all persons born in Germany without German nationality and all persons born in Germany with German nationality but with at least one parent who had immigrated to Germany or who was born there as a foreigner. Among children up to age six, one in three now has a non-German origin or mother tongue.

But this diversity has not been associated with equality of opportunity, understood as providing each individual with the supports needed to develop his or her potential. To the contrary, social and ethnic origin still strongly determines the chances young people have at school and their transition into the labor market. A study by the Social Science Research Center Berlin (WZB), commissioned by the Heinrich Böll Foundation, found that the upper reaches of German society are much less permeable than in almost any other industrialized country. Less than 1 percent of adolescents whose fathers are laborers will have the chance to enter an executive position. While this dilemma affects everyone, it has a particular impact on children in families with a non-German origin. Against the backdrop of the Enlightenment and its call for equal opportunity, it is harmful for a democracy to exclude a significant share of its population from social advancement because of its origins.

Education and the ability to acquire new knowledge now, more than ever, decide individual life chances. Although many unskilled and semi-skilled workers, including many immigrants and so-called guest workers, could enter the labor market during the 1960s and 1970s, rationalization, automation, and the shift from an industrial to a service- and knowledge-based economy have since eliminated these jobs. This is the new context in which the integration of migrants and their descendants is taking place.

Especially in an older and shrinking society, we are more dependent than ever on enabling each individual to maximize his or her talents and abilities. Because we face the threat of a massive shortage of skilled and educated people—and also a homemade lack of innovation and creativity—our aging societies cannot afford to exclude or willfully withhold opportunities from a significant portion of the population. But that is exactly what is happening to many children and young people of non-native origins.

The OECD Program for International Student Assessment (PISA) has found that one in five of Germany's fifteen-year-olds, including many whose mother tongue is not German, cannot meet the minimum standards for successful entry into professional training. Educational attainment is associated with social background in every society, but this nexus is stronger in Germany than in any other OECD country.

Migration research tells us that members of some national-origin groups do better than others in any given social environment and it also shows consistent differences across national settings for any given group. It is well known that the United States is much more at ease with the notion of assimilation, while the debate centers on integration in Europe. It is striking that migrants and their descendants in North America find it easy to feel American without neglecting or denying their connections with their familial country of origin. Neither Germany nor Europe has come to accept the concept of hyphenated identities to the same degree.

Furthermore, religion plays a different role on the two sides of the Atlantic. The United States is a comparatively pious society, but it is much more relaxed about its vibrant religious diversity than most European countries. In the United States, few understand the heated European debates about headscarves. Religion has been successfully privatized in the United States: each individual can live his or her faith, but the shared public sphere is secular and universalistic, a place where no one can be excluded because of origin, color, or creed. This may explain why immigrants identify with the United States more easily and stably than they do in European countries. In the United States, immigrants and their children also become citizens more quickly than in many European settings. All these reasons suggest that national and local environments have as much to do with integration outcomes as the migrants do.

The impact of national context on naturalization rates is particularly striking. Regardless of the particular immigrant population, how high a nation sets the requirements for naturalization, whether it actively asks immigrants to naturalize, and how it treats dual citizenship all significantly affect citizenship rates. Here again, one can understand integration as a process that is not only influenced by individual factors, but also reflects local and national political contexts.

It is obvious that migrant skills, such as education, language ability, and professional qualifications, play a significant role in determining social status and long-term life chances. Accordingly, it should be political common sense (in other words, a "no-brainer") that the second generation is to be encouraged to acquire intellectual and professional qualifications. While some advocate scoring potential immigrants on the basis of characteristics that are considered particularly favorable for successful integration, such an approach would not relieve us of the task of addressing the specific ways that the education system, welfare state structures, and residential segregation hinder or foster immigrant integration.

Against this background, the excellent scientific contributions contained in this volume open up a new chapter of comparative research on migration. The authors share a research strategy in which they analyze how the institutional arrangements in different cities and countries influence the integration of comparably situated members of the immigrant second generation. This enables them to understand the successes and failures in their integration not only in terms of their individual characteristics, but also in how they interact with different institutional settings. If the Turkish-origin second generation is significantly more likely to gain a university education in Paris than in Berlin, that mainly reflects differences in their education systems, not differences in the ethnic, religious, or social characteristics of the two groups.

This comparative research strategy is not only scientifically robust, but also yields insights that are valuable in formulating policies. We should incorporate these visions to strengthen and improve how public institutions treat immigrants and their children, because lack of access to and support from public institutions is a key cause of their social exclusion. This applies first and foremost to the education system. The chapters in this volume point us toward such relevant questions as what kinds of education systems best support children from socially disadvantaged families, foster intercultural competencies, and increase the number of immigrant-origin teachers to serve as role models.

Social solidarity is especially evident when dealing with the public institutions on which people depend to make something of their lives. Of course, private initiatives can also contribute to the inclusive and open ownership of institutions. Nevertheless, the government must guarantee the quality, appropriate access, and financial security of these institutions. This can be summed up in the social justice slogan "institutions matter."

This motto invites us to have the ambition and imagination to ask how we can improve our existing institutions, how we can reshape them to properly fulfill their public functions, and how we can remove the barriers hindering wider levels of opportunity and inclusion. We must think about how our institutions can do a better job of enabling everyone to pursue their life projects, of creating spaces for everyone's ideas and skills, and of empowering everyone to reach their potential.

This book is an important step in moving integration policy in this direction. It documents how cities and countries can learn from each other and highlights how they can translate their successful institutional arrangements to other places. I hope the book will find many readers in the policy world as well as in academia.

Cem Özdemir
Chairman of the German Green Party

PART I

INTRODUCTION

CHAPTER 1

THE SECOND GENERATION

MAURICE CRUL AND JOHN MOLLENKOPF

The children of immigrants are central to the future of the large cities of western Europe and the United States and of the countries surrounding these cities.[1] Not only do young people from immigrant backgrounds make up a large and growing share of their populations, they will also steadily replace the native-born baby boom generation as it ages out of the workplace and positions of influence. It is critical, then, that these young people are prepared—and enabled—to realize their full potential. Their success in school; finding good jobs; forming solid families; identifying strongly, if not uncritically, with their countries of birth; and participating fully in civic and political life augur well for the future. If many drop out of school, lack work, rely on welfare, or form an alienated new urban poor, the chances that western European and American societies can live up to the values they profess will drop sharply.

The large size of the second generation guarantees that these individuals will have a profound impact on the cultural and ethnic differences within their societies. In many places, members of the white majority of native descent feel deep anxieties about this shift. They see people speaking other languages filling their neighborhood schools and shopping places, they encounter minority group members in public spaces, and they may even have new kinds of neighbors. All these make them worry that their way of life is at risk of being displaced. These experiences and reactions make them—especially those in precarious positions—available for anti-immigrant mobilization not only under the right-wing banners of patriotism, protecting a leitkultur, or obeying the law, but also under the left-wing banners of the emancipation of women, tolerance for homosexuality, and secularism.

With an extra push from the current economic and fiscal crisis, the tenor of public debate has already shifted dramatically against immigrants and their children. In the United States, this debate focuses particularly on undocumented immigrants and their children. Some 12 million U.S. residents, or one in twenty-five, are estimated to be undocumented, with far larger shares in immigrant destinations. Many undocumented adults have U.S.-born children, creating a difficult mix in which the children have rights but the parents do not. The great majority of these 12 million are from Mexico. Some see them as highly problematic—using costly social services, committing crimes, taking jobs away from American citizens, lowering wage standards, and being exploited without contributing much. To be sure, their severely disadvantaged position creates major barriers for their children. An important academic strain of thought warns that these children may be subject to segmented assimilation, in which those with disadvantaged and discriminated-against immigrant parents join an alienated and angry native minority underclass.

In Europe, one populist party after another has put the threat of Islam on the political agenda. In Denmark and the Netherlands, success led to minority governments that must rely on votes from legislators from anti-immigrant parties outside of government, giving them a veto power that enables them to highjack the topic of migration and integration and normalize an anti-immigrant discourse that links unemployment, crime, and Islamist extremism with immigrants and their children. Although the murder of sixty-seven Norwegian young people at a Social Democratic party camp by a right-wing zealot in July 2011 is undoubtedly an extreme—and hopefully rare—expression of this tendency, it nonetheless bears witness to the depth of anti-immigrant anxiety.

This trend is pronounced even in the most strongly assimilationist country of Europe, France. The anti-immigrant voice of Marie Le Pen, the popular new leader of the Front National, has gained prominence in the center of the French political arena. Similarly, the relatively moderate leaders of Germany and the United Kingdom, Chancellor Angela Merkel and Prime Minister David Cameron, both recently declared multiculturalism to have failed. Thilo Sarrazin, a former member of the

German Central Bank board from the Social Democratic Party, amplified Merkel's theme in a controversial book arguing that Muslim immigrants did not want to integrate and were happy to rely on criminality and welfare instead. This debate echoes worries about the emergence of a Parallelgesellschaft in which 2 million people of Turkish descent live in a life-world supposedly detached from the wider German society.

What is actually happening to the young adult immigrants is thus a paramount concern to the democratic states of western Europe and the United States. Are media voices correct in asserting that important sections of immigrant communities are failing to integrate and therefore pose a danger to social cohesion? Is classical assimilation theory wrong about the waning of ethnic, cultural, and social distinctions as immigrant ethnic groups become more like the majority—and as the majority in turn evolves as it absorbs new groups? Does the fact that not all immigrants and their children "become similar" and some even resent the host society mean that multiculturalism has failed and cannot succeed?

To answer these questions, the authors of this volume and their colleagues have undertaken a coordinated set of studies to collect data about immigrant and native-origin young people in fifteen major cities in eight western European countries and two major cities in the United States. Our studies focus on young adult children from the most important immigrant groups that have concentrated in these cities over the last fifty years. Described at length in the following chapters, these cities are among the most economically, socially, culturally, and politically dynamic locations within their nations.

Although many suffered from the stresses of deindustrialization, economic restructuring, suburbanization, and group succession, they are also vanguards in the advanced service economy, and all have rebounded from low points reached in the 1960s or 1970s. This dynamism has attracted young people from native-born backgrounds as well as immigrants—these cities provide opportunity, display some degree of tolerance for difference, and host many important institutions. Although we call them world cities in the title of this volume, they are in essence cities of the world, or the world in cities. That is to say, their institutions span continents, not just metropolitan or national borders. Their populations have come from beyond international borders, not just from within their metropolitan areas or national borders. They are laboratories where urban dwellers are experimenting with new patterns and new relationships that will have fundamental implications for their larger national and continental contexts. The trajectories that the young adult children of immigrants wish to take, can take, or are prevented from taking will be central to this story.

A gigantic population turnover is taking place in the cities and metropolitan areas that are the sites of our studies. Statistically, many of their populations have been entirely replaced within one generation. Although most U.S. cities have long been multiethnic—typically since their initial rapid growth in the nineteenth century—the phenomenon that the former ethnic majority group is now rapidly becoming just one more minority group is relatively new in Europe. The authors of the New York study discussed in this chapter (Kasinitz et al. 2008) point out that though non-Hispanic whites are still the largest ethno-racial group in the city, but only by combining all European-origin groups, they are now just one of the city's many ethnic minority groups. (Indeed, fewer than one in five New Yorkers is a native-born non-Hispanic white person with native-born parents.[2]) In most western European cities, people with immigrant origins make up the majority of the population under age fifteen (first, second, or third generation). The reality of a majority-minority population, already prevalent in the United States, will also come to pass in most large western European cities over the coming ten to fifteen years.

The spatial organization of the economies of these cities and metropolitan areas has also undergone a profound transformation in the last half century. Deindustrialization and globalization have vastly diminished the blue-collar jobs that absorbed immigrants in these cities as recently as the 1960s, and central-city economies have increasingly specialized in corporate, professional, social, and individual services, yielding new occupational structures featuring both many positions requiring postsecondary educations and many low-skilled—and low-wage—service jobs. As a result, new barriers have arisen to the upward mobility of those who lack advanced educations needed in the new urban service economies.

The interaction between racial and ethnic succession and economic restructuring poses many challenges. As the old majority group slowly loses its dominant position in the workforce and the larger population, it could well develop a backlash against the new immigrant ethnic groups. However much it resists this trend, the demographic and economic processes seem irreversible. Sooner or later, the old majority group will simply have to adapt to its new minority position within a more diverse terrain of home and work. As it does, the fact that its political and institutional influence will diminish more slowly than its overall population will cushion its decline.

What opportunities does this landscape provide for the young adult children from the rising immigrant ethnic groups? Richard Alba (2009) recently argued that the aging of the baby boomers in the United States (and, by extension, western Europe) provides a unique opportunity for the young adult children of immigrants to rise into the positions being opened up by departing baby boomers. He notes that the supply of native white males in the succeeding generation is simply too sparse to occupy all the positions their fathers held. Prospects are thus potentially bright for well-educated children of immigrants. But social tensions could well grow in places where the descendants of immigrants are barred from these positions by a lack of required credentials or discrimination even when they have them. As the growth of temporary work and flexible labor contracts make low-skilled jobs increasingly precarious, the prospects for those children of immigrants consigned to such positions are uncertain. The resulting lack of social mobility may spill over into feelings of rejection and anger.

The authors of this book use unique new sources of information on how the children of immigrants are actually faring to address these fundamental questions. They and their colleagues have conducted the first large-scale, comprehensive, comparative surveys of the children of immigrants in the two largest destinations in the United States, New York (the Immigrant Second Generation in Metropolitan New York study, or ISGMNY) and Los Angeles (the Immigration and Intergenerational Mobility in Metropolitan Los Angeles study, or IIMMLA), as well as in fifteen cities in eight western European countries with large postwar migration experiences (The Integration of the European Second Generation study, or TIES). These authors closely examine the urban "proving grounds" where the processes of immigrant integration—or exclusion— are most pronounced and most profound. They do so with instruments specifically designed to elicit information not only about the young adult children from the largest immigrant groups but also from comparison groups of native-born young people with native-born parents who reflect the makeup of the majority populations of their countries.

The ISGMNY, IIMMLA, and TIES studies, all carried out between 1999 and 2006, were modeled on one another with the intention of collecting highly comparable data on multiple groups across the most important urban research sites. The result is a groundbreaking effort not just to look at similar outcomes for similar groups across sites in one country but to compare rigorously the European and American experiences.

The chapters in this volume provide ample evidence that second-generation members of immigrant groups show marked variations in their socioeconomic and cultural assimilation or integration across European and American cities. This variation reflects both the characteristic large differences in resources and social position these immigrant groups bring with them on arrival (with groups with higher median levels of education and other assets doing better than those with less) and the specific ways in which these group profiles mesh, or fail to mesh, with the opportunity structure presented by the receiving society. Here, however, we want to focus specifically and comparatively on the groups most disadvantaged in each setting and explain why outcomes differ even when starting positions are similarly disadvantaged.

We identify two main reasons this is so. First, western European societies and the United States have deep-seated differences in how they view immigration, which has important consequences for identity formation and feelings of belonging. Members of the U.S. immigrant second generation, even when they are not always doing well in the labor market, feel more as if they belong, at least to their cities, than their western European counterparts. Second, societies also differ greatly in how their integration contexts, specifically such national and local sorting mechanisms as school systems, housing markets and housing policies, labor markets, and welfare state arrangements, hinder or promote the assimilation or integration of the most disadvantaged second-generation groups. On this score, the U.S. cities are not the unambiguous leaders; indeed, a number of western European cities, particularly Stockholm, have central outcome tendencies that are as good as or better than those of New York and Los Angeles, and far fewer fall to the bottom, as sometimes happens in the United States.

EXPLAINING OUTCOMES ACROSS THE ATLANTIC

Because the United States has a long history of absorbing waves of immigrants, its politicians, policymakers, researchers, and broader public perceive immigration and immigrants differently than their European counterparts. As the authors of the next chapter argue, European nations remain in denial about being immigrant societies. This is reflected, as is debated in the third chapter, in the central concepts of their research debates: assimilation in the United States and integration in Europe. The term *assimilation* implies that immigrants or their offspring can become similar to members of the majority society, who are themselves diverse in terms of race, ethnicity, and class. The assimilation paradigm originates in the historical necessity of creating a common culture out of immigrant elements during the nineteenth and early twentieth centuries, including the initial wave of English and other Europeans as immigrants. As Ewa Morawska (2001) has pointed out, immigrants became Americans by fashioning a hyphenated Americanism.

In Europe, integration focuses explicitly on positions within the social structure, especially with regard to educational attainment and labor market outcomes. Given the stronger welfare state traditions in western Europe, many governments designed active policies to remediate ethnic minority group inequalities (for a catalog of these policies, see Huddleston and Niessen 2011). For Europeans, measuring integration almost automatically means looking at how many immigrants and their offspring are college graduates or hold professional jobs. European policymakers and social research organizations have spent a good deal of time developing such indicators of integration.

The contrasting assumptions embedded in the terms *assimilation* and *integration* reflect different historical discourses and societal responses to a rapidly changing demographic reality. The two chapters that follow discuss these differences at length. One lesson they convey is that scholars on both sides of the Atlantic must be cautious about transplanting American theoretical frameworks to the European context. Rather than remolding historically loaded concepts like assimilation and integration into one general theoretical straightjacket, we take the fundamental differences between the two settings as one important route into understanding how and why outcomes vary across the Atlantic.

Continental Europe and the United States also display many long-embedded differences in the context of integration. Although they certainly vary across the continent, European housing markets, education systems, labor markets, and political structures also differ systematically from those of the United States: western European urban settings have much more social housing and more highly regulated private rental housing; their education systems tend to be stratified more by tracks and less by geography, and the selection point for university educations comes much earlier; their labor markets are more highly regulated, less flexible, and less open to entry; and their political systems are more centralized, with stronger national planning and regulation. At the same time, as the chapters in part II of the book explore, the significant variation across European urban welfare state contexts also has important consequences for the opportunities available to the young adult children of immigrants (for one thoughtful discussion, see Kazepov 2010).

As a result, the authors of this volume seek to think about transatlantic comparisons in ways that are outside the normal American-European box. Although New York and Los Angeles share many American characteristics, they also differ from each other as well as from other U.S. big cities. Similarly, the fifteen cities in the TIES project offer a wide range of local settings. Our comparison thus highlights not only differences between so-called typical American and European assimilation and integration contexts but the way local settings vary around those central tendencies.

Researchers in the United States have paid particular attention to how the national and city contexts affect the forward movement of the second generation. This includes specific modes of incorporation for different ethnic groups (Portes, Fernandez-Kelly, and Haller 2009) as well how finer-grained city and even neighborhood contexts can influence outcomes (Kasinitz et al. 2008, 150–58; Waldinger, Lim, and Cort 2007). They have also extensively studied how school systems and labor markets offer differential access to children from different ethnic groups and social classes, though they have rarely extended this to cross-national comparison. As a result, American theoretical models are still relatively blind to the specifically American contexts of reception that shape second-generation outcomes (for exceptions, see Alba 2005; Foner and Alba 2008; Mollenkopf 2000; Portes et al. 2010). To some extent, this is mirrored in the uncritical importation of American concepts by western European scholars.

The tendency to take U.S. national institutional arrangements for granted in thinking about assimilation or incorporation introduces some serious problems for comparative analysis. When different groups are compared across local contexts, the focus inevitably falls more on the characteristics of the immigrant groups than on the structural features of their settings. Cross-national comparison of similar groups across local settings in turn highlights how national institutional dynamics, varying by urban location, sort groups regardless of their specific characteristics. We do not wish to say that differences across groups—for example, between Dominican and Chinese young people in New York or between Dominicans in New York and Mexican Americans in Los Angeles—are not important. Far from it. But we believe that such differences cannot tell the whole story. The absence of cross-national comparison leaves all the constant factors of U.S. urban settings invisible to such an analysis.

Because European studies of the second generation more often involve cross-national comparison, they pay much more attention to how national contexts shape immigrant integration pathways (Crul and Vermeulen 2003a; Doomernik 1998; Eldering and Kloprogge 1989; Fase 1994; Heckmann, Lederer, and Worbs 2001; Mahnig 1998). The European cases are both differently structured and closely linked, making the distinctive impact of national institutions far more obvious. The European contribution to theoretical debates on integration is thus to highlight how these variations in national context (here extended to the equally important, but more often overlooked, level of urban context) have large impacts on integration outcomes. Second-generation outcomes vary across Europe for many reasons: the quality and funding of different educational streams (vocational or academic), the availability of comprehensive schooling or various post-educational opportunities (apprenticeships), the patterns of neighborhood segregation (inside or outside of social housing), or the type of welfare regime. Such factors not only shape "hard" outcomes like schooling and jobs but also affect identity, belonging, and citizenship. National and local citizenship regimes and the organization of political rights are part of this picture (Hochschild and Mollenkopf 2009) and are frequently reflected in everyday discourse about groups and individuals (Schneider 2002).

In their comparative integration context theory, Maurice Crul and Jens Schneider (2010) call for researchers to explore exactly how national and local institutional arrangements facilitate or hamper participation and access, reproducing or reducing inequality. Failed participation indicates obstacles to access, for example when the late start of compulsory schooling has a disproportionately negative impact on children growing up in households whose members do not speak the national language on an everyday basis. This inverts the normal focus on how individual or family traits may correlate with failure and puts the explanatory burden on how institutions sort groups with such traits toward failure. They also highlight how individuals and groups actively develop options and make choices in the face of restricted opportunities and barriers to mobility. The German half-day primary school system, for example, assumes and expects that parents will actively help their children with homework. Longtime native residents have a much better grasp than immigrant newcomers of the information that is crucial for succeeding within the complex Dutch school system. Such differences structure the subjective and objective options facing individuals as they seek to successfully apply their individual and group resources—economic, social, cultural, and political capital, or lack of it.

The chapters that follow pay close attention to the interaction between institutional constraints and opportunities and the strategies individuals and groups develop in response to them. In so doing, we wish to avoid overemphasizing ethnic background as the main signifier. Instead, we try to tease out the ways in which national and urban arrangements in education, work, housing, social services, and politics shape integration and assimilation outcomes. This does not mean that we ignore the ways in which the migration histories of specific groups in specific places also help explain outcomes, but we can best understand their contribution in terms of how they influence the ways in which groups engage the structural features of the larger setting.

This approach leads us to ask whether the U.S.-centered nature of American theoretical frameworks limits their portability to European settings (Crul and Holdaway 2009; Crul and Schneider 2010). Do not the second-generation outcomes in the United States reflect the distinctively American institutional arrangements in school systems and labor markets? An immigrant group living in a poor neighborhood in a big American city is likely to send its children to poor quality public schools (Portes, Fernandez-Kelly, and Haller 2009, 1081; Suárez-Orozco, Suárez-Orozco, and Todorova 2008, 88–145) from which they have little chance of entering elite private universities. The extreme geographic quality variation in formally similar primary and secondary schools is a distinctively American characteristic (Crul and Holdaway 2009). Although European schools also vary greatly in their performance and linkage to university education, this variation is organized in quite different ways. Theories of assimilation based on an unexamined assumption that other national educational settings will be functionally equivalent to American institutional arrangements are thus on shaky scientific grounds. In each domain explored, we try to strengthen our social-scientific thinking by paying attention to differences in institutional arrangements across and within nations.

Studies of the Second Generation

Increasing numbers of immigrants entered both the United States and western Europe in the decades after 1960. The oldest of their children (the second generation) have now finished their schooling and are entering the labor market in large numbers. This provided the first opportunity to examine their experiences and compare them across settings.

Alejandro Portes and Rubén Rumbaut undertook the first large-scale U.S. study of second-generation outcomes, the Children of Immigrants Longitudinal Study (CILS), in 1992. They followed fifteen-year-old high school students who were born in the United States or arrived as small children into their adolescence. They followed up this initial wave of surveys two more times, creating an unprecedented longitudinal data set. Their work resulted in several highly influential books and journal special issues that framed the subsequent debate (Portes and Rumbaut 2001). To compare a representative sample of the children of major immigrant groups with native-born white and minority peers, a research team led by Philip Kasinitz, John Mollenkopf, Mary Waters, and Jennifer Holdaway fielded a multimethod study of second- and 1.5-generation and native-born groups in the greater New York area in 1999. The ISGMNY study inspired a similar project in Los Angeles (IIMMLA) initiated by a team including Frank Bean, Susan Brown, Leo Chavez, Leo DeSipio, Jennifer Lee, and Rubén Rumbaut of the University of California, Irvine, and Min Zhou of the University of California, Los Angeles, in 2002. Analysis of results from both projects initiated a lively debate about second-generation trajectories in the United States.

At about the same time, scholars in France (Tribalat 1995), the Netherlands (Crul 1994; Veenman 1996), and Belgium (Lesthaeghe 1996) began to study the position of the European second generation. The first European project, Effectiveness of National Integration Strategies toward Second Generation Migrant Youth in Comparative European Perspective (EFFNATIS), compared national approaches to integrating the second generation across Europe. Initiated by Friedrich Heckmann, it compared second-generation groups in France, Germany, and the United Kingdom and reviewed the literature on Spain, the Netherlands, Sweden, and Finland (Heckmann, Lederer, and Worbs 2001; Penn and Lambert 2009). This project was followed by the study of The Integration of the European Second Generation (TIES) on second-generation and native-born comparison youth in fifteen cities in eight European countries. Coordinated by Maurice Crul and Jens Schneider, the TIES team used the New York survey as a starting point, with John Mollenkopf advising the TIES team about the experiences of the ISGMNY and IIMMLA studies. Because the California and European studies were both built on the general approach taken by the New York study, we can now make transatlantic comparisons involving two American cities and fifteen cities in eight European countries on the same topics with data gathered in closely parallel ways. The ISGMNY, IIMMLA, and TIES studies provide the empirical basis for the following transatlantic comparisons.

The New York ISGMNY

With guidance from the Russell Sage Foundation and its advisory committee on immigration research, the New York team began a series of pilot projects for the final study in the mid-1990s. This facilitated a large-scale telephone survey (in 1999 and 2000) of 3,415 young adult children in representative samples of five immigrant-origin groups (Dominicans; Anglophone Afro-Caribbeans; Chinese; Colombians, Ecuadorans, and Peruvians; and Jews from Russia and elsewhere in the former Soviet Union) and three comparison groups (whites, African Americans, and

Puerto Ricans with native-born parents). With additional support from national foundations and the National Institutes of Health, the research team complemented the survey with in-depth, in-person interviews of 330 survey respondents and with ethnographies of key sites of interaction between young people from second-generation and native backgrounds. The results are reported in a coauthored volume (Kasinitz et al. 2008), an edited volume of the ethnographies (Kasinitz, Mollenkopf, and Waters 2004), and many journal articles and papers.

The Los Angeles IIMMLA

With ISGMNY well under way, the Russell Sage Foundation launched a comparison study in the other large gateway for contemporary immigration to the United States, Los Angeles. The University of California, Irvine, team designed a similar sampling frame to that of New York with several modifications: it extended the age range to capture a broader range of experiences and sampled both first-generation Mexican immigrants and third-plus-generation individuals of Mexican background. The study covered other major groups in Los Angeles, including Salvadorans and Guatemalans, Chinese, Koreans, Vietnamese, Filipinos, and a sample of all other immigrant backgrounds, comparing them with whites and African Americans with native parents. The IIMMLA survey was carried out in 2004. The results have been reported in a series of journal articles.

The European TIES

The TIES project officially started in 2005 with support from the Volkswagen Stiftung in Germany and the Swiss foundation Stiftung für Bevölkerung, Migration und Umwelt (BMU). The project was initially managed by Maurice Crul and Hans Vermeulen at the University of Amsterdam, with Jens Schneider becoming cocoordinator when Vermeulen retired. Liesbeth Heering and Jeannette Schoorl from the Netherlands Interdisciplinary Demographic Institute (NIDI) coordinated the international TIES survey. Senior researchers from nine research institutes participated: Rosa Aparicio-Gomez (IEM, Madrid); Michael Bommes and Maren Wilmes (IMIS, Osnabrück); Maurice Crul and Jens Schneider (IMES, Amsterdam); Rosita Fibbi (SFM, Neuchâtel); Liesbeth Heering, George Groenewold, and Laurence Lessard-Phillips (NIDI, The Hague); Barbara Herzog-Punzenberger (ÖAW, Vienna); Karen Phalet (ERCOMER/KUL, Leuven); Patrick Simon and Christel Hamel (INED, Paris); and Charles Westin, Alireza Behtoui, and Ali Osman (CEIFO, Stockholm).[3]

The TIES study compares second-generation young adults who were eighteen to thirty-five years old at the time of the survey (during 2007 and 2008) across fifteen cities in eight European countries. Sampled groups included the children of immigrants from Turkey, the former Yugoslavia, and Morocco as well as young people with both parents born in the survey country. The sites include Paris and Strasbourg in France, Berlin and Frankfurt in Germany, Madrid and Barcelona in Spain, Vienna and Linz in Austria, Amsterdam and Rotterdam in the Netherlands, Brussels and Antwerp in Belgium, Zürich and Basel in Switzerland, and Stockholm in Sweden. The interviews were conducted face to face among almost ten thousand respondents. The TIES team faced a major challenge in developing comparable samples across these settings. Municipal registers provided samples in the Netherlands and Sweden. Though population registers were also available in Belgium, France, Germany, Switzerland, and Austria, they were difficult to access because of privacy rules and regulations (Belgium) or lacked information on the birth place of both respondents and their parents (France, Germany, Switzerland, Austria). In Austria, France, Germany, and Switzerland, the TIES teams compiled sampling frames of the ethnic origin groups by analyzing ethnically distinctive surnames and forenames (onomastic sampling) on up-to-date listings of names and addresses from electricity board registers, telephone listings, and city registers.

The TIES team can thus compare young people from the same ethnic backgrounds and starting positions (all born in Europe) across cities and countries. The primary project focus of TIES was thus to analyze how specific city and national contexts promote or hamper the integration of the same second-generation groups. To pursue this objective, the national TIES partners spent a great deal of effort gathering additional information on national and local institutional arrangements in school and the labor market as well as citizenship policies and antidiscrimination measures. The project resulted in an international comparative volume (Crul, Schneider, and Lelie 2012), numerous separate country publications, articles, and papers.

THREE MAIN COMPARISON GROUPS

All the chapters of this volume focus on the most disadvantaged groups in each of the settings, even though ISGMNY, IIMMLA, and TIES looked at a number of different second-generation groups. As will be elaborated subsequently, we focus on these groups not because they represent the entire second-generation experience but because they represent the most challenging case and thus the strongest test of whether individuals and groups can be upwardly mobile. On the American side of the Atlantic, chapters focus on Dominicans in New York and Mexicans in Los Angeles, and Turks in western European cities are the focus on the European side.[4] Because the Mexican and Turkish second generations are by far the largest second-generation groups in the United States and western Europe, any assessment of failed or successful integration must include them. (Some 32 million Mexican-origin individuals live in the United States, and Europe is home to 4 million first-, second-, and third-generation Turks. Although the Mexican population of New York has risen rapidly in the last two decades, the biggest single national-origin group in the city is its 577,000-strong Dominican population.)

Because Mexicans and Turks hold similar positions in their respective settings, earlier researchers have already compared them (Faist 1995). Both groups came from rural areas that had poor schools, little access to secondary education, and no universities. They arrived in the United States and western Europe to do unskilled jobs that native workers often no longer wished to do, filling the lowest positions in the labor market and living in poor working-class neighborhoods. At the same time, both groups have a tradition of setting up small businesses that provide one pathway for upward mobility. (Dominican migrants to New York followed a roughly similar path to Mexican migrants to Los Angeles, though their country had suffered more recently from dictatorship and U.S. occupation.)

Although members of these first-generation groups all occupy low social positions, they do differ in some respects, especially in educational attainment. Far more Turkish parents have no more than a primary school education (sometimes no schooling at all) compared with the Dominican and Mexican parents (see tables 1.1 and 1.2). Some Turkish mothers are illiterate and their children often grow up surrounded by adults with only primary school educations. Only in Stockholm did a significant share of Turkish fathers have a postsecondary education. Most Turkish parents in Amsterdam and Berlin had no more than a primary school education. In the United States, by contrast, more Mexican and Dominican parents had postsecondary educations and fewer had only primary school educations. The Turkish mothers were even more disadvantaged than the Dominican or Mexican mothers (see tables 1.3 and 1.4). Given the importance of parental education for their children's progress, we would therefore expect that the Dominican and Mexican second generation should slightly outperform the Turkish Europeans in school, all other things being equal.

TABLE 1.1   Father's Education, Second-Generation Turks

	Amsterdam	Berlin	Brussels	Paris	Stockholm	Vienna
Primary school or less	54.1%	74.7%	36.4%	41.5%	38.5%	31.1%
Secondary school	40.6	24.4	55.0	46.8	44.6	57.4
Postsecondary	5.3	0.9	8.6	11.7	16.9	11.6

Source: Authors' compilation based on TIES survey 2007, 2008 (data not yet publicly available).
Note: The TIES survey comprises eight separate national data sets, collected by Institute for Studies on Migrations (IEM), Comillas Pontifical University, Spain; Swiss Forum for Migration and Population Studies (SFM), Neuchâtel, Switzerland; Netherlands Interdisciplinary Demographic Institute (NIDI), The Hague, Netherlands; Austrian Academy of Sciences (ÖAW), Vienna, Austria; the European Research Centre on Migration and Ethnic Relations (ERCOMER), Katholieke Universiteit Leuven, Belgium; National Institute for Demographic Studies (INED), Paris, France; Institute for Migration Research and Intercultural Studies (IMIS), University of Osnabrück, Germany; Centre for Research in International Migration and Ethnic Relations (CEIFO), Stockholm University, Sweden. The TIES national surveys will be made publicly available by the national TIES partners individually, but were not yet available at the time of publication.

TABLE 1.2   Father's Education, Second-Generation Dominicans and Mexicans

	New York	Los Angeles
Primary school or less	14.9%	29.0%
High school graduate	42.4	47.7
Post–high school	25.7	23.3

Source: Authors' compilation based on ISGMNY (Mollenkopf, Kasinitz, and Waters 1999); IIMMLA (Rumbaut et al. 2004).

TABLE 1.3   Mother's Education, Second-Generation Turks

	Amsterdam	Berlin	Brussels	Paris	Stockholm	Vienna
Primary school or less	68.4%	78.5%	48.2%	50.2%	35.0%	56.4%
Secondary school	28.8	21.5	46.9	43.6	56.3	39.1
Postsecondary	2.8	0	4.9	6.2	8.8	4.5

Source: Authors' compilation based on TIES survey 2007, 2008.

TABLE 1.4   Mother's Education, Second-Generation Dominicans and Mexicans

	New York	Los Angeles
Primary school or less	13.7%	28.4%
High school	57.6	50.9
Post–high school	27.7	20.7

Source: Authors' compilation based on ISGMNY (Mollenkopf, Kasinitz, and Waters 1999); IIMMLA (Rumbaut et al. 2004).

Although some Turkish parents came as refugees or students, most came as labor migrants. Although many entered on temporary visas, almost all eventually were legalized. It would be exceptional for an illegal Turkish parent to raise a child born in western Europe. This was much more common in the United States, however. In a nontrivial number of cases, the parent of a Mexican American or Dominican American young person arrived without authorization. Although the 1986 Immigration Reform and Control Act (IRCA) legislation enabled many of them to gain legal status, at least a few of these parents continue to be undocumented.

First-generation parents had to apply for citizenship in both the United States and Europe (see tables 1.5 and 1.6). Although the United States considers itself a country of immigration, the citizenship chapter demonstrates

TABLE 1.5   Citizenship of Parents of Second-Generation Turks

	Amsterdam	Berlin	Brussels	Paris	Stockholm	Vienna
Father	76.8%	44.4%	56.5%	21.0%	NA	67.2%
Mother	77.1	43.6	55.8	24.4	NA	68.4

Source: Authors' compilation based on TIES survey 2007, 2008.
NA, not applicable.

TABLE 1.6   Citizenship of Parents of Second-Generation Dominicans and Mexicans

	New York	Los Angeles
Father	61.3%	67.6%
Mother	75.0	68.1

Source: Authors' compilation based on ISGMNY (Mollenkopf, Kasinitz, and Waters 1999); IIMMLA (Rumbaut et al. 2004).

TABLE 1.7   Citizenship of Second-Generation Turks

	Amsterdam	Berlin	Brussels	Paris	Stockholm	Vienna
Citizens	94.5%	89.3%	96.3%	92.7%	98.8%	88.1%

Source: Authors' compilation based on TIES survey 2007, 2008.

that even long-term immigrant parents do not always become U.S. citizens. In fact, the immigrant parents in Amsterdam and Vienna were as likely to become citizens as the Mexican and Dominican parents in Los Angeles and New York.

American-born children with immigrant parents all have the great advantage of birthright citizenship. The European cities present a mixed picture. In some cases, the children were citizens at birth because their parents had already naturalized. In France, the second generation also receives citizenship automatically at age eighteen. As table 1.7 shows, however, in the end, regardless of their location, almost all members of the Turkish second generation did become citizens in young adulthood. Even in Germany and Austria, where second-generation Turks must apply for citizenship, almost as many did so as in the other cities. The legal situation of the parents and children in the United States and Europe thus ends up differing far less than we might have expected based on the long immigration tradition in the United States.

The second generation grows up in quite different family settings on the two sides of the Atlantic (see tables 1.8 and 1.9). Marriages among the Mexican and Dominican parents sometimes dissolved early in the respondent's childhood, or never took place. It was also fairly common for one parent never to have come to the United States. Members of the Dominican and Mexican second generation therefore often grew up in more fluid and less traditional family situations than their Turkish counterparts did. With the exception of those in Amsterdam, second-

TABLE 1.8   Percentage of Second-Generation Turks Whose Parents Are Separated

	Amsterdam	Berlin	Brussels	Paris	Stockholm	Vienna
Parents no longer together	20.3%	4.7%	9.5%	3.1%	12.4%	6.7%

Source: Authors' compilation based on TIES survey 2007, 2008.

TABLE 1.9   Percentage of Second-Generation Dominicans and
Mexicans Whose Parents Are Divorced or Separated

	New York	Los Angeles
Parents now divorced or separated	52.4%	34.4%
Did not grow up with both parents	35.8	NA

Source: Authors' compilation based on ISGMNY (Mollenkopf, Kasinitz, and Waters 1999); IIMMLA (Rumbaut et al. 2004).
NA = not applicable

generation Turks overwhelmingly grew up in two-parent families that remained intact into their adulthood. In the United States, one-third of the respondents grew up in separated families, a factor that can have important negative consequences for the children. We would thus expect the family backgrounds of the Turkish respondents to work in their favor.

The disadvantaged groups we examine across these settings, then, were comparable without being the same. The European second generation grew up with parents in less favorable labor market positions and less human capital than their U.S. counterparts but in more secure environments, in the sense of intact families living in secure housing and neighborhoods. All these second-generation youngsters experienced some disadvantages, but of somewhat different kinds.

OVERVIEW

This volume has a simple design. We asked teams of researchers who are experts on specific themes (such as education, the labor market, or identity) to pair up across the Atlantic. Although all had research experience in their own settings, none had previously worked together on transatlantic comparisons. It was therefore challenging for us to synthesize findings across settings despite having parallel data sets, not least because each national survey took a somewhat different approach to each topic. Religion (Islam) was a big issue in the European surveys, for example, whereas language (Spanish) was a central focus in the United States. Despite the lack of previous experience in working together, however, the researchers went through a long process of finding common ground. The Rockefeller Foundation and the Russell Sage Foundation enabled us to launch this process at the Rockefeller Foundation's Bellagio Conference Center, an ideal place for extended reflection. Each team worked hard to reconcile differences in the ways surveys explored themes, operationalized concepts, and categorized answers. We undertook new analyses to fashion common variables and commensurable answer categories with increasing enthusiasm about being able to synthesize our findings.

The volume is divided into three parts. The first expands on the themes introduced here concerning the historical and the theoretical debates about the second generation in the United States and Europe. The second describes the empirical results of the transatlantic comparison. The third synthesizes our overall findings.

The volume opens with three introductory chapters on the historical differences between Europe and the United States concerning immigration. They explain the factors that were crucial to the emphasis and design of the various surveys.

In chapter 2, Nancy Foner and Leo Lucassen show how the discussion of immigration has very different starting points on the two sides of the Atlantic. Foner highlights the great extent to which contemporary U.S. studies of immigration have been influenced by the literature on the assimilation of descendants of earlier immigrants—as well as on the negative racialization experienced by African Americans and certain other groups. The continued disadvantage among African Americans led to a focus on how segregation and discrimination yielded a black urban underclass that has no parallel in Europe. This accounts for why the U.S. studies include native-descent blacks and whites as well as Puerto Rican and third-generation Mexican native comparison groups and the TIES survey examines those of native-born parentage in an undifferentiated way.

Lucassen argues that Europe has a historical amnesia about its earlier waves of migration. European scholars do not label intra-European migrants or returnees from former colonies as immigrants. Despite this amnesia, however, European countries took widely varied approaches toward the immigrants of the 1960s and 1970s in terms of both integration policies and gathering statistical information about ethnicity. Before the TIES study, it was quite difficult to compare or even describe the second generation across Europe. European countries also have different policies regarding survey questions about race, ethnicity, religion, or sexuality. Even certain questions (racial identification) were considered taboo for TIES and not asked at all or asked only in certain countries (some religion and sexuality questions).

In chapter 3, Richard Alba, Jeffrey Reitz, and Patrick Simon build on chapter 2 to describe the theoretical debate around integration and assimilation. Developed in the American context, assimilation theory holds that becoming similar to the mainstream is an empirical and normative part of the American framework. This classical approach, however, has been revised by contemporary analysts partly to better explain differences in current outcomes and partly to account for the remaking of the mainstream itself. They describe and discuss the two most important theories, new assimilation theory and segmented assimilation theory.

The Canadian and western European literatures see assimilation as just one possible outcome among others, like pluralism or marginalization. Following French sociologist Émile Durkheim, they define integration as equal participation of immigrants in different social spheres. This emphasis on equality fits with Europe's more developed welfare states. The Durkheimian concept of integration also leaves room for solidarity with one's community as a key part of psychological and emotional well-being for immigrants and their children, an important pillar for multiculturalist approaches in Canada and some European countries.

On the basis of these introductory chapters, the chapters in part II delve into specific explorations of education, the labor market, gender, neighborhoods, citizenship, and identity. Because educational attainment is pivotal for all assimilation and integration outcomes, the second part opens with a chapter on this topic. In chapter 4, Maurice Crul, Min Zhou, Jennifer Lee, Philipp Schnell, and Elif Keskiner compare second-generation Mexicans in Los Angeles with second-generation Turks in western European cities. More precisely, they focus on the success stories, those who are studying at a college or university or have completed a bachelor's degree (BA). The outcomes in this chapter foreshadow a trend visible in other chapters. The rate of college attendance in the United States positions it between the relatively positive European cases (Sweden and France) and those with considerably worse second-generation educational outcomes (Germany and Austria). On both sides of the Atlantic, successful students often had to take an alternative—and often longer—route to higher education (for instance, through community college). Help from committed parents, older siblings, or teachers and mentors also played a significant role in their success. In the United States, low or uneven primary and secondary school quality and the cost of higher education can block success; in western Europe, early tracking selection and/or a high need for practical support from parents who cannot provide it block success.

Two chapters on the labor market follow. The first focuses on men and women and the second specifically on women.

In chapter 5, Liza Reisel, Laurence Lessard-Phillips, and Philip Kasinitz compare labor market outcomes across the western European and U.S. cities. The authors compare the NEET (not in employment, education, or training) rates, percentages in professional jobs, and incomes. The groups vary most in terms of NEET rates. It seems that the most negatively stereotyped minority individuals are usually at the end of the hiring queue. Because native black groups occupy this least favorable position in the two U.S. cities, disadvantaged second-generation groups often occupy a somewhat more favorable position in the hiring queue. In Europe, however, Turks often occupy the least favorable position in the hiring queue, especially in Berlin, Brussels, and Vienna. Counter to the usual stereotype about the urban underclass, women have the highest NEET rates in western Europe.

In chapter 6, Thomas Soehl, Rosita Fibbi, and Constanza Vera-Larrucea look at gender differences on the labor market. Picking up on the high NEET rates among women discussed in chapter 5, the authors analyze how welfare regime treatment of care work and paid work influences labor force participation. The authors show that welfare regimes afford second-generation women very different chances to participate in the labor market. Sweden provides the best opportunities through a welfare system wholly geared toward enabling women with children to work full time. Despite often coming from strongly traditional families, second-generation Turkish women join Stockholm's labor market in massive numbers. This raises interesting questions about the potential role of welfare systems for the emancipation of women from conservative (immigrant) communities.

In chapter 7, Van Tran, Susan Brown, and Jens Schneider discuss the often neglected aspect of the neighborhood where the second generation lives. The authors geocoded the home addresses of second-generation respondents and linked them with neighborhood and city statistics from census sources. Because this is an elaborate task, the authors were able to compare only the two U.S. cities and Berlin. Berlin was chosen as the "Turkish capital of Europe." With up to 300,000 people with partial Turkish ancestry living in its neighborhoods, Berlin would be the European city most likely to show clear neighborhood effects. This chapter shows that the Mexican and the Dominican second generations live in far more disadvantaged neighborhoods in Los Angeles and New York than Turks in Berlin do. Both objectively and relatively, the Mexican and Dominican second-generation youths perceive a lot of disorder (among other things, crime and gangs) in their neighborhoods. Their Turkish counterparts in Berlin (the most deprived second-generation group in the western European cities) live in far better neighborhood conditions. Levels of disorder are much lower and differences minimal in how the Turkish second-generation and native-descent respondents perceive neighborhood disorder.

In chapter 8, Barbara Herzog-Punzenberger, Rosita Fibbi, Constanza Vera-Larrucea, Louis DeSipio, and John Mollenkopf discuss differences in citizenship regimes and participation across the Atlantic. For the comparison with the United States, the authors chose western European countries with big differences in their citizenship regimes. For historical reasons, the U.S. context should be much more favorable because it provides unconditional birthright citizenship. Although this holds for the second generation at birth, the differences are much less pronounced by the time these youngsters come of age. Differences are also much less pronounced among the parents. Indeed, many immigrant parents in the United States have a much more precarious legal situation. Parental illegality can also affect members of the second generation, even when they hold citizenship. The political and civic participation (the broader aspects of citizenship) of the second generation is substantial, both in mainstream as well as in community organizations and engagement, along with citizenship, and seems highest in the United States and Sweden.

In chapter 9, Jens Schneider, Leo Chávez, Louis DeSipio, and Mary Waters describe a wide range of topics around identity and belonging. The data on this topic were most difficult to compare across the Atlantic because of differences in both questions and answer categories. It is probably a sign in itself that the context and outcomes on this topic differ significantly across the Atlantic. As the authors put it, historically being of immigrant descent is not a major obstacle for becoming an American, whereas in western Europe having immigrant parents almost automatically makes it problematic to identify with being, for instance, German or Dutch. Religiosity, especially having a visible Muslim identity, is a further major obstacle in western Europe but in the United States has a bridging function for the largely Catholic immigrants. The authors, however, also show that the American second generation does not simply dissolve in the mainstream but rather remakes it.

Part III and its single, final chapter draws larger conclusions about the transatlantic comparison and synthesizes the findings of the previous chapters, underscoring how local and national institutional contexts of integration shape second-generation outcomes. In it, Maurice Crul and John Mollenkopf revisit the trajectories of second-generation Turks in western Europe and second-generation Mexicans and Dominicans in the United States. They find that the Turkish second generation, in most cities of western Europe, achieves considerable upward mobility compared with their parents and that national welfare systems usually prevent the lagging part of the group (which differs considerably in size across Europe) from completely falling through the cracks. By contrast, the more open U.S. labor market and its weaker welfare system compel disadvantaged immigrant groups and their children to find upward mobility through work. A great many members of disadvantaged immigrant minority groups manage to do so. Those who are stuck in low-paying jobs or are not in the labor force, however, can end up in worse material conditions facing greater personal insecurity than their low-achieving counterparts in the European cities. However, U.S. cities are more open to the disadvantaged second generation in terms of belonging and identity formation. Although the European cities vary on this point, it is problematic to be a Muslim in any of them. Historical differences in the incorporation of immigrants and their children and differences in welfare state regimes have important consequences for the position of the second generation across the Atlantic.

NOTES

1. We define the immigrant second generation as the children born to first-generation foreign migrants in the countries where they have moved, regardless of the nationality status of these children. When specifically noted, we also include the children of first-generation immigrants who migrated into the host country along with their parents at a young age and mostly grew up there, often called the 1.5 generation.

2. In the United States, the word *Hispanic* refers to people who identify themselves as being descendants of those born in Spanish-speaking countries and is used interchangeably with *Latino*. Because the U.S. Census defines Hispanic as an ethnic rather than a racial category, Hispanics can be of any or multiple races. U.S. researchers often distinguish five mutually exclusive categories: non-Hispanic whites, non-Hispanic blacks, non-Hispanic Asians, non-Hispanic others (that is, Native Americans), and all Hispanics (of any race).

3. IEM = Instituto Universitario de Estudios sobre Migraciones
   IMIS = Institut für Migrationsforschung und Interkulturelle Studien
   IMES = Institute for Migration and Ethnic Studies
   SFM = Swiss Forum for Migration and Population Studies
   OAW = Austrian Academy of Science
   ERCOMER = European Research Centre on Migration and Ethnic Relations
   KUL = Katholieke Universiteit Leuven
   INED = Institut National Etudes Démographiques
   CEIFO = Centrum för forskning om internationell migration och etniska relationer or Centre for Research in International Migration and Ethnic Relations.

4. Normally, in the U.S. context, we would use Dominican American or Mexican American to describe these and other second-generation groups, but here we shorten this to national origin for the sake of brevity. Turkish-German or Turkish-Dutch are less common usages in Europe.

CHAPTER 2

LEGACIES OF THE PAST

NANCY FONER AND LEO LUCASSEN

T he present, it is often said, is a product of the past, and nowhere is this truer than in contemporary studies of the second generation. On both sides of the Atlantic, debates about the children of immigrants and the themes studied have been strongly affected by legacies of the past and scholars' engagement—or lack of engagement—with earlier periods of immigration. Not surprisingly, the past has influenced present-day research on the second generation in different ways in western Europe and the United States.

This chapter seeks to interrogate how this has happened, and with what consequences. In Europe, what stands out is the degree of amnesia about the immigrant past, which helps explain the social panic and widely held idea in the scholarly literature that something unprecedented happened there after World War II (Castles and Miller 1993). Although from the 1980s onward many historians stressed the longtime presence of migrants in western Europe (Holmes 1978; Bade 1983; Noiriel 1984, 1988; Lucassen and Penninx 1985; Green 1986), the message barely reached social scientists, let alone the larger public. One result of this failure of communication was that Europeans regarded the idea of a multicultural society as something new. European concepts and methods for studying the second generation have also been influenced by historical relations between Europe and its colonies and the continued impact of particular national models of integration that developed in previous eras.

If the west European denial or lack of attention to past immigration has given a particular cast to second-generation studies there, contemporary second-generation studies in the United States are deeply and often explicitly rooted in analyses of the experiences of earlier second generations, especially the children of turn-of-the-twentieth-century immigrants. The classic mid-twentieth-century sociological works on assimilation set the stage, as it were, for much of the writing about the present-day second generation and, along with historical studies of the earlier second generation, have helped shape central issues and arguments in the literature today. The past is also alive and well in the ways in which America's history of slavery, segregation, and the civil rights movement have influenced studies explaining the patterns of incorporation among the children of immigrants.

WESTERN EUROPE

From the late 1970s onward, historians began uncovering Europe's migratory past, and recently a thousand-page encyclopedia was published on the history of migration and integration in Europe since 1600 (Bade et al. 2007, 2011). Such publications, however, have remained rather isolated. Except for emigration to other parts of the world, most Europeans have not considered migration as an integral part of European history. Most historians did not realize that the past offered relevant precedents for the large-scale labor and colonial migrations from the late 1960s into the 1980s. It should not come as a surprise, then, that the social science that boomed in that period and greatly influenced national debates and policies (Scholten 2011; Lucassen and Lucassen 2011) was barely influenced by a long-term historical perspective. Indeed, most social scientists lacked historical knowledge about European immigration and—like the broader public—assumed that it was a relatively new phenomenon emerging from the post–World War II decolonization movements that brought West Indians, Indians, and Pakistanis to Britain; Algerians to France; and the Indo-Dutch to the Netherlands. The National Demographic Institute (INED) in France did, however, begin producing regular studies of the labor migrants who settled there in the interwar period (especially Poles, Italians, and Spaniards) in the 1950s (Girard and Stoetzel 1953).

To the extent that sociologists, anthropologists, and political scientists were aware of Europe's previous migration experiences, most assumed that earlier migrants were so different in phenotype and culture that their settlement processes were of little use in understanding those of the present (for a critical discussion, see Lucassen 2005). This was an attitude shared by many American scholars, who, though having an all-pervasive awareness of the United States as an immigrant country, also tended to emphasize the newness and unprecedented nature of the post-1965 immigration, including transnational connections that differed from earlier eras owing to technological change and the nature of today's global economy.

To be sure, much is new about recent immigration, but parallels with the past are also significant. Migration scholars in the United States have examined the assumption of unqualified newness, underlining the continuities and similarities between the two great waves of immigration, from 1880 to 1920 and from 1965 to the present. This effort has been led not by historians but by social scientists, including an author of this chapter (Foner 2000). Earlier pleas for systematic comparison across time also came from Ewa Morawska (1990, 1997) and Joel Perlmann (1988). This has brought about a fruitful exchange of knowledge and insight between historians and social scientists, a departure from an earlier period in which American social scientists studying immigration showed a lack of interest in historical studies (Morawska 1990).

Europe's dominant discourses, which saw migration as exceptional and recent, did not provide a favorable climate for an interdisciplinary, long-term perspective (Noiriel 1988; Lucassen and Lucassen 1997, 2009). Insofar as European historians paid attention to pre–World War II migration, they focused on refugees—such as Belgians during World War I, stateless refugees afterwards, and Jews in the 1930s—or forced population exchanges—such as between Greece and Turkey in the early 1920s. This myopic perspective reinforced the idea that, unlike the Americas and the so-called white settler colonies, Europe was demographically static, except for the mass emigrations to other parts of the world from 1860 through 1920 and again in the 1950s. European scholars simply forgot or ignored the hundreds of thousands of Irish who settled in Britain, similarly numerous Polish-speaking migrants in Germany, and Italians in France (Lucassen 2005; Lucassen, Feldman, and Oltmer 2006). They gave little better treatment to the millions of internal migrants moving into large European cities during the nineteenth and twentieth centuries, who experienced integration hurdles similar to those of foreign migrants

(Moch 1983, 2003). In addition, the official discourse of many western European states—until quite recently—denied they were de facto immigration countries. Taken together, these dynamics stunted the study of the migrants and their offspring from the 1950s onward. Most conspicuously, hardly any attempts have been made to use earlier periods to gain insight into today's second generation (for an exception that proves the rule, see Lucassen 2005).

The Invisibility of Returnees

Another way history is linked to contemporary second-generation studies is that relations with sending societies and populations in earlier periods made the children of migrants in a number of groups invisible in official statistical data. After World War II, western European countries confronted large-scale migrations from their colonies and former colonies, and many of the newcomers were defined as people who belonged to the mother country. The Netherlands, for example, defined its Eurasian colonial migrants from Indonesia, many of whom were of mixed descent, as returnees and thus not as immigrants. The Dutch government used the term *repatriates*, a deliberately inclusive construction of migrants as an integral part of the nation, although the overwhelming majority had never set foot on Dutch soil and had Indonesian as well as Dutch parentage (Willems 2003). The same holds true for the 500,000 to 1 million *retornados* from the African former colonies to Portugal and France's Algerian *pieds noirs*, who entered France during and after the war of independence (1954 to 1962). In these cases, official categorizations avoided the terms *migrants* and *migration* and officially classified the newcomers as part of the national community (Smith 2003).

A similar reaction occurred with regard to ethnic Germans who "returned" to Germany after World War II (Aussiedler and Volksdeutsche). Considered part of Germany's national heritage, many so-called returnees were descendants of German colonists who had settled in Russia and eastern Europe as early as the eighteenth century. Most of the Aussiedler had never been in Germany and many did not speak German. Nevertheless, Germany entitled them to citizenship with all its rights and obligations (Bade and Oltmer 1999; Dietz 2006). Their numbers ranged from tens of thousands in the 1920s (Oltmer 2006) to millions after 1945. Around 4.5 million Aussiedler entered Germany between 1950 and 2007, 3 million after the Iron Curtain was lifted.

Officials defined all these returnees as belonging to the German people and adopted policies aimed at the swift inclusion and assimilation of the first generation. Their children were assumed to be natives by definition, though more recently it has become clear that the children of the German Aussiedler have integration problems similar to those of other migrants. So far, however, we know little about how the children of returnees have fared, and only lately have they captured the attention of policymakers and researchers (Wierling 2004; Vogelgesang 2008).

Visibility of Colonial Migrants of Color in Government Statistics

A second category of immigrants from the colonies was phenotypically and culturally too different to be defined as lost tribes, so to speak. Yet most retained the nationality of the mother country and, like the Aussiedler, were at least officially defined as belonging (Hansen 2000; Lucassen 2005). At the same time, however, their passports did not automatically lead to their acceptance within the metropole.

European governments adopted a variety of approaches to such people in their official statistics, depending on national political traditions about highlighting ethnic differences. Broadly speaking, there is a continuum from denial to deliberate social construction of ethnic difference. France, with its laïcist ideology, refused to differentiate along ethnic lines. Only West Indians or Algerians born in the (former) colony or holding a foreign passport appeared on the state's statistical radar screen. When they began to arrive, officials deemed them to be citizens free to settle in the mother country, an approach promoted by the colonial ideology of Francophonie (Silverstein 2004; Beriss 2004).

The Netherlands took a different approach. It has not taken a national census since 1971, but government research institutes began to produce a wealth of longitudinal data and microdata on migrant populations beginning in the 1980s, as mass immigration of colonial—mainly Surinamese—and labor migrants took place. Since 1993, the government has issued yearly reports on the integration of foreign national-origin groups that differentiate between the first and second generation. These data were restricted to those groups policymakers targeted as problematic or needing assistance, such as Surinamese and Antilleans, both important nonwhite colonial groups.

Integrating Immigrants and Their Children

Whether migrants to Europe had their origins in colonies (or former colonies) or arrived as guest workers, the longer they stayed, the more state policies focused on integration—especially as they began to have European-born children. This stimulated the development of studies of the second generation. In this sense, recent historical changes have certainly had an impact. Colonial migrants were not the only object of integration policies. As governments slowly realized that guest workers might not return, but instead were adding to their numbers through family reunification, they began to focus on policies dealing with ethnic diversity and integration.

A telling example is the Dutch "ethnic minorities policy" (Minderhedenbeleid). Confronted with the massive Surinamese arrival in the wake of independence in 1975 and increasing family reunification among Turks and Moroccans, the Dutch government, not wishing to be caught unprepared, decided that it needed an explicit integration policy. This was reinforced by the terrorist actions of Moluccans in the 1970s, whose colonial soldier parents had been transported against their will to the Netherlands in 1951 after Indonesia's independence. In the face of highjacked trains and hostage-taking of schoolchildren, the government felt an urgent need to develop a response. Influenced by various Dutch anthropologists, it accepted the basic principle that it needed new programs to integrate colonial and labor migrants from non-European destinations yet allow them to maintain their "own identity" (Scholten 2011).

In the spirit of the age, the Netherlands rejected the concept of assimilation. Instead, policy stressed structural integration in the labor and housing market as well as in the educational system, inspired by the principles of equality and nondiscrimination within an all-embracing welfare state. As long as new immigrant groups did not achieve structural equality, the prevailing technocratic ideal was the progress of migrants and their children with worrying social positions, especially Moluccans, Surinamese, Turks, and Moroccans, within a broader social engineering project. Policymakers ignored others, such as the Chinese and Indonesians, who did much better in the labor market and at school and therefore did not need specific policies. Instead of using color to define ethnic or cultural minorities (as Britain did), the Netherlands used socioeconomic criteria.

Since the late 1980s, the Netherlands' monitoring process has produced numerous reports and data sets highlighting the second generation. In 1989, a more universalist framing of integration policies made ethnic minorities—renamed *allochtones* (those born abroad or with at least one parent born abroad)—one of the most "legible" (Scott 1998) categories in the Netherlands (Scholten 2011). The Central Bureau of Statistics and various academic surveys and panels made their employment, education, housing, marriage, friendship, and organizational patterns the object of measurement. In 1988, an important longitudinal survey was set up at the University of Rotterdam to measure the social position of minorities. This survey was taken up by the Central Bureau of Statistics, which published yearly overviews after 1995, and later on by the Social and Cultural Planning Office. Both institutions were closely linked to policymakers in various ministries and reflect the state's desire to understand and assist in the integration of these groups.

An unintended downside of this focus on ethnic minorities was an increasing elite and popular discomfort with integration policies that were perceived to be failing. From the late 1980s onward, studies placed a major stress on how migrants and their children were lagging behind, exemplified by their disproportionate share among the unemployed, criminals, and school dropouts. The problematization of Muslims since the Salman Rushdie affair in 1989 and the rise of anti-Muslim populist politicians such as Pim Fortuyn and later Geert Wilders added an ideological ingredient to the growing "democratic impatience" in western Europe with the lagging integration of Turks and migrants from Northern Africa.

In western Europe, the growth in the number of children of immigrants and, perhaps even more, the desire to understand and develop policies to respond to their problems and needs spurred social research on these questions. By the 1980s, it was clear that guest workers had become a permanent presence—and family reunification was fueling further immigration. Unlike southern European guest workers, who had free entry as European Union citizens, Turks, Algerians, and Moroccans decided to stay and bring in family members because returning meant shutting the door to Europe behind their backs. The majority in western Europe saw these continuing inflows, and low average human capital of the first generation, as sources of concern.

Especially after the recession of the early 1970s, the problems of immigrant integration and the growing second generation became more visible. In the 1980s, European economies experienced another downturn and immigrant unemployment skyrocketed to almost 50 percent for Moroccans and Turks in the Netherlands. The inner-city and banlieu riots in 1980 in Britain and France put the problems of schooling, residential segregation, criminality, and unemployment among the children of immigrants high on the political—and scholarly—agenda (Wacquant 2008), triggering the establishment of longitudinal data sets that enabled researchers to distinguish between generations—a development that further encouraged studies on the second generation.

National Models

As is already clear, distinctive national policies and attitudes toward ethnic and cultural differences have affected approaches to studying the second generation. These differences can be broadly analyzed under the rubric of models of integration, which are rooted in specific national historical traditions (Brubaker 1992; Ireland 1994).

The national differences in migration experiences and ideas about categorizing and treating migrants across Europe have played an important role in framing research responses (Scholten 2011). Whereas the Nordic countries (especially Sweden) created early monitoring systems that highlighted their second generations, Germany and France were slower to do so. Notwithstanding a strong welfare state and social engineering tradition in these two countries (Lucassen 2010), national statistics only listed the migrants themselves or those who had a foreign nationality, without distinguishing between the generations.

The reasons for this purposeful partial blindness differ but are linked to specific notions of nationality and citizenship. In France, the laïcist republican ideals of equality and secularism deterred the collection of census data on the basis of ethnicity. French government statistics classify those with a foreign passport as foreigners, even if they are born in France. Given French nationality law, based on a partial jus soli principle (nationality based on the country of birth), the children of immigrants born in France generally remain foreigners until the age of eighteen (Hamilton and Simon 2004). This has made it virtually impossible to use official statistics to study the second generation. When INED took the initiative in the early 1990s, with Michèle Tribalat (1995) as a key figure, to build its own data set using ethnic categories and differentiating between immigrant parents and second-generation children, it was highly controversial, even though it provided valuable new information about intergenerational integration processes (Le Bras 1998; Green 2002). Recently INED and the National Institute for Statistics and Economic Studies (INSEE) launched the Trajectoires et Origines (TeO) survey, which includes migrants born after 1958 and their French-born children, thereby highlighting the second generation (Borrel and Lhommeau 2010). These initiatives show that despite national differences the European research landscape is slowly converging.

The quite different German model (Brubaker 1992) led to similar outcomes. Germany's jus sanguinis tradition, in which a parent's citizenship determines the child's, required the German-born children of immigrants to naturalize to become citizens. Only since 2000, after changes in the law, have German-born children of (former) guest workers obtained the right to German citizenship at birth, but this is provisional and a person must decide by the age of twenty-three whether to retain German citizenship. Most early guest workers were Turks, whom the government expected to return to Turkey. Whether Turks were first or second generation, official statistics listed those who did not become citizens as foreigners, and thus in Germany, as in France, it was not possible to distinguish the first from the second generation (Heath, Rothon, and Kilpi 2008). Although the new national sample survey conducted since 2005 has introduced the concept of migrant background, it lumps generations together, including those born abroad and those with non-German citizenship who naturalized or had at least one parent who was or still is a foreign national or immigrated to Germany (Schönwälder and Sohn 2009, 1441). As in France, German scholars took the initiative to create their own panel studies and surveys. The most important is the Social and Economic Panel (SOEP) of the German Institute for Economic Research in Berlin (Deutsches Institut für Wirtschaftsforschung, or DIW), which has gathered data on some 20,000 individuals in Germany since 1984, including special samples of immigrants. Although financed by state agencies since 2003, DIW is an independent academic institution, and by distinguishing between genera-tions at the outset it has provided one of the most important sources for second-generation research in Germany (Münz, Seifer, and Ulrich 1997). Similar data were gathered between 1998 and 2001 in a European-wide project at the University of Bamberg under the title "Effectiveness of National Integration Strategies Toward Second-Generation Migrant Youth in Comparative European Perspective," commonly referred to by its acronym EFFNATIS (Worbs 2003; Heckmann and Schnapper 2003).

These bottom-up academic initiatives made it possible to gather insights into the most problematic second-generation groups (Turks in Germany; Algerians, Moroccans, and southern European migrants in France). That these initiatives emerged and have become so important in European second-generation studies makes clear that national approaches to defin-ing and categorizing groups linked to historical models of integration only partly explain how migration studies developed. Still, as the conflicts around Michèle Tribalat's second-generation research at INED in the early 1990s or the unwillingness of government bodies (or government-supported bodies) in some countries to engage in certain kinds of second-generation research suggest, elements of what we might call an official invisibility policy persist. This national variation has posed a serious hurdle for comparative research on the integration process of the second generation (Lucassen and Laarman 2009).

THE UNITED STATES

Memories of past immigrations, especially the last great wave of European immigrants, are alive and well in the United States. They provide background for most contemporary second-generation studies and are front and center in many. Indeed, the major theoretical approaches to the contemporary second generation have been formulated in direct response to, or in dialogue with, earlier models of assimilation developed to explain the trajectories of the children of early twentieth-century European immigrants. Moreover, discussions of the role of race among the second generation often draw on historical studies of "whiteness" achieved by the descendants of early twentieth-century arrivals.

This is not surprising. Between 1880 and the 1920s, more than 23 million immigrants arrived in the United States. By 1910, the nation's population was almost 15 percent foreign born, a height it has not yet reached since, though it is coming close. (The numbers are much larger now, of course, rising from 13.5 million foreign born in 1910 to 40 million in 2010.) The earlier immigrants, mostly from southern, eastern, and central Europe, had a lasting impact on the nation. A large historical literature documents their experiences. The classic studies of the Chicago School (at the University of Chicago, which established the nation's first sociology department) gave rise to many concepts and theories used today, including assimilation (Waters 2000; Alba and Nee 2003; chapter 3, this volume). These studies focused on European immigrants to the Northeast and Midwest: in 1910, 87 percent of the foreign born came from Europe and more than 80 percent lived in these regions (Alba and Denton 2004). Only recently have the experiences of the children of the early Mexican and Asian immigrants on the West Coast and in the Southwest received much scholarly attention (Sánchez 1993; Telles and Ortiz 2008).

One issue in the contemporary sociological literature is how well theories developed to explain trajectories of the early twentieth-century European second generation apply to their present-day counterparts—and whether current developments require us to revise or even scrap the old assimilation model. How much should we stress continuity with, as opposed to differences from, the past? Will today's second generation also become mainstream Americans? Will the American immigrant story continue to feature large-scale upward mobility? In short, is the past a reliable guide to understanding the present as well as to predicting the future?

In their study of Newburyport, Massachusetts, William Lloyd Warner and Leo Srole (1945) elaborated the old conception of assimilation, and Milton Gordon refined it in *Assimilation in American Life* (1964). Warner and Srole described the intergenerational progression of ethnic groups from the residential and occupational segregation of the first generation to the residential, occupational, and identificational integration and Americanization of later generations. In what has been called a "canonical synthesis" (Alba and Nee 2003, 23), Gordon set out several stages of the assimilation process, beginning with identification with cultural patterns of the host society. Once structural assimilation, or integration into primary groups, occurred, then other types of assimilation would follow, including intermarriage, the waning of a separate ethnic identity, and decline not only of prejudice and discrimination against the group but even of ethnic distinction.

Over the years, American sociologists and historians have raised many objections to these conceptions, among them that assimilation is presented as inevitable, that middle-class whites of British ancestry set the norm by which other groups are assessed, that minority groups are assumed to change in order to assimilate and the majority culture remains unaffected, and that there is no room for the positive role of ethnic and racial groups (for a summary, see Alba and Nee 2003, 3–5).

As the post-1965 second generation has come of age, Alejandro Portes and his colleagues have articulated a segmented assimilation model that, they contend, explains the more mixed outcomes they see now taking place among the children of immigrants. They argue that the conventional assimilation model does not apply today: "Given the momentous changes wrought in the structure of the American economy and labor market during the twentieth century, it is implausible that the difficulties and barriers faced by today's second generation should be the same as those confronted by the children of Europeans" (Portes and Fernandez-Kelly 2008, 15). The argument is that because members of today's second generation face an increasingly bifurcated labor market—low-paid service jobs on one side and high-paid jobs requiring advanced education on the other—many will be hindered by their parents' lack of resources and subordinate racial and class locations, as well as by discriminatory responses by the larger society, and end up experiencing stagnation or downward mobility (Portes and Fernandez-Kelly 2008; see also Portes and Zhou 1993; Portes and Rumbaut 2001; Telles and Ortiz 2008).

The pessimism of this approach—and the notion that today's second generation faces greater obstacles than before—has triggered a reassessment of the historical trajectories of the earlier European second generation to critically examine assumptions about the extent, pace, and nature of mobility in the past. Distance and nostalgia, Roger Waldinger and Joel Perlmann state, should not blind us to the significant difficulties the European second generation encountered in the past (1998, 11). Contrary to what the segmented assimilation model assumes, Waldinger and Perlmann argue that the children of European immigrants faced disadvantages as great as those the children of the post-1965 immigration have confronted. Indeed, they think the picture is far rosier today because American society is more receptive to immigrant incorporation and more contemporary immigrants come from middle-class backgrounds than a century ago (20). Waldinger (2007) has recently challenged the view that well-paid, low-skilled manufacturing jobs were the key to upward mobility for the children of the 1880 to 1920 immigration. In *Italians Then, Mexicans Now*, Perlmann (2005) compared the progress of two major past and present low-skilled groups and concluded that both are characterized by slow but steady advancement over the generations, though intergenerational progress may be slower for the Mexicans.

Nancy Foner and Richard Alba (2006) have also argued that upbeat portrayals of the past misrepresent the complexities of earlier second-generation mobility paths. To be sure, most of yesterday's European second generation did show overall progress and advancement, but the climb was often slow and gradual. Far from being able to "claw their way . . . into economic affluence" (Portes and Rumbaut 2001, 53) or make giant leaps forward, second-generation Europeans in the past usually made modest upward moves from their parents. A good number stayed at the same level and some suffered painful setbacks and difficulties, especially the cohort that matured during the Great Depression in the 1930s.

If critiques of the segmented assimilation model emphasize continuities between past and present, so do modern-day assimilation approaches. Most prominent among them is Richard Alba and Victor Nee's revised theory of assimilation in *Remaking the American Mainstream* (2003). Based on a detailed analysis of, among other things, intermarriage and linguistic acculturation, they argue that assimilation was not only the master trend for the children and grandchildren of the earlier European immigration but also the most likely path for most descendants of the post-1965 immigration (see chapter 3, this volume). Although assimilation remains a powerful force, they argue, it also needs to be reconceptualized. In their view, ethnicity does not inevitably disappear or weaken as assimilation takes place, and immigrants and their descendants change the mainstream culture at the same time that they are incorporated into it.

Many contemporary studies that are less concerned with or only give a nod to the experiences of yesterday's second generation still show the historical continuity of assimilation; the children of today's immigrants generally have attained higher economic, occupational, and educational levels than their parents, are proficient in English, and show other signs of generational progression seen for the children of European immigrants in the past (Farley and Alba 2002; Kasinitz et al. 2008; Bean and Stevens 2003; White and Glick 2009).

Race is bound up with the assimilation of today's second generation, which has led present-day studies to engage with the historical literature on whiteness among the old European immigrants (for example, Barrett and Roediger 1997; Foner 2000; Foner and Fredrickson 2004; Gerstle 2001; Guglielmo 2003; Jacobson 1998). Indeed, a volume sponsored by the Social Science Research Council (SSRC), *Not Just Black and White: Historical and Contemporary Perspectives on Immigration, Race, and Ethnicity in the United States* (Foner and Fredrickson 2004), brought a distinguished group of social scientists and historians together to reflect on the relationship between race, immigration, and ethnicity in the United States from the end of the nineteenth century to the present (see also two other SSRC-supported historical comparison volumes, Gerstle and Mollenkopf 2001; Alba, Raboteau, and DeWind 2008).

Although eastern and southern European immigrants were initially considered racial inferiors whose status as whites was often doubted, the second generation by and large and the third certainly were considered part of an all-encompassing white racial majority. Historical analyses of how and why this happened make dramatically clear that racial categories are changeable. The gradual inclusion of these groups has helped shape sociological perspectives on race and racial change among the current second generation.

Social scientists are now asking many questions that engage with or are influenced by the historical literature: Will the factors responsible for enabling Jews and Italians to meld into the white majority operate in changing ethno-racial boundaries confronting descendants of Latino, Asian, and black immigrants? Will any groups currently thought of as non-white, as well as nonblack, come to be seen as white? Or will ethno-racial boundaries and meanings shift in a different way? Given how prominent color is in today's racial discourse, will intermarriage be a more important agent of racial change than in the past (Foner 2000, 2005; Lee and Bean 2010; Perlmann and Waters 2007)? Will, as Richard Alba (2009) argues, members of the second generation in racial minority groups be able to take advantage of non–zero sum mobility—ascending socially without adversely affecting the life chances of the established majority? Whatever the particular arguments or predictions, it is clear that research on ethnoracial change in the past is informing and affecting contemporary studies of the second generation.

America's original sin of slavery—followed by nearly a century of legal segregation in the South, rolled back finally by the civil rights movement of the 1960s and the resulting legislation—has also heavily influenced studies of the contemporary second generation. It explains why color-coded race plays a fundamentally different role in the analysis of assimilation in the United States than in continental Europe and why the American black experience looms so large in U.S. second-generation studies (Foner 2005; Lucassen 2002; Lucassen and Laarman 2009). Indeed, American scholars often measure the progress of the second generation in the United States by comparing them with native blacks.

The historical legacy of institutionalized racial oppression in the United States and the continued realities of racial prejudice and exclusion have been problematic for nonwhite immigrants and their children. Indeed, second-generation studies designed to examine the impact of racial discrimination and prejudice show just how persistent the barriers are that the children of Latino, black, and Asian immigrants experience because of their race and ethnicity (Portes and Zhou 1993; Portes and Rumbaut 2001; Kasinitz et al. 2008; Telles and Ortiz 2008). As the quintessentially racialized Americans, people of visible African ancestry face especially acute difficulties. Black immigrants and their children are still more residentially segregated than Latinos and Asians and less likely to marry outside their group than other ethnic and racial minorities. In the New York second-generation study, young adult West Indians worked in predominantly black work sites, whereas second-generation Chinese and Latinos were more likely to work in racially mixed workplaces (Kasinitz et al. 2008, 198). Black as well as Latino second-generation students often ended up in predominantly minority schools in poor neighborhoods, with less experienced teachers, more limited curricula, higher turnover, and more dangerous environments.

The children of West Indian immigrants, admittedly a small second-generation group, have attracted considerable scholarly attention precisely because they are overwhelmingly black and share a racial status—and stigma—with African Americans. Because a central question is whether they will become African Americans, how they identify takes on special significance (Waters 1999, 2001; Butterfield 2004; Vickerman 2001; Bashi-Bobb and Clarke 2001; Foner 2010). So far, second-generation West Indians have had trouble "marshalling their West Indianness in a society that racializes blacks with little regard to ethnicity" (Bashi-Bobb and Clarke 2001, 233). Without an accent or other clues to reveal their ethnic status, second-generation West Indians, it has been said, are likely to fade to black (Kasinitz, Battle, and Miyares 2001). Those who continue to identify with their ethnic backgrounds are aware that unless they actively convey their ethnic identities, others will see them as African Americans and that will be all that matters in encounters with whites, and they will be subject to the same racial prejudice and exclusion that black Americans face (Waters 1994, 1999).

That many second-generation young people live near poor native blacks in inner-city neighborhoods is central to the segmented assimilation model and studies influenced by it. The argument is that children of immigrants whose parents lack resources and share a racial or ethnic similarity with native minorities are at risk of adopting a peer culture said to be widespread among inner-city minority youth that devalues educational achievement and encourages behavior impeding academic success (Portes and Zhou 1993; Portes and Rumbaut 2001). Research to evaluate this claim, however, finds that identifying with African Americans often does not lead to downward assimilation; members of the Afro-Caribbean second generation, as a whole, not only have better educational and occupational outcomes than their parents but also do better than their African American peers (Farley and Alba 2002; Kasinitz et al. 2008). Moreover, adopting aspects of black American culture, such as listening to hip-hop music or affecting a ghetto presentation of self, should not be taken as evidence that such persons are engaging in self-defeating behavior (Kasinitz, Mollenkopf, and Waters 2004, 396).

America's racial history has had some positive consequences for the second generation (Foner 2005; Foner and Alba 2010; Kasinitz et al. 2008). They have benefitted from government policies developed to redress and overcome institutionalized black disadvantages following slavery and legal segregation. The literature on the U.S. second generation has explored how the children of black and Latino immigrants have profited from "the institutions, political strategies, and notions of rights developed in the aftermath of the civil rights movement precisely because they have been nonwhite" (Kasinitz et al. 2008, 303).

Originally set up to promote greater African American representation in higher education and public service jobs, affirmative action was subsequently extended to other groups, especially Latinos. The New York second-generation study contends that these programs have worked better for the black and Latino children of immigrants than for the native minorities for whom they were designed (Kasinitz et al. 2008). The children of immigrants may not know how much they have benefitted from African American struggles against racism, but they are well positioned to take advantage of the results. Although many suffer from racial discrimination, substandard schools, and lack of knowledge of America's educational system, they come from families that invest a great deal in the success of their American-born children (Kasinitz et al. 2008, 366). A recent study of freshmen at thirty-five selective colleges and universities found a substantial overrepresentation of immigrants and their children among black students (Massey et al. 2007). In much the same way, the children of an ever-broadening category of Latino immigrants have used programs designed for Mexican Americans and Puerto Ricans (Kasinitz et al. 2008, 332).

The children of immigrants have also benefitted from the growth of schools, clubs, and curricula (for example, ethnic studies programs) to meet the needs of African Americans, Latinos, and Asians; these have helped the second generation increase its chances for mobility and promoted a sense of ethnic and racial pride (on West Indians, see Foner 2001; Kasinitz 2001).

The second generation has also derived political benefits from civil rights legislation. The 1965 Voting Rights Act, a hallmark law designed to enfranchise blacks who had been deprived of political power, was amended ten years later to enhance the representation of Spanish- and various Asian-language minorities (Mollenkopf and Hochschild 2010, 27–28). As Mollenkopf and Hochschild observe, the civil rights movement of the 1960s "has canonical status as a model for combining vigorous protest with political mobilization and electoral success," serving as "a vivid model of how to mobilize politically and attain at least some power, often locally" (28–29).

CONCLUSION

Our analysis of how the past has affected present-day research on the second generation highlights fundamental differences between Europe and the United States. In the United States, contemporary studies have been heavily influenced by the literature about the descendants of earlier immigrants—on racialization as well as assimilation—and lively discussions take place about what is new about the current situation. In Europe, by contrast, the past has actually contributed to making some second-generation groups invisible or harder to study.

The legacy of slavery in the United States, followed by Jim Crow segregation laws and ultimately civil rights legislation, has had a strong impact on scholarship there. Although colonialism and slavery in far-off possessions gave rise to racist attitudes and structures in Europe, these had much less impact on race relations within the mother countries than internal slavery had in the United States. The American legacy of slavery and presence of a huge African American population—now about 13 percent of the U.S. population and much higher in many gateway cities—means that race-as-color is a prominent feature of American society and, as a consequence, in research on the second generation. Color-coded race has played a less central role in the analysis of the second generation in mainland Europe. Not only was large-scale slavery practiced at a distance, but the Holocaust and World War II make race a suspect concept. Members of the U.S. second generation, unlike their European counterparts, have profited from affirmative action mechanisms set up to help native-born minorities gain access to higher education and better employment. Whereas the children of immigrants in the United States may compare themselves favorably with African Americans (who are below them in the social hierarchy), the European second generation has no equivalent native minority group, ruling out this dynamic.

We have stressed history's role in framing debates and shaping what is studied, or ignored, in second-generation research today, but other factors are of course also crucial in explaining the transatlantic contrasts. The focus on Islam in Europe, for example, reflects large Muslim immigrant flows with low human capital, in contrast with the United States, where the overwhelming majority of immigrants and their children are Christian (Foner and Alba 2008). In fact, the influx of Muslim immigrants in Europe has affected the significance of color as a basis for racialization there. It has been argued, for example, that first- and second-generation Caribbean migrants of African ancestry in the Netherlands and France are less stigmatized than Muslims, who differ much more from the native population in cultural and religious terms (Lucassen 2005).

Because western European countries have more highly developed welfare states and programs than the United States it is also not surprising that the European second-generation literature is more often, and more directly, geared to providing advice to governments on policy issues—although here, too, history has clearly had a hand. The relatively strong welfare states in contemporary Europe have their origins in historical developments there, particularly in the early post–World War II period. Historically, as well, class inequalities have played a larger role in public debates, political movements, and self-identity in Europe than in the United States. How this historical legacy has shaped studies of, and realities among, the second generation in contemporary Europe compared with the United States is an important subject for future analysis.

History clearly helps us understand which concepts and theories are used to study the second generation in the United States and Europe and helps us make sense of contemporary outcomes on the two sides of the Atlantic (chapter 10, this volume). As we enter the second decade of the twenty-first century, and as scholarly research on the second generation develops and changes, we will need to explore in more detail how—and why—the past sheds light on the current content and focus of this research. Systematic historical comparisons between past and present developments among the second generation will help us delineate more clearly the significance of the continuities and contrasts (Foner 2000; Lucassen 2005) and thus test what are often too easy and unproven assumptions about the past that affect how we view and understand the present.

CHAPTER 3

NATIONAL CONCEPTIONS OF ASSIMILATION, INTEGRATION, AND COHESION

RICHARD ALBA, JEFFREY G. REITZ, AND PATRICK SIMON

Models of incorporation provide the touchstones for social science research on immigration, offering hypotheses to guide empirical analysis. These models address the following central questions: How will immigrants and their children, the second generation, shed their status as outsiders (or newcomers) and become recognized as insiders? What place will they assume in society when they do? In addition, the models often address how societies manage increasing diversity and what determines their success in bringing new groups into a more integrated society.

As chapter 2 noted, these models are not the exclusive products of science but are framed by national concerns, which complicates the task of cross-national comparative research. As Nancy Foner and Leo Lucassen so clearly put it, the history of the societies in which academics are thinking and writing frames their concepts and theories. Comparative research must overcome the fact that the distinctive concepts and theories developed in each unique national context of immigration make it hard to transfer them from one context to another. This chapter examines the national social-scientific approaches to immigrant integration in some depth in order to clarify their differences and to seek out common themes and approaches that may allow us to bridge them.

It is not surprising that social scientists are influenced by the public discourses and policy debates that have arisen within their national settings. Social scientists generally want to affect how lay audiences and policy-makers think about the place of immigration in national life, so they couch their ideas in ways that make sense to these individuals. Even when addressing other social scientists, they are usually aware of how this audience will translate their ideas into public and policy discourses. If for no other reason, this roots them in their national approaches to immigration and minority issues. For instance, anyone today who reads Milton Gordon's classic book *Assimilation in American Life* (1964), an inspiration for much comparative research, cannot fail to recognize how clearly it reflects the mid-twentieth-century understanding of the U.S. experience of assimilating European immigrant groups.

The major theoretical approaches to immigrant integration are also entangled in normative concerns about how incorporation should ideally work in each national setting. National philosophies not only shape public discourses about and perceptions of immigrant incorporation, they deeply influence how social scientists design their theories and concepts (Favell 2005). Even as social science becomes more internationally integrated, such idiosyncrasies still prevail in many domains. Thinking about the assimilation or integration of immigrants and their descendants is obviously one of them.

In each setting, various actors have different points of view. Members of the host society usually think first about how immigrants will affect their society and their own place within it. They may see immigrants as an opportunity or a threat, and their criteria for evaluating their incorporation will vary accordingly. Immigrants themselves are likely to assess their success within their adopted homeland in terms of their own life goals, usually that of achieving a higher standard of living. Particular groups may also be concerned with minority status, religion, or culture. For their part, the children of immigrants share many of their parents' concerns but may possibly also be concerned with longer-term prospects and critical problems for their group emerging over longer periods. In this way, different host societies bring different criteria to the question of what is expected of immigrants. All of these actors have some influence on how social scientists interpret the world.

This chapter delves into the main models of incorporation in each setting and asks what they imply for conducting comparative research.

We believe that social science can move beyond national idiosyncrasies and identify recurring frames that can be the basis for a more general comparative analysis of immigrant incorporation while taking into account historical and national integration differences.

ASSIMILATION IN THE UNITED STATES

The United States has long used the concept of assimilation to understand immigrant incorporation. This extends back to the colonial period, when immigrants from northern and western European countries—primarily the British Isles, France, Germany, the Netherlands, and Sweden—intermixed to form a new society. The idea of assimilation is incipient in the oft-quoted words of J. Hector St. John de Crèvecoeur's *Letters from an American Farmer* (1782), defining the nature of a "new man" emerging under New World conditions.

The ultimate markers of the success of assimilation, however, stem from the mass incorporation of the Catholic and Jewish descendants of the Irish and the southern and eastern European immigrants in the mid-twentieth century. Until this point, the Protestant old-stock ethnic groups who made up the core of the American mainstream viewed these groups as inferior and kept them at the margins. This mass assimilation, which was most concentrated between 1945 and 1970, removed this stamp of inferiority. The efficacy of this assimilation was especially convincing because its scope included both eastern European Jews, whose rapid educational and economic ascent challenged the dominance of Protestant whites, and southern Italians, whose slow educational progress seemed to mark them out as permanent denizens of the working class.

The canonical theory of assimilation is concerned especially with the processes by which members of originally low-status and ethno-racially excluded groups—such as southern Italians and European Jews then or Mexicans now—enter the societal mainstream and attain life chances on a par with members of the dominant group. The theory envisions change not just at the individual level but, possibly, at the group level. Because the social distinctions that afflict immigrants and their children are not just anchored in social-class disadvantages but typically also involve racial, ethnic, and religious aspects, assimilation theory must therefore address how such social boundaries change and even fade.

The most encompassing contemporary restatement and refinement of the canonical concept can be found in Richard Alba and Victor Nee's definition of assimilation as the "decline of an ethnic distinction and its corollary cultural and social differences" (2003, 11). In this context, *decline* means that a distinction becomes less salient and that its relevance becomes less frequent and is confined to fewer domains of social life.

This definition leaves room for assimilation to be a two-sided process, whereby the immigrant minority influences the societal majority group rather than simply being influenced by it. The Alba and Nee account envisions that assimilation can involve a culturally or ethnically distinct group's entry into a mainstream (a term that probably should be put in the plural to recognize that advanced societies have socially heterogeneous and culturally layered mainstreams) as distinct from members of that group being accepted into the ethno-racial majority itself. The mainstream can be thought of as encompassing those social settings where the presence of members of the majority population (with the appropriate age, gender, social class, and so on) is unproblematic or taken for granted. Although the majority group defines mainstream settings by its presence, others who enter and whom they accept in these settings also become part of the mainstream, at least for part of their social lives; mainstream culture thus comes to incorporate elements from the new arrivals, lending it a variegated character.

The Alba-Nee approach specifies mechanisms that under the right conditions bring about assimilation into the mainstream. The core mechanism involves the aspirations of immigrants and subsequent generations to improve the material and social circumstances of their lives. This mechanism does not require that individuals intend to take assimilatory steps. Often assimilation is an unintended consequence of practical strategies taken in pursuit of highly valued goals—a good education, a good job, a nice place to live, interesting friends and acquaintances.

Behind this mechanism lies a highly stratified society in which a dominant ethno-racial group has most of the valued social goods. In the United States, the search for a desirable place to live—with good schools and opportunities for children to grow up protected from the seductions of deviant behavior—leads many socioeconomically successful ethnic families into largely white communities, because resources and amenities tend to be concentrated in such places. One consequence of such moves, whether intended or not, is that the ethnic families will interact with majority group families; such increased contact tends to encourage acculturation and social integration, especially for children.

This restatement of assimilation theory posits that cultural and social assimilation, on the one hand, are related to entering the mainstream and approaching its life chances, on the other. But it does not presume that these dimensions of assimilation follow a specific sequence. It argues that individuals and families undertake various forms of cultural and social assimilation in a search for greater opportunities and that achieving social mobility through mainstream institutions this way often obliges them to mold their behavior in assimilative ways (for example, in language and speech patterns). The greater linguistic assimilation among second-generation Asian groups, which are enjoying relatively great success in U.S. educational institutions and the labor market, offers empirical evidence for this posited relationship, as does the strong link between educational attainment and the likelihood of marrying a white partner (Alba 2004; Qian and Lichter 2007).

Not everyone will assimilate into the mainstream, however, and Alba and Nee dispense with the classical assumption that assimilation is inevitable. The most complete statement of alternative outcomes is provided by segmented assimilation theory (Portes and Zhou 1993). According to it, groups can be assimilated into different sectors, or segments, of the receiving society, and assimilating individuals and groups can therefore take one of several distinct trajectories. One trajectory leads to the mainstream; this is assimilation addressed by neo-assimilation theory. But another leads to incorporation as an ethno-racial minority whose members suffer from systemic disadvantages compared to members of the mainstream. Applying this concept to U.S. society, Alejandro Portes and Min Zhou (1993) describe this trajectory as downward and likely to be followed by many in those second-generation groups who are hindered by their parents' humble starting points in the United States and who are barred from entry to the largely white mainstream by their darker skin. There is also a pluralist alternative to either upward (mainstream) or downward (minority) assimilation. Some individuals and groups are able to draw on their ethnic group's distinctive social and economic advantages, especially in the form of ethnic economic niches. Under optimal circumstances, exemplified perhaps by the Cubans of Miami, immigrant-origin groups may even attain socioeconomic opportunities through their ethnic communities and networks that are equal to those afforded by the mainstream.

The Alba and Nee approach to assimilation theory is concerned not just with individual assimilation but also with the changing distance of immigrant-origin groups from the mainstream. The theory draws on ideas about social boundaries to identify different ways such changes can occur. A social boundary can be conceptualized as a social distinction that individuals make in their everyday lives and that shapes their actions and mental orientations toward others (Lamont and Molnar 2002). Obviously, ethnic and racial distinctions can be viewed as social boundaries, and Alba and

Nee's definition of assimilation involves the decline of a boundary's relevance for a group (in relation to another group) or for some individuals within the group. However, this decline of relevance can come about in one of three ways (Zolberg and Long 1999). Boundary crossing corresponds to the classic version of individual-level assimilation: someone moves from one group to another, without the boundary itself changing in any real way (although if such boundary crossings happen on a large scale in a consistent direction, then they are altering the social structure). Boundary blurring implies that a boundary has a less distinct social profile: the clarity of the social distinction involved has become clouded. Finally, boundary shifting involves relocating a boundary so that populations once situated on one side are now included on the other: former outsiders are thereby transformed into insiders.

Specific structural conditions in the labor market and in other key societal institutions can favor the large-scale blurring or shifting of boundaries. Alba's (2009) analysis of the mass assimilation of the so-called white ethnics in the United States in the quarter century following World War II points to the critical role of what he calls non-zero-sum mobility, where members of disadvantaged groups can move up without appearing to threaten the life chances that members of the dominant group take for granted for themselves and their children. An extraordinary period of prosperity made this mobility possible in the postwar era. For instance, the number of places in colleges and universities, especially in the public sector, increased fivefold between 1940 and 1970, making postsecondary education available on a mass scale.

Corresponding changes occurred in the occupational structure, expanding the occupational tiers appropriate to postsecondary credentials. In addition to this vertical mobility, young members of disadvantaged groups also experienced horizontal forms of social mobility as many of them drew socially closer to the mainstream population. This happened in part through postwar suburbanization, which lured many young families out of the urban ethnic areas where they had grown up and into ethnically mixed residential settings. This social melding ultimately yielded higher rates of intermarriage across ethnic and even religious lines. Undoubtedly, cultural changes helped these mobility processes along. In particular, white Protestants came to hold more positive attitudes toward the white ethnics, at least those who were largely acculturated, during World War II as a result of the calculated emphasis on how diverse parts of the white population contributed to victory. Novels and films helped Americans digest the wartime experience and reinforced this cultural shift.

One other lesson can be drawn from close analysis of this important case of large-scale assimilation. In contrast to the simplistic view that sees assimilation as requiring assimilating minorities to surrender their cultural differences, the postwar case involved, at least for religion, incorporating cultural differences into the U.S. mainstream. That mainstream was once defined as Christian, a term defined partly in opposition to Roman Catholicism. Hence, the mainstream saw Jews and Catholics as outsiders and defended the Protestant and non-Protestant boundary by such actions as restricting admission of Jews to elite universities where privilege was minted and mobilizing white Protestants to defeat the Catholic presidential candidate, Al Smith, in the election of 1928.

Yet, in the end, the mainstream redefined itself as Judeo-Christian, a key achievement of the post–World War II mass assimilation. During that period, Judaism and Catholicism did undergo changes in the United States that made them more closely resemble American Protestant models. But the fundamental point is that the once-salient boundaries separating Protestants from Jews and Catholics faded without these aspirants to the mainstream remaking themselves into carbon copies of those who possessed it as a birthright.

Intergenerational changes are critical to assimilation theory, which recognizes that first-generation immigrants, who typically arrive as young adults after being socialized in another society, have limited potential for assimilation. It envisions the second generation as an in-between generation. Raised in immigrant homes but also socialized by mainstream schools, mixed public spaces, and mainstream mass media, its members still generally bear the traces of their families' recent immigrant origins; but they are much more likely than their parents to be culturally and socially equipped to function within mainstream institutions. Because of their ethno-racial distinctiveness, they frequently face prejudice and discrimination from members of the mainstream society. At the same time, their socialization, especially their schooling, enables them mostly to take large steps beyond their parents' status.

Members of the second generation occupy a wide variety of social positions, especially when they are the children of low-wage immigrants. Many advance towards, if not into, the mainstream, moving up socio-economically, moving out of immigrant contexts, moving into mixed neighborhoods, and even marrying into mainstream families. At the same time, many others, either because they are blocked by ethno-racial exclusion or held by preference, may remain strongly attached to the social and cultural contexts in which their parents raised them. Some do both.

The third generation, defined by having immigrant grandparents, is usually seen as the generation with the potential to complete the entry into the mainstream. In the mid-twentieth-century experience of mass assimilation in the United States, that generation largely completed this step. However, doubts have been raised about whether the United States can sustain this pace of assimilation today. Frank Bean and Gillian Stevens (2003) argue that Mexican assimilation will take at least an additional generation. Alba (2009) argues that, under conditions of constrained social mobility, portions of the descendants of contemporary immigrant groups will assimilate into the mainstream and other portions will experience the systemic disadvantages associated with ethno-racial minority status.

INTEGRATION VERSUS MULTICULTURALISM IN EUROPE

In Europe (and Canada), scholars use the concept of integration rather than of assimilation to define the outcomes of the immigrant experience. The European Union has now identified integration as a policy challenge by adopting the Common Basic Principles on Integration (CBP). The process of defining and implementing common integration policies in the European Union of twenty-seven member states (EU27) has made integration into one of the most widespread sociological concepts in European public discourse. This has somehow blurred the canonical distinction among European models of incorporation: the republican-assimilationist model (France), the multicultural-pluralist model (United Kingdom, the Netherlands), and the cultural-ethnic model (Germany, Austria). The French model is now evolving toward a more integrationist approach (Simon and Sala Pala 2009), but the United Kingdom and the Netherlands have seen a backlash against multiculturalism (Vertovec and Wessendorf 2009). The German debate has turned toward the idea of a lead culture (Leitkultur) and the creation of a ministry for integration. The very notion of national identity and the need to set limits on the tolerance of diversity have recently fostered hot debates in the United Kingdom, France, Germany, and the Netherlands, echoing similar debates in Canada (Bloemraad 2007).

Christian Joppke (2007) has described these convergences as a shift toward civic integration. The link between immigration and integration policies has gained importance in the last decade, and most western and northern European countries have conditioned the admission of immigrants on the fulfillment of certain integration obligations. Linguistic training has been made mandatory for receiving residence permits. Immigrants must also show they accept a set of core values that shape fundamental rights in western democracy. As Joppke puts it, the "coexistence of civic integration and antidiscrimination reveals that the liberal mantra of two-way integration, according to which not just the migrants but also the receiving societies must change in the process of immigration, consists in reality of two separate one-way processes" (2007, 248).

In other words, the liberal conception of integration has given way to a more authoritarian approach that sounds more like old-school assimilation than the contractual approach.

The Canadian version of multiculturalism had integration as an objective, but in Europe, multiculturalism and integration came to be seen as more and more opposed to each other. The contemporary rejection of multiculturalism in the United Kingdom, the Netherlands, and Germany is therefore mainly an assertion that greater efforts at integration are needed. Canadian multiculturalism had its roots in the English-French duality of Canada and the emergence of national aspirations of Francophones in Quebec in the 1960s. Their new demands for federal bilingualism and biculturalism, however, seemed to threaten the so-called other ethnic (immigrant) groups. In 1971, therefore, Prime Minister Pierre Trudeau offered multiculturalism to secure immigrant-group support for bilingualism and to reassure immigrants that they too would have a prominent place within the mainstream. Internationally, multiculturalism became associated almost entirely with accommodating minority cultures, reflecting philosophical defenses by Will Kymlicka (1996) and Charles Taylor (1994), and quite disconnected from efforts at immigrant integration.

Whereas assimilation defines immigrant success in terms of the reduction of an overall ethnic difference, the alternative European concepts—variously labeled integration, incorporation, or adaptation—focus specifically on the relation between immigrants and core institutions of the host society. Integration or incorporation may include successful participation in labor markets, in housing markets, in schools, and in politics. It may also include participation in informal social relations in local communities. These perspectives judge immigrant success in terms of the differential representation of immigrant groups in these sectors of the host society. Some authors focus on labor markets as the most critical domain, but others include broader aspects of inclusion.

This perspective considers the cultural characteristics of immigrants, such as their identity, their ethnic social and community attachments, their religion, and their retention of ethnic culture over time, to be distinct topics, separate from the question of structural integration. This allows for the possibility that retention of ethnic characteristics may be independent of socioeconomic integration.

TABLE 3.1   Integration and Ethnic Distinctiveness

	Ethnic Attachment	
Mainstream Integration	High	Low
High	pluralism	assimilation
Low	ethnic enclave	marginality

Source: Authors' compilation.

A pluralistic approach ideally values both socioeconomic integration and ethnic attachment, but in reality the two dimensions can vary independently to create the four ideal types depicted in table 3.1 (Breton et al. 1990; Berry 1980). As explained in a study of immigrant ethnic groups in Toronto, immigrant success may be assessed as a progression from ethnic characteristics toward either pluralist or assimilationist outcomes (Breton et al. 1990, 261). Under certain circumstances, marginality may result instead, but little attention has been given to this outcome.

Differentiating these two dimensions has had two primary implications for the theoretical agenda in Europe. One is that each dimension should be analyzed separately. Although gauging the degree of integration into mainstream institutions is important, so is analyzing the social, institutional, and organizational dimensions of the ethnic community and the determinants of its survival. This latter task is potentially complex. First, key ethnic characteristics include not only size, level of residential or regional concentration, and ethnic resources but overall level of institutional development; institutional completeness; and racial, linguistic, or religious distinctiveness. All these elements can contribute to ethnic retention. Second, it is important to see how relations among subgroups within the ethnic community, based perhaps on class, specific regions of origin, arrival cohort, or generation (among other characteristics), may affect the overall development of the community. In particular, conflicts over economic resources, political issues, or cultural aspects may divide it. Finally, the ethnic community's relations with the host society need to be examined, for example, the political influence of ethnic elites.

The other major implication is that we need to analyze the relations between the two dimensions. How does ethnic retention affect integration, and how does integration in turn affect ethnic retention? Assimilation theory suggests that a high degree of ethnic retention may reduce integration into the mainstream society. For example, it may deter members of the immigrant group from developing the degree of cultural conformity to mainstream values or social practices necessary for economic opportunity. Employment in an ethnic enclave economy may limit opportunities compared with those in the mainstream. However, ethnic retention may also have positive impacts on overall group incorporation, leading to greater pluralism. These positive effects may be individual, such as when an ethnic business succeeds within the mainstream economy, or group-based, such as when an ethnic organization promotes educational attainment by community children or influences political decision-making about providing public benefits to the group.

These positive effects arise primarily for instrumental reasons, but ethnic retention may promote social integration for affective reasons. Ethnic identity retention may enhance psychological or emotional well-being (Taylor 1994), particularly when the majority positively recognizes a minority group or the latter achieves relatively high status in mainstream institutional arenas (Kymlicka 1996). Individual identity with the group may then foster self-esteem and a sense of inclusion. This in turn may promote a more positive identification with the broader society than attachment to a stigmatized minority group.

VISIBLE CLEAVAGES AND SOCIAL COHESION

Much of the European approach to social cohesion is rooted in the thinking of Emile Durkheim. The dialectical relation between integration into society and the integration of society lies at the heart of Durkheim's thinking in the nineteenth century. He considered society to be integrated when all its constitutive parts, either groups or individuals, worked to reinforce its cohesion. Durkheim never attempted to measure individual integration because he considered the notion of integration to be a property of systems of relationships, power relations, and stratifications. One can nevertheless infer the definition of individual integration simply by turning the definition of an integrated society around. In other words, an individual has a certain degree of capacity or opportunity for evolution within society. Durkheim's approach identified institutions as the main conveyors of norms and therefore of integration.

In this approach, the purpose of integration is to create compatibility between the values and desires of immigrants (or outsiders) and those of members of the mainstream society, which in turn ought to increase social participation among immigrants. Aiming at this compatibility does not entail that immigrants be absorbed into mainstream society and completely lose their group identity. The objective is rather for significant groups within society to achieve a functional complementarity with the rest of society, which does not necessarily require the society to be culturally, socially, or politically uniform with them. The degree to which immigrants and subsequent generations have to converge with the mainstream population for society at large to be cohesive depends greatly on the particular normative expectations expressed and disseminated in its laws, institutions, policies, and public discourse. Societies adopting a multicultural approach (normative pluralism) will set different benchmarks for integration than those promoting cohesion through the reduction of ethnic or race-based differences with the mainstream (Bloemraad 2007). From this perspective, a multiculturalist approach may offer ethnic communities more opportunities for recognition and success than assimilationist or republican universalist approaches that actively seek to achieve cohesion by reducing ethnic distinctiveness (Heckmann and Schnapper 2003).

The purpose of such normative definitions is to frame the adjustments that insiders and outsiders will both have to achieve to be able to live together. The definitions reveal uneasy questions regarding what price both groups will have to pay, what consequences policies acknowledging the existence of ethnic communities will have, and what risks will be posed by too much reciprocity between the settlement society and the groups to be integrated. Most controversies surrounding immigration issues can be understood as conflicts over the definitions of core norms and values. One of the crucial debates in contemporary European political life is how far mainstream society should accommodate outsiders' cultural traits, beliefs, and practices (Koopmans et al. 2005; Bail 2008).

The degree to which immigrants' and minorities' cultural and religious practices and references are dissonant with the mainstream has long been central to the assimilation process. Milton Gordon (1964) points out that acculturation is one dimension among others of assimilation and that the process sometimes never goes beyond this stage. One may even expect that structural assimilation can be achieved despite a persistent ethnic dissonance with the mainstream. Dissonance does not always generate negative receptional attitudes from the mainstream population. The issue of visibility is particularly important. The more visible the differences, the more likely that society will pin them down as both the source and the expression of integration difficulties. But visibility does not proceed from predetermined characteristics that create "natural" boundaries within society. If traits such as phenotype, accent, dress codes, or religious tags create more potential for generating prejudices and stereotyping, their salience and significance nonetheless vary across societies. To return to the differences between assimilation and integration theories, the construction of visibility sorts out which groups can join the mainstream population, conditional on the reduction of some of its distinguishing dissonances. The reproduction of visible distinctiveness across generations cannot be explained by resistance to cultural changes (language maintenance, cultural resistance, or symbolic ethnicity) but rather by the persistence of social processes of othering. In this context, scholars should approach the situation of postcolonial minorities in Europe and racial minorities in the United States with different conceptual tools than they use to analyze the assimilation of immigrants.

The main approaches on the two sides of the Atlantic reflect different historical experiences and different goals for achieving immigrant integration into the mainstream, along with different constructions of visible differences between the mainstream and immigrant ethnic groups. We can use the variation in these approaches to widen the range of indicators useful for comparative research.

RECONCILING THE APPROACHES

In the search for common ground, we need to consider each perspective from the standpoint of the others.

Critique of Assimilation

From the perspective of the integration approach, assimilation theory overemphasizes one dimension of ethnic change—whether an immigrant group moves toward membership in the mainstream—and underemphasizes the possibility of plural or multiple group membership. Assimilation theory asks whether and how ethnic group membership itself is an obstacle to full membership in the host society, forcing individuals to choose between loyalty to their ethnic group and its ancestral heritage and becoming a full member of the adopted host society. Members of immigrant ethnic minorities may think they face such a choice. However, the integration-pluralism approach creates a conceptual space allowing for the possibility of stable multiple group memberships. Whether this possibility exists in reality may depend on such factors as the distribution of resources across groups and the institutional and cultural opportunities offered within the host society. In the right circumstances, members of immigrant ethnic groups may achieve full membership in the host society yet retain various specific ethnic attributes.

This focus on plural group memberships shifts our attention to social dynamics that favor the persistence of ethnic minority groups and whether they promote or obstruct progress toward inclusion in or attachment to the host society. From a normative point of view, this focus values the principle of cultural freedom. It matters not only whether minorities become assimilated but also why they do or don't. Members of immigrant minority groups may seek mobility through cultural assimilation, but whether cultural conformity is in fact a requirement for mobility remains an important theoretical and empirical question.

Critique of Integration

Compared with assimilation, the integration approach underplays the importance of group social boundaries that impede inclusion in highly unequal and race-conscious societies in which a dominant group retains the power to exclude members of identifiable minority groups from important arenas. Evidence from the United States underscores the importance of exclusionary mechanisms anchored in boundary setting by the dominant majority, which uses such mechanisms to maintain its advantages.

Residential segregation is a prime example. The inequalities across residential contexts—for example, in school quality or the risk of teenagers being recruited into illegal activity—play a key role in transmitting social disadvantages across generations (Krivo, Peterson, and Kuhl 2009; Sampson and Sharkey 2008). Moreover, because the dominant white population monopolizes neighborhoods with the best resources and amenities, gaining access to these resources depends largely on the ability to integrate socially with the majority population. Considerable research demonstrates that economic success does not guarantee that minorities will gain such access. The evidence is clear that, because of individual and institutionalized discrimination, members of some minorities, especially those in which African descent is prominent (not only African Americans, but also many Puerto Ricans and Dominicans), have limited ability to settle in white neighborhoods.

The assimilation perspective thus underscores how important it is to reduce the salience of ethno-racial boundaries and undercut the exclusionary processes rooted in them. Eastern European Jews and Japanese Americans are two groups whose position shifted through such a process. These examples lead to a second criticism of integration theory: namely, if socioeconomic success yields some degree of social integration with the mainstream majority, assimilation may be just a matter of time.

The case of American Jews seems especially telling in this respect. Their initial economic successes frequently came through entrepreneurial activities in specific niches that depended on a sense of shared ethnicity. They also devoted considerable energy to establishing the institutional foundations for a Jewish social world that would confine the social relationships of their children. Nevertheless, after remaining low through the early post–World War II period, the Jewish intermarriage rate rose sharply in the 1960s, reaching about 50 percent in the last decades of the century. A great deal of research has measured the religious affiliations of intermarried families and finds that the majority are detached from the Jewish group to a greater or lesser extent.

These mutual critiques hint at a possible resolution. The integration approach may work best in selective immigration settings where groups bring significant human capital and other resources (most notably Canada) or where welfare states reduce inequalities (some western European and Nordic countries). The assimilation approach may work best in immigration settings that reward groups that quickly adjust to mainstream norms and values regardless of whether they bring in high human capital (most notably the United States). As noted in the first two chapters, these main differences are related to historical differences in the conception of migration and differences in national institutional arrangements that originate from different conceptions of the role of the nation-state in creating equal opportunities for their citizens.

Critique of Cohesion

Assimilation and integration perspectives both see overall social cohesion as a goal but rarely study it because their methods address cohesion only at the individual level. Public attitudes may set cultural prerequisites for cohesion in an arbitrary manner, subject to value judgments and personal bias. This is evident in recent European experiences of backlash against multiculturalism. Instances of unrest or violence within immigrant communities have led the mainstream to question whether particular groups hold values that are incompatible with mainstream values, for example, regarding the status of women or the role of religion in public life. Research on the prevalence of particular values within minority groups may reveal something about the impact on individual assimilation or integration but provides little evidence of the implications for social cohesion.

The concept of integration should encompass not only questions of equal participation but also feelings of belonging or commitment to the host society, based on concerns about overall social cohesion. Clearly equality and social cohesion are quite different criteria, though very likely related. Huge inequality, however, may threaten feelings of belonging and therefore cohesion, though loyalty to the host society could override discontent based on a sense of being unfairly treated.

IMPLICATIONS FOR COMPARATIVE RESEARCH

Can we apply the same analytical grid to the experiences of the children of immigrants in western Europe and United States? The welfare state and public policies definitely play a crucial role in Europe, but their role is relatively neglected in the United States. Most European countries have targeted integration policies toward immigrants, sometimes explicitly at their second generations. Conversely, affirmative action and equality policies implemented in the United States have a significant unintended impact on the outcomes of immigrants and second generations (Kasinitz et al. 2008; Alba 2009). The U.S. literature merely mentions the problematic role of citizenship, but it is a key dimension in European studies (Bauböck 2006; Bloemraad 2007). In Europe, different citizenship regimes create different statuses for the second generation that influence their access to formal rights. These regimes have shaped political participation and political expression, which in turn explain variations in civic assimilation. Conversely, the role of illegality, that is, the situation of undocumented migrants, tends to be critical in the United States but is practically ignored in Europe.

These contrasting institutional frameworks influence the socioeconomic trajectories experienced by immigrants and their children and channel how they organize themselves, in part by defining their access to political representation and determining their impact on public policy. Theories of incorporation should thus account for the consequences of policies and laws and institutional differences across countries.

Comparisons across countries also recognize how nations differ in assessing the success of the immigrant settlement process. However, comparison may occur in different modalities. An observer situated within one national context can learn about it by comparing it with others. Less frequently, an observer situated above all the cases can attempt to arrive at broader generalizations. In the first case, the researcher may use her own national yardstick, because national context determines the issues of concern. The second requires researchers to employ multiple concepts and theories so that the analysis reflects the perspectives and issues significant within all the national situations.

With this difference in mind, empirical indicators need to be viewed in terms of their relevance or importance according to the different approaches. Ideally, one should not restrict analysis to those indicators for which data are most easily available but consider the indicators that are important or relevant. Benefitting from roughly comparable data gathered for just such a purpose, this volume uses indicators of labor market status, educational attainment, residential location, citizenship (for immigrants), political participation, identity, and social-cultural orientation. Here, we comment on the relative importance of two research topics—labor markets and cultural differences—and how they compare with the others.

Many studies focus on the labor market status of immigrant minorities as a significant aspect of assimilation, integration, and social cohesion. Commonly used indicators include labor force participation, occupation, earnings, and career mobility. In addition, comparative researchers keep a close eye on gender differences in how educational attainment relates to job opportunities across settings for immigrants and their children. At the same time, the significance of these indicators may vary across settings. For example, unemployment and self-employment have different social meanings and entail different material conditions in the United States as compared with Europe, because social benefits differ and entrepreneurship plays different roles. Poverty levels are important across all settings, but in Europe the policy goal lies more often in preserving the welfare state, whereas the goal in the United States is to avoid welfare dependency.

Cultural indicators such as minority identities, community attachments, or residential locations may be important across all contexts but may have potentially more negative implications for social or economic inclusion in some settings than others. Our discussion of assimilation, integration, and social cohesion suggests how scholars in different settings have different views about these matters. Overall social distance may matter more in societies that expect immigrants to assimilate, whereas pluralist societies may value cultural differences. Societies that value cohesion may interpret or value specific cultural differences in terms of their perceived implication for cohesion. When they view immigration positively, they may be more concerned about whether immigrants are satisfied, not just whether immigrants meet social expectations.

The chapters that follow compare education and labor market outcomes as well as social and cultural trends across the Atlantic. Education and labor market indicators are somewhat easier to transfer across the Atlantic, though their consequences vary a good deal. Common indicators for social and cultural incorporation are much more difficult to establish across the

Atlantic, and different national contexts view and judge the outcomes in very different ways.

This chapter has interrogated the concepts of immigrant assimilation and integration, the so-called dependent variable. However, comparative research also requires careful analysis of the independent variables, including characteristics of the host society as well as of the various immigrant groups. Which independent variables have salience can affect the choice of dependent variable. One important comparative challenge is how to commensurate minority groups from quite different national origins. In the United States, minority groups include not only African Americans, Puerto Ricans, and Mexican Americans that have been citizens for many generations but recent immigrants from Latin America, East Asia, South Asia, the Middle East, and many other parts of the world. Europe lacks native minority groups of similar scale, so its minorities include Turks, Moroccans and other North Africans, and sub-Saharan Africans. To control, however roughly, for this great heterogeneity in immigrant and minority experiences, we focus on children of immigrant parents with similarly disadvantaged socioeconomic backgrounds: second-generation Mexicans and Dominicans on the U.S. side and second-generation Turks on the European side. By comparing similarly situated groups, we will be better prepared to face the conceptual and analytic challenges outlined here.

PART II

RESULTS

CHAPTER 4

SUCCESS AGAINST ALL ODDS

MAURICE CRUL, MIN ZHOU, JENNIFER LEE, PHILIPP SCHNELL,
AND ELIF KESKINER

Scholars have given considerable attention to the educational pathways of the new second generation, the children of immigrants to the United States and western Europe who came of age at the turn of the twenty-first century. Social scientists on both sides of the Atlantic have consistently reported significant differences in academic outcomes among second-generation youth and across national-origin groups. Some do extraordinarily well, yet others fail to graduate from high school. Outcomes vary systematically by group. Second-generation Mexicans in the United States and second-generation Turks in northwestern Europe tend to fall toward the low end. Researchers have studied both groups extensively because a great many of them are dropping out of high school (in the United States) or failing even to complete lower secondary education (in Europe). Despite high dropout rates, a small but visible group of young people from these backgrounds manage to beat the odds and achieve university educations. Although they may be anomalous, they are too numerous to ignore, yet researchers and policymakers continue to focus on failures.

Our aim is to use these success stories to better understand the pathways and mechanisms that enable the second generation to achieve a good education (or prevent it), drawing on our previous research (Crul 2000a; Crul and Vermeulen 2006; Crul and Heering 2008; Zhou and Lee 2007; Zhou et al. 2008). Specifically, we compare successful second-generation Mexicans in Los Angeles with their Turkish counterparts in Berlin, Frankfurt, Rotterdam, and Strasbourg. The strategy behind this comparative approach is to identify similarities and differences across national contexts.

We foreground the experiences and practices of successful immigrant youth to demonstrate how institutional arrangements in school and external resources account for their success (Crul and Holdaway 2009; Crul and Schneider 2009; Crul, Schneider, and Lelie 2012). Crucial to this effort are a detailed reconstruction of school careers and, more precisely, an inventory of the opportunities and constraints these students face during their education and the pathways they take to adulthood (Crul 2000b; Zhou and Lee 2007; Zhou et al. 2008). We analyze both quantitative and qualitative data to explain what enables some immigrant youth of severely disadvantaged backgrounds to succeed, how they have tapped into additional resources in their quest to get ahead, and which institutional and social settings have helped promote their success.

Our comparative analyses are twofold. First, we analyze survey data collected in Los Angeles and select cities in northwestern Europe to look at the pathways successful second-generation youths have taken. Second, we turn to qualitative data from in-depth, life history interviews to highlight illustrative cases of high academic achievement despite disadvantaged backgrounds. The interviews allow us to examine closely the choices made, the conditions under which they were made, and the resources that allowed for these choices. Combining the quantitative and qualitative data allows us to identify some key mechanisms for success. We gain analytical mileage from comparing similarly situated groups across different contexts in making more general claims about the mechanisms of success than if we focused on only one national setting or on only one ethnic group.

Data

We draw on two large surveys of the new second generation: the IIMMLA and TIES. We also analyze face-to-face, in-depth interview data from two qualitative studies, as well as census data.

As outlined earlier, we chose to compare the experiences of second-generation Mexican and Turkish youths because of their similarly disadvantaged backgrounds. Although these groups differ in important ways—most notably religion—both have parents who were poor labor migrants who arrived in their host countries with low levels of education into contexts where manufacturing employment was declining. The media and public policy debates have negatively stereotyped both groups. Examining the successful outcomes of young people from such backgrounds allows us to assess how different educational systems sort people across opportunities and, most important, to identify the unique pathways and mechanisms for succeeding within them.

We study second-generation Mexicans in one metropolitan context, Los Angeles. They come from by far the largest immigrant group in the United States and in Los Angeles. Mexicans make up more than 30 percent of immigrants to the United States and 32 percent of immigrants in greater Los Angeles. Los Angeles is particularly interesting because nearly two-thirds of Los Angeles's residents (62 percent) are either immigrants or the children of immigrants.

We compare the second-generation Turks in Europe across four metropolitan settings—Berlin, Frankfurt, Rotterdam, and Strasbourg. These are the largest Turkish communities in Germany, the Netherlands, and France, and their educational systems contrast in interesting ways with that of the United States. The German case differs most because of its strongly vocationally oriented system. The French case is most similar because its primary and secondary system is largely comprehensive and its higher education is selective. The Dutch case is a mix of the German and French systems, including both a vocationally oriented track and elements of a comprehensive school system, such as intermediary classes and access to higher education through middle vocational education.

In a comparison of the U.S. and European settings, the two-year community colleges (or junior colleges) in the United States serve similar roles as the middle vocational colleges in the Netherlands; both institutions potentially provide students access to higher education through less competitive, more inclusive channels. By contrasting the U.S. and European school systems, we show the impact of different institutional arrangements but also highlight how each educational system provides some opportunities for educational mobility to second-generation Mexicans and Turks.

MEXICAN MIGRATION TO LOS ANGELES

Mexican migration to the southwest United States was an integral part of the development in commercial agriculture, mining, light industry, and the railroad in the late nineteenth century. At the outset, Mexican immigrant

labor was needed for economic expansion, but later it became a conve-
nient scapegoat during periods of economic contraction (Daniel 1981;
Sánchez 1993). The increasing demand for unskilled migrant labor during
World War II attracted a continual flow of Mexican immigrants to cross
the border—with or without legal documentation (Durand, Malone, and
Massey 2003; Massey and Espinosa 1997; Monroy 1999). U.S. ambivalence about Mexican migration was epitomized by Operation Wetback in
1954, when the authorities apprehended Mexicans—regardless of their
legal status—and forcibly deported them (Lee and Bean 2010). The Mexican population in Los Angeles grew rapidly over the past century, tripling
from 1920 (30,000) to 1930 (97,000) before World War II and growing
exponentially since the U.S. immigration reform of 1965. Today, 3.1 million of Los Angeles County's 10 million residents are of Mexican origin.

Past and contemporary Mexican immigrants largely hail from rural
backgrounds and arrive with little education and or job skills. Until recently,
many sojourning workers were concerned primarily with job opportunities
(Massey 1986; Sánchez 1993). Mexican immigrants tend to find work in
agribusiness and construction in the Southwest, as well as in textile mills
and chicken processing plants in other parts of the United States (Massey
1986). Mexican Angelinos—native or immigrant, mestizo or mulatto—have
faced structural barriers to mobility (Acuña 1996; Monroy 1999; Sánchez
1993; Telles and Ortiz 2008).

As it has been for the children of all immigrants, education has always
been the key to social mobility and the American Dream for the children and
grandchildren of Mexican immigrants (Valencia 2002). However, Mexicans
face unique challenges in their quest for a quality education. They are highly
concentrated in inner-city neighborhoods plagued by poverty, inadequately
funded schools, family disruption, single parenthood, teenage pregnancy,
youth gangs, violent crimes, drug abuse, and alcoholism. Although second-
generation Mexicans often live in families with both parents, most work full
time—or even hold multiple jobs, working different shifts—in low-wage
industries. The parents' severe lack of human, social, and cultural capital
leaves them dependent on their children as translators and cultural brokers
with the outside world (Lee 2002). In addition, the parents' low levels of
human capital and their need to juggle the demands of work and household
responsibilities often prevent them from giving much tangible help to support their children's education. Adding to their disadvantage, most second-
generation Mexicans attend poorly performing public schools with high
dropout rates and a large concentration of minority students from low-
income families. Most second-generation Mexican students in Los Angeles

face a daunting cumulative disadvantage that can severely truncate their educational and social mobility (Zhou 1997; Zhou and Lee 2007).

TURKISH MIGRATION TO WESTERN EUROPE

The first Turkish labor migrants came on their own initiative to Germany in the 1950s and to the Netherlands and France at the beginning of the 1960s. The continuing demand for low-skilled workers in the textile and metal industries triggered a chain migration by relatives and friends, and official labor migration agreements with Turkey were signed at the end of the 1960s. European industries needed a new source of low-skilled labor and recruited the majority of these first-generation Turkish guest workers from the lowest socioeconomic strata in their home country. Labor recruitment was aimed only at men; women came only much later to join their spouses. The peak of labor migration occurred between 1970 and 1974, after which official migration halted (Crul and Doomernik 2003). An estimated 4 million people of Turkish descent now live in Europe, half in Germany (Crul and Vermeulen 2003a). The recession in the 1980s hit the industrial sector hard, and many first-generation Turkish men lost their jobs. Because most Turkish women were not employed, many Turkish immigrant families came to depend on welfare as a result.

The change in the political climate in Europe since 9/11 and the wars in Iraq and Afghanistan have made matters even more difficult for Turkish immigrants and their children. As one of the largest Muslim populations in Europe, the Turkish community (along with other Muslims) has increasingly been the target of hostility, racism, and discrimination. The rise of anti-immigrant populist parties across Europe sends the message that many Europeans believe that Muslims do not belong in Europe. These sentiments are similar to those expressed by some in the American Tea Party Movement who hold strong anti-immigrant sentiments, aimed primarily at Mexican immigrants.

Like children of Mexican immigrants in Los Angeles, second-generation Turks are from poorly educated families. Table 4.1 shows the educational levels of the fathers and mothers in three categories: primary school, secondary school (high school), and postsecondary school (university or higher vocational). The majority of parents had only a primary school education and mothers generally had even less education than fathers. First-generation Turks in Berlin and Frankfurt are, on average, the least educated among those in the four cities. Like their Mexican counterparts, many Turkish immigrant parents are unable to help their children with

TABLE 4.1   Parents of Second-Generation Turks

	Berlin	Frankfurt	Rotterdam	Strasbourg
Speaking the national language				
Father hardly or not at all	1.6%	3.2%	5.7%	15.4%
Mother hardly or not at all	19.4	18.0	26.0	31.4
Father's education				
Primary school at the most	74.3	72.6	50.5	54.4
Secondary school	24.7	22.6	40.8	41.5
Postsecondary	1.0	4.8	8.8	4.1
Mother's education				
Primary school at the most	77.8	72.3	68.9	70.2
Secondary school	22.2	26.9	25.8	28.4
Postsecondary	0.0	0.8	5.3	1.4
Parents married	95.3	95.6	82.5	93.3

Source: Authors' compilation based on TIES survey 2007, 2008 (data not yet publicly available).
Note: The TIES survey comprises eight separate national data sets, collected by Institute for Studies on Migrations (IEM), Comillas Pontifical University, Spain; Swiss Forum for Migration and Population Studies (SFM), Neuchâtel, Switzerland; Netherlands Inter-disciplinary Demographic Institute (NIDI), The Hague, Netherlands; Austrian Acad-emy of Sciences (ÖAW), Vienna, Austria; the European Research Centre on Migration and Ethnic Relations (ERCOMER), Katholieke Universiteit Leuven, Belgium; National Institute for Demographic Studies (INED), Paris, France; Institute for Migration Research and Intercultural Studies (IMIS), University of Osnabrück, Germany; Centre for Research in International Migration and Ethnic Relations (CEIFO), Stockholm University, Sweden. The TIES national surveys will be made publicly available by the national TIES partners individually, but were not yet available at the time of publication.

school work. In fact, many parents have difficulty speaking and read-ing the national language, which further disadvantages their children because European school systems expect parents to guide and support their children in school matters—a responsibility for which these Turk-ish parents are woefully ill equipped.

MEXICANS IN LOS ANGELES

U.S. Census data offer a comprehensive profile of the socioeconomic sta-tus (SES) of young Mexican Americans (native and immigrant) in Los Angeles. As table 4.2 shows, young Mexican Angelinos (age twenty-five to thirty-nine) are disadvantaged compared not only with non-Hispanic whites ut also in some instances with non-Hispanic blacks. They have less education, lower rates of labor force participation (but higher rates

TABLE 4.2   Socioeconomic Characteristics of Young Mexican
Americans in Los Angeles

	Mexican	Non-Hispanic Black	Non-Hispanic White
Education			
Percentage no high school diploma	55.4	18.1	9.7
Percentage high school diploma	22.1	27.8	21.1
Percentage some college (including associate's degrees)	15.9	35.0	29.3
Percentage bachelor's degree or higher	6.6	19.1	40.0
Labor market status			
Percentage in labor force	65.8	73.4	80.4
Percentage working full time (thirty-five hours or more per week)	86.8	84.3	83.3
Percentage unemployment	5.3	9.1	4.4
Income			
Median family income in 1999 (in dollars)	$37,600	$40,100	$64,700
Earnings (full time, thirty-five hours or more per week)			
Percentage earning $30,000 or less	82.8	57.6	39.2
Percentage earning $30,001 to $49,999	12.0	26.6	29.0
Percentage earning $50,000 to $74,999	3.8	11.3	18.7
Percentage earning $75,000 or more	1.4	4.5	13.1
Home ownership	42.6	34.0	51.1
Family situation			
Percentage married couple families	69.1	37.3	56.4
Number of children under eighteen in household			
Percentage with no child	27.8	46.0	54.8
Percentage with one child	17.6	20.0	15.8
Percentage with two or more children	54.6	34.0	29.4
Incarceration (percentage institutional group quarter)	0.8	3.8	1.2
Total N in sample	1,075,922	263,339	964,025

Source: Authors' compilation based on Census 2000, 5 Percent Public Use Microdata
Sample (U.S. Census Bureau 2000).

TABLE 4.3   Parents of Second-Generation Mexicans

Parents	Second-Generation Mexican	Native Black	Native White
English proficiency			
Father with no English proficiency	7.6	—	—
Mother with no English proficiency	10.7	—	—
Father's education			
Father with no high school diploma	47.3	10.9	3.5
Father high school	29.7	44.1	31.5
Father post high school	22.9	45.0	65.0
Mother's education			
Mother with no high school diploma	48.2	9.0	4.4
Mother high school	31.7	34.3	36.7
Mother post high school	20.1	56.8	58.8
Family situation			
Parents married	66.4	43.3	51.9
Parents owning a home	71.0	67.5	89.2

Source: Authors' compilation based on IIMMLA (Rumbaut et al. 2004).

of full-time employment and lower rates of unemployment) than blacks, lower earnings among those who worked full time, and lower median family household incomes. They fared slightly better than blacks in terms of home ownership, however. One advantage they have over blacks and whites is their intact family structure, despite the higher likelihood that their families include young children. They were also less likely to be in local jails than blacks or whites. These figures suggest that, on average, young Mexican Angelinos may be moving ahead of their parents, but they cluster in working-class positions rather than achieve middle-class status.

IIMMLA data for the U.S.-born children of Mexican immigrants confirm some of these general patterns. Table 4.3 shows that second-generation Mexicans came from families with very low human capital; about half of their parents had not completed high school, but they seemed to benefit from an intact family structure, in which both parents were present.

Table 4.4 shows how the children of Mexican immigrants fared as they entered adulthood. The most striking finding is the enormous intergenerational mobility evinced by the second generation; nearly half of Mexican immigrant mothers and fathers lack a high school diploma, but the figure drops to 12.5 percent in one generation. Moreover, close to one-

TABLE 4.4   Outcomes of Los Angeles's Second Generation

	Mexican	Native Black	Native White
Education: highest diploma or present level of schooling for those still studying			
No high school diploma	12.5	10.6	5.8
High school (diploma)	36.5	35.1	30.3
Trade school (diploma)	11.3	6.9	3.8
Two-year college (associate's degree)	16.7	20.2	10.5
Four-year college or graduate school (BA or MA)	23.0	27.2	49.6
Labor market status*			
Unemployment	10.7	12.1	4.7
Earnings			
$20,000 or less	74.4	73.7	60.2
$20,001 to $30,000	17.4	17.8	21.7
$30,001 to $50,000	7.6	6.9	12.2
Over $50,000	0.7	1.7	5.9
Home ownership	27.4	18.0	35.6
Family situation			
Married	37.1	25.9	44.6
Mean age when first child was born	22.1	22.3	25.4
Having children at teen age	14.8	12.0	2.9
Incarceration	11.2	19.3	10.6
Total in sample	553	401	402

Source: Authors' compilation based on IIMMLA (Rumbaut et al. 2004).
BA = bachelor's degree; MA = master's degree.
*Among those who are in the labor force.

quarter graduate from a four-year college, and another 16.7 percent earn an associate's degree. The clear pattern of intergenerational mobility is often missed when examining educational attainment cross-sectionally rather than intergenerationally. The gap in college education with whites, however, remains large (26.9 percentage points). Early childbearing may be problematic because it poses risk factors for social mobility, especially among women (Shearer et al. 2002; Portes and Rumbaut 2006). Mexican second-generation young people are as likely to have had children as teenagers as blacks and are five times more likely than whites. However, incarceration rates among second-generation Mexicans are relatively low and closely resemble those of native-born whites (Rumbaut 2005).

Pico Union, an inner-city neighborhood in downtown Los Angeles, is typical of the neighborhoods where second-generation Mexicans grow up. The 2000 census reports that more than three-quarters of the residents are Hispanic (40 percent Mexican, 14 percent Central American, 24 percent other Hispanic, along with 12 percent Asian, and few whites). More than three-quarters of neighborhood residents are foreign born, and a significant portion are undocumented. Two-thirds of Pico Union's residents have not completed a high school education, and 42 percent of the families live in poverty; the median household income is less than $18,000 (versus $42,000 for Los Angeles County). Most residents of Pico Union live in overcrowded rental housing. They are aware of the neighborhood's adverse reputation because of the high frequency of car thefts and burglaries and the visibility of hot spots for prostitution, gangs, drug-dealing, and public alcohol consumption and urination (Zhou 2009).

The local public schools are overwhelmingly Hispanic. For example, 88 percent of the nearly 5,000 students enrolled in one neighborhood high school are Hispanic, the majority of whom are Mexican. Nearly half (45 percent) of the students are classified as English-language learners (formerly limited English proficiency), and more than 75 percent qualify for free or subsidized lunches—an indicator of family poverty. Not only is the school understaffed, but its poor Hispanic students are also low achieving. Fewer than 13 percent of ninth, tenth, and eleventh graders score at or above the 50th national percentile ranking on the 1999 Stanford 9 test for reading (and less than 28 percent do so for math). Additionally, the high school dropout rate among Hispanic students—82 percent—is astronomically high (Zhou 2009). More students in this school are likely to drop out than to graduate.

Furthering the disadvantages they face in the school context is the situation of the immigrant parents. Mexican immigrants in Los Angeles have low socioeconomic backgrounds and often less than an elementary school education. In some cases, they are in the United States illegally. California has recently passed a number of initiatives that have negative consequences for the children of immigrants, including Proposition 209, which abolished affirmative action in college admission, and Proposition 227, which dismantled bilingual education. Funding for public education has also been cut back (Acuña 1996; Padilla and Gonzalez 2001; Telles and Ortiz 2008).

Remarkably, despite these huge disadvantages, about one in five second-generation Mexicans has either enrolled in a four-year college or graduate school or already earned a BA or master's (MA) degree. When we examined this group more closely, we found that its members followed a starkly different life course than the average second-generation Mexican in our sample. For instance, they marry later, postpone having children, and have fewer children. They are more likely to marry a non-Hispanic partner who also has some college education: two-thirds of these partners had at least some college education. Their higher levels of education also resulted in better labor market outcomes; both partners usually work full time, and about 40 percent have an annual household income greater than $70,000.

One-third of the successful group of second-generation Mexicans work in the educational or social service sectors, and many (about 30 percent) volunteer in community organizations. Only a few (10 percent) work in professional jobs. That is, the educational mobility of the most successful second-generation Mexicans has not yet translated into prestigious jobs. However, nearly one-third are homeowners, and few have ever been arrested or incarcerated. In sum, the mobility pathways and future prospects for this group and their children look very different compared to those for other 1.5- or second-generation Mexicans in Los Angeles.

SECOND-GENERATION TURKS IN EUROPE

Members of the Turkish second generation in Rotterdam, Strasbourg, Berlin, and Frankfurt also overwhelmingly grow up in the poorest neighborhoods in these cities. Although these neighborhoods had large concentrations of Turkish inhabitants, in no case did Turks form the majority. Most neighborhoods have a mix of immigrant and non-immigrant inhabitants. One example is Het Oude Noorden in Rotterdam, which has 18,000 inhabitants and ranks as one of the poorest in the Netherlands. More than three-quarters of the apartments are social housing (similar to public housing in the United States). Children from the larger Turkish families usually do not have their own bedroom or a separate place to study. The neighborhood is also home to one of the lowest performing schools in the city. Moreover, many neighborhood residents are unemployed and Het Oude Noorden has a higher crime rate than the rest of the city. The police have therefore marked the neighborhood as a high risk zone, which allows them to search residents for weapons and drugs without cause in the street.

Given these poor neighborhood and family conditions, it comes as little surprise that many second-generation Turkish children perform poorly in school. As noted in table 4.5, about one-third of the second-generation Turks in the four cities do not study beyond compulsory lower secondary school (which is the equivalent to middle school in the

TABLE 4.5   Outcomes for the Second-Generation Turks

	Berlin	Frankfurt	Rotterdam	Strasbourg
Citizenship status				
Citizenship	89.7	77.5	94.0	98.4
Citizenship by birth (versus naturalization)	91.1	83.0	49.5	48.9
Education: highest diploma for those who left school or present level of schooling for those still studying				
No lower secondary diploma	4.7	1.4	12.0	6.7
Lower secondary school (diploma)	29.4	26.7	19.0	12.2
Apprenticeship and CAP/BEP (diploma; equivalent to trade school)	48.3	56.9	13.3	31.1
Upper secondary and MBO (diploma; equivalent to associate's degree)	10.9	8.2	28.1	21.1
Higher education (BA or MA)	6.7	6.7	27.6	29.0
Labor market status*				
Unemployment (ILO definition)	14.2	9.2	9.9	11.9
Home ownership (house owned by parents in parentheses)	12.3 (8.8)	14.7 (12.5)	19.5 (8.8)	10.3 (33.9)
Total in sample	253	250	263	240

Source: Authors' compilation based on TIES survey 2007, 2008.
BA = bachelor's degree; MA = master's degree; CAP = Certificat d'aptitude professionnelle; BEP = brevet d'etudes professionelles; MBO = middelbaar beroeps onderwijs
(middle vocational education); ILO = International Labour Organisation.
*Among those in the labor force.

United States). European Union jargon refers to them as early school
leavers and officially labels them as at-risk youth. Additionally, many of
these pupils attended elementary schools where the majority of children
were of immigrant origin. Those who make it to secondary school often
end up in vocational schools with an even higher concentration of children of immigrants. Popularly referred to as ghetto schools, schools with
many second-generation students are known for high levels of violence
and high dropout rates.

Table 4.6   Higher Education, Second-Generation Turks
and Comparison Group of Native Parentage

	Berlin and Frankfurt		Rotterdam		Strasbourg	
	Percentage	N	Percentage	N	Percentage	N
Tertiary education						
Turks	6.7	34	27.6	72	29.0	78
Comparison group	19.7	96	56.9	144	69.8	111
Among those whose parents had primary school education at most						
Second-generation Turks	2.5		19.5		29.4	

Source: Authors' compilation based on TIES survey 2007, 2008.

This poor academic performance translates into poor employment outcomes: unemployment rates are high, especially among the early school leavers (see table 4.5). Many second-generation Turkish girls who leave school early never enter the labor market and instead become homemakers. The majority marry coethnic partners with similarly slim educational credentials. These young couples usually build their lives in the same working-class neighborhoods as their parents and, as a consequence, remain surrounded by people of Turkish origin.

Despite this bleak portrait, we can also point to a growing group of well-educated second-generation Turks who, like their Mexican-origin counterparts, achieve academic success in spite of the odds. Table 4.6 shows how many students are pursuing higher education at the time of the survey or already have a higher education diploma (BA or MA); their profiles also differ from those of their fellow ethnics. This group also postpones marriage, and both partners stay active in the labor market after marriage. As urban professionals, they earn considerable incomes. Like their Mexican American counterparts in Los Angeles, many high-achieving second-generation Turks work in the public sector as policymakers, social workers, and teachers. However, a growing group also work in finance, law, and economics—the three university subjects second-generation Turks most often study at university. They are among the few who are able to buy their own house or apartment in the city, and they often move to better parts of their parents' neighborhood or into less segregated neighborhoods altogether. They are assuming leading positions in community organizations and becoming more visible in local political parties (Crul and Heering 2008).

The size of the successful group differs considerably across European cities (see table 4.6). Turkish educational outcomes rank highest in Strasbourg and Rotterdam but lowest in Berlin and Frankfurt, as found in the TIES survey. (We combine the Berlin and Frankfurt samples to get a large enough group for comparative analysis.) In Strasbourg, four times as many second-generation Turks are in the higher education category than in Berlin and Frankfurt. The outcomes for the comparison group (people whose parents are both native born) show that this largely reflects national trends on tertiary education attendance, which in general is higher in France and the Netherlands than in the German-speaking countries. The differences between the cities remain equally large when we look only at those children whose parents did not attend school beyond the primary level.

THE STUDY OF SUCCESS

Maurice Crul and Jens Schneider (2010) argue that international comparison reveals the importance of the interplay between agency and institutional arrangements that have a major impact on educational and labor market outcomes. The local or national specifics of a national educational system become evident only when it is compared with school systems in other countries. Adopting this comparative approach enables us to point to both the institutional hindrances as well as the role of supportive educational institutional and familial systems in each national or local setting.

Mexican Angelinos in the United States

The children of Mexican immigrants are often considered to be at a higher risk of failure than other immigrant groups in the United States, not only because many arrive with little education but also because many enter as unauthorized migrants (Bean and Stevens 2003). Because Mexicans often start much further behind other immigrants, some observers fear that they will never be able to catch up to native-born Americans. This concern generates anxiety about whether Mexican Americans will become mired in the bottom rungs of the occupational and pay structure and form a permanent and largely undocumented urban underclass (Borjas 1999; Huntington 2004). However, in the IIMMLA survey, about one in five second-generation Mexicans defies this trajectory. This group has attained extraordinarily high levels of education, especially given their parents' poor human capital and the disadvantaged neighborhoods in which they were raised.

The results from IIMMLA survey show that the school careers of these successful students differ in three important ways from those of many of their second-generation Mexican peers. First, the successful students were significantly less likely to be placed in ESL (English as a second language) classes. Although all second-generation Mexicans are by definition U.S. born, many are placed in ESL classes in high school. Second, Mexicans who excelled in school were also significantly more likely to attend private or parochial schools. Despite their limited resources, some Mexican immigrant parents were able and willing to make a large financial investment in their children's education because they considered the local public schools to be of such poor quality.

Third, they were also more likely to be placed in honors or Advanced Placement (AP) classes in high school; the IIMMLA data show that about three-quarters of the students who went to college were placed in these more competitive tracks, providing second-generation Mexicans a different reference group than that available to those in the regular tracks. This informal tracking taught them to view college as an attainable goal, and the information that they gained in the honors and AP tracks also better prepared them to apply to college. Most, but not all, students who earned strong grades (As and Bs) were placed in honors classes or AP programs, though a small group report they mostly got As in high school but were not placed in an honors program or the AP track. This may be because the schools these students attended did not offer these programs, the respondents did not pursue these possibilities, or the students did not know about them. Of this smaller group, only one has a BA or MA diploma or is studying in a four-year college.

When we look at those who were in the honors program or AP tracks but did not enter a four-year college, we find that the majority finished high school but chose to attend a two-year community college rather than a four-year university. Some (13.3 percent) earned an associate's degree but did not transfer to a four-year university. The largest group, however, dropped out of community college in the first or second year without a degree. The critical point is that the success or failure of Mexican children is determined first in honors classes in high school but again later, in the initial years of college; many drop out of college at age eighteen or nineteen.

The IIMMLA data also reveal that neighborhood and community characteristics explain an important part of the college dropout patterns. The males in honors or AP classes who continued on to a four-year college were only a third as likely as those not in these classes to say that gangs and drugs had been a big problem in their neighborhood. Those who did not continue in college were twice as likely to have been arrested as those who did. Of the females who did not pursue further education, one-quarter married before they were twenty years old, and about 40 percent had a child by that age, which meant they had to juggle school and child care or drop out of school altogether. In short, neighborhood disadvantages, early marriage, and pregnancy among women had a significant impact on the success of second-generation Mexicans who enrolled in and completed college.

A further remarkable finding is the large group of older, part-time students enrolled in four-year colleges and graduate schools, most of whom reentered school while working (which is true for most working-class students in general). This finding reflects the determination of these students as well as the flexibility of the U.S. educational system that offers the possibility of a second chance at a college degree if a student did not pursue one immediately after high school.

In the sections that follow, we present two life histories of the Los Angeles respondents whose educational pathways diverged at critical junctures, which consequently lead to dissimilar outcomes.

Case Study, Danielle: No Excuses   Danielle is a thirty-four-year-old Mexican woman who immigrated to the United States at the age of one. Her parents entered the United States illegally but legalized themselves and their children after the Immigration Reform and Control Act (IRCA) immigration reform in 1986 when she was in the tenth grade. Danielle's legal status has therefore never hampered her educational opportunities. Given that her parents have only a general equivalency diploma, Danielle's educational intergenerational mobility is extraordinary. Not only has she graduated from college, but she has also earned a teaching certificate and holds a master's degree. We detail how she was able to achieve what she did despite poor parental human capital.

After leaving Mexico, Danielle's parents settled in a working-class neighborhood near Los Angeles and held blue-collar jobs. Her father worked in manufacturing and her mother worked in a factory as an assembler. Having witnessed how hard they labored and how little they earned in return, Danielle knew early on that she wanted to take a different path and become a professional.

Danielle's parents always stressed education and instilled the importance of attending college: college was simply expected. They knew that a college education would open doors for her that had been closed to them. Danielle also knew that she would need a college degree to fulfill her professional goal of becoming a teacher—a dream that her mother also had but was unable to realize. As Danielle explains, because her parents were unable to go to college, they were all the more adamant that all four of their daughters seize the opportunity.

Danielle enjoyed school, did well in her classes, and became actively involved in extracurricular activities such as softball and the drill team. A teenager with abundant energy, Danielle wanted to work part time during high school and got a job at a local car dealership to cover her personal expenses. Having witnessed her parents' struggle to make ends meet, Danielle could not imagine asking them for extra spending money. However, before she was allowed to accept the job, her father had a serious talk with her and made it very clear that she would be allowed to work only under the condition that she kept up her high grades. Vividly recalling this conversation, Danielle recognized the lesson: school should be her highest priority.

Danielle's efforts in high school earned her a 3.5 grade point average, and with guidance from her school's College Bound program, Danielle earned admission to several top four-year universities, including a University of California (UC) school. The College Bound program offered in Danielle's high school was critical because it helped guide her with information about the SAT exams as well as the college application process. This educational support system was critical because Danielle's parents (like many Mexican immigrant parents) did not know how to navigate the college admissions process, even though they desperately wanted their children to attend.

Although Danielle earned admission to a UC school, she decided to attend community college for a few years instead, given her family's limited financial resources. Not only was tuition much cheaper at the community college, but Danielle also saved money by living at home. Although she had to work part time during college to pay for her tuition, her parents helped as much as they could; they gave her $1,000 toward a car and also paid for her car insurance, which provided the means to go to classes. Danielle excelled in community college and eventually transferred to a four-year college where she received her bachelor's degree. After graduating from college, she earned her teaching credentials and a master's degree and then landed her dream job as a kindergarten teacher with an annual salary of $65,000 (more than her parents' combined salaries).

Danielle has achieved everything that she wanted—a college education, an advanced degree, a job as a teacher, and economic independence. What makes these achievements even more meaningful is that Danielle achieved what her mother had not been able to do for herself. Although Danielle recognizes that she has worked hard to get where she is, she firmly believes that the path to mobility is a simple one—education—open to all Americans. In fact, Danielle is extremely critical of Hispanics who do not prioritize education, including two of her siblings who did not make it to college. She is doing what she can to ensure that her youngest sister, who is still in high school, follows Danielle's path.

Although Danielle takes a strictly individualistic approach to her educational success and maintains that there are no excuses in life for not getting ahead, she had several important advantages. First, her parents were determined that she attend college and always reminded her that college was expected. Second, they prioritized school over work. Third, her high school provided a program—College Bound—that helped her through the admissions process. Finally, her parents were willing and able to help her financially while she attended college. Although Danielle might have succeeded without these advantages, it seems clear that they were essential to her paving her path to educational mobility.

Case Study, Armando: Family Obligations   Armando attended high school in a low-income neighborhood of Los Angeles where the majority of students were Latino or African American (Zhou et al. 2008, 52–53). "It was just basically a low end high school," Armando explained. "It's just baby-sit them [the students] and ship-them-out kind of place." Most students who attended Armando's high school did not take school seriously and were not college bound. Armando was an exception, even though his parents never pushed him to attend college. In fact, his parents were delighted that he graduated from high school—which neither of them had done. Armando always knew that he would go to college because he dreamed of becoming a doctor and knew that going to college and medical school was the only way he could reach this goal.

Because Armando's parents did not expect him to attend college, it is all the more remarkable that he learned about the college track in his high school and, furthermore, insisted on being placed in AP classes. The classes were a world apart from the regular ones in Armando's school; the students were serious and determined to go to college, and the teachers were eager to help them achieve their goal. Even today, Armando recalls the impact that his AP teachers have had in his life; they taught him not only how to write but also the importance of writing well. He fared well in his classes and received several awards for academic achievement.

His friends in his AP classes were also a pivotal part of his success and became the reference group by which he measured his success. Because of the competitive nature of AP classes, Armando felt that he had to do well. As he put it, "It was a little bit of keeping up with the Joneses kind of deal," with respect to grades. "They did that well. I am going to do that too." With friends who excelled in their classes, Armando felt he had no choice but to perform just as well because he did not want to be an out-sider. These two school resources—the AP classes and his AP friends—were instrumental in keeping Armando on track during high school.

Armando's efforts earned him admission into several top four-year uni-versities, including an Ivy League university and a high-ranking UC school. Weighing his college options, he chose to attend a UC school because it was the only affordable option, given his family's limited financial resources. He also calculated that he would be able to live at home while attending the UC school. During his first two years of college, Armando immersed himself in course work to fulfill his premedical requirements and chose to major in biology. He worked part time to pay for his tuition, which he fully covered himself, without any financial help from his parents.

Although Armando skillfully juggled the demands of work and school during his first two years of college, he veered off course during the third. In his junior year, his parents decided to start their own business and expected Armando to do the books and taxes and his sisters to answer phones and deal with customers. Initially, Armando was excited about his parents' new business venture because he thought that this would enable them to secure a better future. The demands on Armando's time increased as his parents' business grew, and because he was optimistic about the prospects of his family's business, he decided to go to college only part time. Armando poured his time and energy into the family business, gave up his dream of becoming a doctor, and switched to what he felt was a less demanding major, art history. In his view (and that of his parents), a college degree became secondary because the business was growing and profitable. Here, we see an enormous difference between Armando's and Danielle's parents' priorities and trajectories; whereas Danielle's parents insisted that she prioritize school over work, Armando's parents insisted that he prioritize work over school.

Unfortunately, Armando's bet did not pay off: things did not turn out as he had hoped. After a few years, Armando's parents separated, and his father took the business, which was in his name, leaving nothing for the rest of the family. With the family business gone, Armando decided to return to school full time, but having limited college to part time for years, he found the transition to full-time college far more difficult than he had anticipated. Although Armando eventually graduated, it took him eight years to do so. Moreover, his bachelor's degree was not in biology, as he had originally planned, but in art history. With that major, Armando had a difficult time landing a job. Eventually he was hired as a bus driver for the Los Angeles Metropolitan Transport Authority (MTA). Armando recently learned that he has a heart condition that makes him ineligible to drive a city bus, so he is currently unemployed and receives support through disability and Social Security.

At the age of forty-two, Armando lives with his mother and is now taking accounting classes at a local community college, with the hope that someday he may find work as an accountant. Reflecting on his college years, Armando wishes he could turn back time and do things differently. If given the chance, he would have chosen to attend the Ivy League school because he would have lived on the East Coast and not have felt such a strong obligation to help his family with the business. As Armando thinks about what might have been, he believes that he would have stayed in school full time, majored in biology, gone to medical school, and become a doctor.

Our analysis of these life histories of second-generation Mexicans reveals some significant mechanisms that serve to neutralize advantages or circumvent disadvantages (Zhou et al. 2008, 57–59). First, family educational expectations can have varied effects on children's outcomes. On the positive side, high expectations often contribute to desirable academic outcomes. Almost all of our respondents reported that their parents valued education and, moreover, expected that their children's education would exceed their own. However, family educational expectations can be at odds with other family obligations, such as the need to work to supplement the family household income. In low-SES families in particular, economic survival often stands in the way of laying a strong foundation for economic mobility, creating a conflict between working and school. As our study reveals, the burden of work often impedes or stalls educational achievement. For the children of Mexican immigrants, working during school was customary, not only for pocket money but also to help support their families. For second-generation Mexicans, having to work to support oneself and one's family while attending school can interfere with one's educational trajectory. Second, access to public resources is of paramount importance, especially for national-origin groups who are disadvantaged by low parental SES.

Our study confirms two major findings from existing research. First, most immigrant children from low-income families attend urban public schools, but those who have access to more competitive academic tracks, AP courses, and quality after-school programs tend to fare much better than their peers. This suggests that access to rigorous academic programs and supplementary after-school resources matters, especially for disadvantaged immigrant youth. Second, community colleges serve as bridging mechanisms for upward social mobility (Callan and Finney 2003; Portes and Fernandez-Kelly 2008; Szelényi and Chang 2010). Many of our respondents reported having taken the route of community colleges, either as steppingstones to four-year colleges or universities or to earn certificates and licenses that enabled them to seek jobs in skilled trades (for example, as teacher's assistants, lab technicians, dental assistants, and paramedics) or to develop their own businesses.

Second-Generation Turks in Europe

In the case of second-generation Mexicans, informal selection into the AP or honors tracks in high school, the neighborhood and community context, and the financial situation of the families are important factors in explaining success and failure. We now contrast the American case with that of the second-generation Turks in three European countries. The case that differs most starkly is Germany. In contrast to the United States, the German school system selects a formal track for children as early as age ten; they are selected either for Gymnasium or for Hauptschule or Realschule (the two last tracks both potentially lead to apprenticeships afterward). Fewer than 10 percent of second-generation Turks enter Gymnasium (the academic track). Of the 10 percent who take the academic track, even fewer actually make it into higher education. Of the second-generation children from poorly educated families, the majority have Turkish parents who attended only primary school or, at most, a few years of secondary school. Few survive further selection in the academic track. Early selection makes the period of preschool and elementary school the most important factor in determining academic success in the German system.

Among European countries, the school system in France is most similar to that of the United States. In Strasbourg, as in the rest of the country, selection does not take place until age fifteen (the end of college, which is similar to high school). At that point, students are selected into either a general or technological lyceum or a vocational track. Almost half of the second-generation Turks go to a general or technological lyceum, which, in principle, gives direct access into university. The group in lyceum is equal in size to the group of second-generation Mexican students (about 40 percent) that is tracked into an honors or AP program. Both comprehensive school systems enable children of disadvantaged family backgrounds to attend more academically rigorous tracks in secondary school. The most notable difference is that French students usually gain direct access to university, whereas second-generation Mexican students in the United States generally first attend a community college and often drop out before they graduate. The choice of a two-year college rather than a more prestigious

four-year university is due partly to the less rigorous admissions requirements and partly to the lower cost of community colleges, the latter of
which is not a salient factor in France because its educational system is
heavily subsidized by the government.

Like in the United States, neighborhood contexts play an important
role in students' ability to continue in higher education and obtain a
degree. Unfortunately, the TIES survey did not ask about incarceration.
However, we can get some idea of students' high school environment to
gauge their school and neighborhood context. Almost half the students
on the academic track in Strasbourg who did not continue into higher education attended schools where more than three-quarters were of immigrant origin. This was true for only 15 percent of the students on an
academic track who continued into higher education. The TIES survey
also includes a question about peers in high school who dropped out of
school; those with a peer in secondary school who dropped out are three
times more likely to not pursue higher education or to drop out themselves. The neighborhood and peer context appears to play a similar role
in France and Los Angeles.

The case of Rotterdam (the Netherlands) falls somewhere between the
comprehensive system in France and the vocationally oriented system in
Germany. One characteristic of the Dutch case is that half of the higher
education students of Turkish descent made it into higher education
through the vocational route. The largest group on this alternative route
first went to a four-year middle vocational school (between the ages of
sixteen and twenty) before entering higher education to get a BA. Middle
vocational education in the Netherlands is partly modeled after the idea
of the community colleges in the United States. The importance of the
community college route in the United States makes the school careers
of the successful second-generation Mexicans more similar to those of
second-generation Turks in the Netherlands than one might expect.
However, the indirect route in the Netherlands takes at least three years
longer than the direct route. These students often come from large families in which both parents attended at most primary school. The indirect
route seems to be an important alternative for persistent and smart children of disadvantaged families. The same seems to be true of the American
students who use the two-year community college as a steppingstone to
a four-year university.

In all three European countries, selection in secondary school plays
an important part in whether students can enter higher education. However, national institutional arrangements take different approaches to

determining who gets to enter an academic track in secondary school. These differences involve preschool attendance, school segregation, and late selection.

In Strasbourg, as in the rest of France, preschool attendance is almost universal. Children of immigrants as well as children of native parentage go to preschool at age two and half or three, almost without exception. As a result, Turkish children in France begin to learn French in an educational environment from a very early age. In the Netherlands and Germany, preschool attendance before the age of four and six, respectively, is optional, and as a result, many second-generation Turkish respondents do not attend preschool at all. In Germany, this means that a sizable group of second-generation Turkish children speak Turkish fluently but have a poor command of German when they enter school at the age of six. Those who attend preschool in Germany are significantly ($p < 0.01$) more likely to be placed in an academic track. Similarly, children of disadvantaged immigrants in the United States do not attend preschool, placing them at a disadvantage with respect to the French system.

Moreover, the quality of schools matters (more so in the United States than in Europe) and is related to the neighborhood SES and the degree of ethnic segregation—factors that sometimes, but not always, overlap. The Turkish group is the most segregated of all ethnic groups in the four western European cities, but segregation there has a totally different flavor than in Los Angeles. The neighborhoods in which Turks reside are more ethnically mixed than those dominated by ethnic minorities in Los Angeles and many other American cities. However, in the three large cities under study (Berlin, Frankfurt, and Rotterdam), Turks tend to concentrate in neighborhoods with the largest immigrant communities. In Berlin and Frankfurt, pupils in more segregated schools have significantly ($p < 0.05$) less access to an academic track. In Rotterdam and Strasbourg, there is no significant effect of school segregation. The mother's ability to speak German is a strong indicator of the decision to send a child to preschool and the choice of primary school in Germany. In families in which the mother does not master German, the children are less likely to attend preschool and more likely to attend primary schools with many other migrant children.

Another major difference between the three European cases is the timing of selection for academic or vocational tracks. In France, children are selected twelve to thirteen years after they have started school. In Germany, they are selected after only four to six years. The Netherlands is in between, with, on average, eight years between the start of schooling and selection.

Children from families with less education are better able to reach an academic track with a longer stretch of time between the start and selection into tracks. The obstacles second-generation Turks in the two German cities face are much greater than in the Dutch and French cities. On average, Turkish children start education later and are selected into less competitive tracks earlier. In this compressed time frame, the effect of segregated schools holds them back even further.

The different institutional school settings in the three countries require different forms of support from the parents. Because of the short period between the starting age and the selection age in Germany, and the fact that children in primary school only go to school half days, parents need to play an active role in their child's education. Parents are expected to provide practical help with homework and assist their children in reading and writing. According to their children, only a small group of Turkish parents in the two German cities were able to help often with homework. Even so, only 14 percent of these children of highly supportive Turkish parents were able to go to Gymnasium. This number is not much higher than the 10 percent who do not receive help from parents but nevertheless gain entrance to the academic track. Both cases show that the extra help that Turkish parents provide is not enough to compensate for their disadvantaged position and get their children into Gymnasium. The results in the Netherlands and France show the same difficulty; however, 25 percent of the Turks in the Netherlands and nearly 50 percent of those in France who do not receive help still manage to get into an academic track. The more stratified school system of Germany severely disadvantages and punishes children whose parents are unable to provide effective supplemental support.

The practical support of parents with homework requires knowledge of the national language and content of the homework. Parents can, however, also talk about the importance of school. For this, parents need less knowledge of the content. In all three countries, children whose parents often talk about school are much more often tracked (between one and a half and two times more often) into an academic track. The most open school system, in France, relies least on effective practical support with homework. Talking about school and meeting often with teachers are the most powerful factors in explaining differences among the students. The importance of support from older siblings is also remarkable in all three countries. For both sorts of help (talking about school and practical help) the help of older siblings is as important as the support of the parents. This supports the findings of earlier research among second-generation Turks (Crul 1994, 2000b), which underscores the importance of the support of older siblings in a situation in which parents often are not able to help.

The results in the four cities show that even successful students face challenging pathways. In Berlin, only the top students from relatively well-educated parents make it into higher education. In the other two cities, the university-going group is larger and more diverse. Because of an earlier start and later selection in France, many more above-average students can also take a direct route to higher education. In the Netherlands, students who test above average who are persistent enough can also enter higher education through a longer or alternative route. But in the two German cities, we find that even the brightest children of poorly educated parents do not make it to university. The academic track of the German school system gets progressively more selective until virtually all children from poorly educated Turkish parents are shunted off it.

Case Study, Zeliha: Familial Support   Zeliha is a second-generation Turkish woman in France with a remarkable educational career that she combined with an early marriage and motherhood. Zeliha's father came to Strasbourg as a guest worker in construction; her mother is a housewife. Having suffered from the lack of educational opportunities in Turkey, her parents were motivated to provide better opportunities for their children. Zeliha started preschool (école maternelle) at the age of three. This was where she, like her two older siblings, learned to speak French, because her father had a very low proficiency in French and her mother did not speak it at all. Fortunately, the school did not expect frequent visits from parents except for the annual parental meetings. According to Zeliha, her parents handled bureaucratic affairs quite well without speaking French. The four brothers and sisters helped one another with their homework, and their parents managed to pay for some short-term private courses.

Zeliha's parents were fortunate to find social housing in the center of Strasbourg, unlike many workers who reside in the remote parts of the city or in villages dominated by large Turkish populations. Because school selection is determined by postal code, the center city location was a great advantage for Zeliha and her siblings. They had access to prestigious public schools in the neighborhood. Even though their house was quite small, Zeliha's father did not want to move because of the opportunities the location provided. Zeliha had only a few Turkish students in her lower secondary school class (collège), and she was the only Turkish pupil in the lyceum (lycée).

Zeliha had good grades and after lower secondary school (collège) went to a general lycée, at the end of which she earned a baccalaureate degree in economics and social sciences. She decided to pursue her dream to become an English teacher. However, things did not go as she had planned. On the first day, she was disappointed to enter a large amphitheater where a professor taught the entire course in English. She had not been aware that English proficiency was required to begin this course of study. Thus, in the second semester, she changed her major and transferred to French as a Foreign Language (FLE). She relates that, of the 250 students who had enrolled in the English department, only 100 remained. She believes that this dropout rate shows that most students did not receive enough guidance before choosing their major. Nevertheless, the flexibility of the system made it possible for her to transfer to another department without losing ground.

Although her older siblings pursued their education in the vocational field, Zeliha was the first to attend university. Her family was very proud and supportive of her educational career. Yet, in the midst of her undergraduate education, Zeliha made an unexpected decision. During the family's summer vacation in Turkey, she met a relative and decided to get married at age twenty. Zeliha's parents did not oppose her decision but warned her against the hardship of studying while married. Indeed, things did not go as easily as she had expected, but family support mechanisms eased the way. Her husband, who initially did not speak any French, found a job in the construction business through her father. The couple moved in with Zeliha's parents, which made it easier for her to attend school while her mother ran the household. Two years later, she became pregnant, but with the support of her mother, who took care of the baby, she was able to go back to school one month after giving birth. Zeliha also received a great deal of help from friends at school who covered her absences and assisted her with course work. And, finally, she earned a (professional) MA degree in French.

Zeliha received considerable support from her family in all her decisions. Access to public resources, such as government aid for low-income families, and public schools made it possible for her parents to support their children, despite their precarious economic situation and low human capital. Even though she took a large risk by getting married and having a child before she graduated, these personal decisions did not deter her educational pursuits. Thus, in an interaction with the institutional and social structures, Zeliha managed to pursue a successful career in education. After four years of intensive effort to finish her studies while raising her child, she decided to take a short break before starting to work.

Her husband then started his business in a village of Strasbourg, which improved their financial situation and enabled them to move into their own apartment. Zeliha is thinking of looking for a part-time job "to keep the balance between family and work." She acknowledges the difficulties of finding a job as a woman wearing a head scarf, especially after the hardships she has experienced finding an apprenticeship. However, due to her positive experience at a company in which she worked as an apprentice, she was recently offered a part-time job there, and she is now more optimistic about her chances in the labor market.

Case Study, Volkan: Sports and School   Volkan is a second-generation Turk in the Netherlands studying business economics in higher vocational education (a postsecondary institution specializing in training people for a profession). Volkan's mother arrived in the Netherlands in her early twenties. Unlike many Turkish immigrants, she tried to attend vocational education and, as a result, gained good command of the Dutch language. She later married a man from Turkey, and the couple opened a dry cleaning business. As a working mother, Volkan's mother has frequent access to Dutch society and she was actively involved in Volkan's school activities. Both parents not only supported their children's education financially but also helped them to pursue their objectives in life.

Initially, Volkan was not a motivated student. His grades were average, and at the end of secondary school, he was advised to go to the lowest track in secondary school (lower vocational education). He was not bothered by this low recommendation because his dream was to become a professional soccer player, and his mother supported his passion for sports. Volkan played during his teenage years in a semiprofessional league with other talented players. Volkan and his family lived in a highly segregated neighborhood where many young children were drawn into drugs and crime. Volkan's parents saw his involvement in sports partly as a way to keep him away from dangerous street life. Volkan always had a full schedule of studying, school, and sports practice on most days. Because of the low level of vocational education, he never experienced any problems doing his course work and playing sports. After finishing lower vocational education at age sixteen, he continued toward a four-year middle vocational education school.

Volkan's ambition of becoming a professional soccer player was checked by an injury he suffered. After this incident, he decided that betting on soccer as his only career choice was too risky. He finished his four years of middle vocational education (MBO), earning an associate's degree, but believed that to be successful and earn a decent income, he needed to further his education. Hence, he decided to continue toward a four-year higher vocational (HBO) education school. Almost all of his friends and some of his cousins were studying economics at the time, and, considering the prospects of expanding the family business, Volkan decided that business economics would be a good choice. His family supported his decision. He signed up for the most prestigious business economics school in Amsterdam. Fortunately for Volkan, most youth who pursue noncompulsory schooling after the age of eighteen in the Netherlands are automatically entitled to a scholarship that continues for the entire four years of study. Volkan pays for his additional living expenses through his part-time job working as a gym instructor.

Like many students who take the long route into higher education in the Netherlands, Volkan had difficulty with some of the course work that presumes secondary school academic preparation. Even though the middle vocational diploma gives access to higher vocational training, the students lack some of the academic preparation necessary to excel in school. Because his friends and cousins were also studying economics, he was able to turn to them for help with his schoolwork, and his parents helped by providing extra assistance through a paid tutor. At the time of this writing Volkan is in his third year and has managed to pass all his courses by working hard, remaining dedicated, and accepting the help and support of his family and friends. Volkan now aspires to follow the university preparatory track (HBO propedeuse) and continue toward an MA university business degree. Volkan has decided that, once he finishes his studies, he will explore different job opportunities to gain further experience and extend his horizons.

Case Study, Derya: Parental Ambitions   Derya is a successful second-generation Turkish woman in Germany with an MA in linguistics. Her father completed higher vocational school in Istanbul in the 1960s but, despite his advanced degree, had difficulty finding employment. Weary of trying to find a job through employment agencies, he decided to join the many guest workers migrating to Germany and found a job in the German telecommunication company. During visits back to Istanbul, he met Derya's mother, then a Turkish literature teacher in a high school in Istanbul, and they soon married. Derya's mother arrived in Germany in 1981, and Derya, their only child, was born two years later. Derya's mother attended a language school after her arrival in Germany. Over the years, both of her parents have acquired an average level of German, and they settled in a working-class German neighborhood.

Although it was not obligatory in the German system, Derya attended kindergarten at the age of three. Because Turkish was spoken at home, her parents wanted her to become familiar with the German language while socializing with other children. As a result, she did not have much difficulty with German when she began primary school. She remembers asking her mother certain questions about German grammar, but otherwise she did not receive much assistance from her parents throughout her schooling. Derya was a good student; she studied hard and did her homework regularly. She remembers that most of the students in her class (who were predominantly working class) were not nearly as studious and seemed rather careless about their future careers. This made it easy for her to stand out as a good student, and at the end of primary school, she and only one other student from her class were recommended to go on to Gymnasium (academic track).

Her positive school experience continued in Gymnasium, where the student body was more ethnically diverse. She had colleagues of Afghan and Persian backgrounds, as well as a few Turks, although most were German. Derya does not recall receiving any help from her parents with courses, but they would always ask whether she had completed her homework, and they asked her questions about school. She emphasizes that working together with her German friends improved her German language skills considerably.

Toward the end of high school, Derya experienced difficulties with her courses for the first time. She felt tired and worn out because of exams and classes, and her grades dropped. However, streaming down to a vocational track (as many others would do in that situation) was not an option; her parents would not have accepted the move. Because Derya did not aspire to go to medical or law school, her lower grades did not obstruct her university career. With a final push, she obtained her high school degree (Abitur), in part because she did not want to be the only one among her friends to fail.

When Derya graduated from high school, she was unsure about what subject to study in university, so she decided to take a year off to go abroad. This "social year" is popular among young people in Germany. Her mother was not pleased with the idea because she thought it was too early for Derya to leave home, but in the end both parents accepted her decision. In high school, Derya's favorite subject was French, so she decided to go to France as an au pair, with the intention of improving her language skills. She spent one year in Paris, where she enhanced her language skills considerably. When she returned to Germany, Derya decided to make use of these skills and proceeded to study French as her major. Even though she has pleasant memories of her university years, she regrets having stayed in her hometown for school; she thinks she could have become more independent had she studied in another German city. Nevertheless, she is also happy that she can live with her parents.

In the first year of her university studies, Derya secured a mentoring job through her mother's contacts at work. This mentoring project was an initiative to provide course work aid to second-generation students by second-generation mentors who could also act as role models. After two years as a mentor, Derya was invited to join the organizational team and immersed herself in the project. Through this experience, she acquired skills in project management, organization, public relations, and communication, as well as more self-confidence and better presentation skills— all of which she believes will be useful in her future career. While working on this project, Derya began to reconsider her experience at school and the experience of immigrant children in general. She believes that such a mentoring project could have been very helpful for her in choosing her area of study and occupation.

Today, Derya has successfully finished her studies and is ready to enter the labor market. Even though she regrets not studying for a specific profession, such as the law, she is aware of the flexibility afforded by her skills when choosing among different sectors and companies.

SUCCESS AGAINST THE ODDS

In our comparative study of Mexicans in Los Angeles and Turks in western European cities, we find discernible pathways of mobility among the second generation in their respective host societies. Both second-generation Mexicans and Turks come from low socioeconomic family backgrounds, their parents arrived in their host countries as low-skilled labor migrants, and they face a disadvantaged family situation in which both parents must work to make ends meet. Hence, despite stable households, most parents are unable to provide extra resources for their children's education. Despite similarities in family SES, the pathways and mechanisms that contribute to success vary in different national and local contexts. Comparative integration context theory posits that national institutional arrangements in school significantly shape the challenges faced by second-generation youth but also emphasizes that students can maximize opportunities within school systems, especially when there are windows of opportunities for active and persistent second-generation students, especially those who have supportive parents or siblings (Crul and Schneider 2010; Crul, Schneider, and Lelie

2012). In the United States, access to more competitive tracks in public schools, programs like College Bound that help students navigate the complex college system, and community colleges provide a pathway for second-generation Mexicans who are unable to turn to their parents for support. The U.S.-European comparison highlights this interplay between family SES and institutional and community resources and characteristics.

From the international comparison, we can deduce several important lessons. The best institutional setting for children from immigrant families with low parental human and cultural capital is provided by school systems in which all children start school at an early age, schools are ethnically diverse, and selection into tracks (formal or informal) is postponed until students are able to compensate for their disadvantaged starting position. The United States and Europe differ considerably in how they select children in high school or secondary school. In the United States, urban school systems are typically comprehensive, but the quality of individual schools differs enormously. In Europe, by contrast, school quality does not differ as much. This greater uniformity in school quality works to the advantage of second-generation youth in Europe, but early tracking in Germany and the Netherlands reduces their opportunities with respect to the more comprehensive school situation in the United States. However, honors classes and AP courses provide an informal variant of tracking in the United States that allows the brightest children from underprivileged families a chance to excel and move beyond high school. Still, most poor immigrant children in the United States find it hard to attend selective colleges and universities.

In the United States, the Netherlands, and France, children who were not able to access selective colleges or universities have found alternative routes. Vocational pathways in the Netherlands and France can be an alternative long route to higher education, as can community colleges in the United States. On both sides of the Atlantic, researchers often do not highlight these alternative routes because they still consider education to be a linear development from high school to college or from upper secondary school to university. However, many respondents who have beat the odds and attained higher education have used these alternative ways to mobility and have achieved success on their own terms.

The supportive role of parents in low-SES families is crucial in both Europe and the United States, but in a different way than that of more educated parents. These immigrant parents are usually unable to give practical help with homework and the college admissions process because of their low level of human capital, poor command of the native language, and scant understanding of the school system. However, second-generation children whose parents hold high expectations—who consistently talk about the importance of school, who prioritize school over work, and who support choices that give their children the best educational opportunities—exhibit better educational outcomes than their counterparts whose parents do not. The support of older siblings and cousins also proves to be critical; they often help with homework and with the college admissions process, which compensates, in part, for their parents' severe lack of human capital.

There are other important structural differences across the Atlantic. One of the most notable is the clear relationship between the family's financial situation and the higher education opportunities available in the Los Angeles case. Families whose parents migrate to the United States illegally are usually in a precarious financial situation (Zhou and Lee 2007). The situation in Europe is quite different; schooling children rarely places financial demands on the families, even at the highest level, because higher education receives deeper public subsidies. (Of course, this also helps the young adult children of more affluent majority families.) This extra hurdle in the United States also comes with second-chance possibilities, however. Some IIMMLA respondents successfully managed to reenter the educational system after a hiatus from school, often in conjunction with work. In Europe, second-chance schooling opportunities are extremely limited; the TIES respondents almost never returned to school after entering the labor force.

In Europe, also, the inability of poorly educated immigrant parents to provide practical help with homework has consequences similar to the financial hurdles that poor immigrant parents in the United States face. Some European school systems (most notably in Germany, but also in Austria and Switzerland) rely heavily on the parents' ability to assist their children with homework. When parents are unable to do so, their children suffer, because they are underprepared and therefore underperform.

The cross-Atlantic comparison demonstrates that support from parents and siblings, the influence of the peer and neighborhood context, and access to alternative resources and routes all play important roles in shaping outcomes, despite large differences in how school systems are organized. At the same time, it highlights the ways in which each educational system either holds back (late start, early selection, or the funding of the higher education system) or advances the position of the second generation (preschool, late selection, honors or AP programs, alternative routes or second chances). Finally, the international context provides a glimpse of why second-generation Mexicans and Turks make the choices they do in the face of limited opportunities and enormous constraints and how they navigate this field in their quest to get ahead.

CHAPTER 5

ENTERING THE LABOR MARKET

LIZA REISEL, LAURENCE LESSARD-PHILLIPS, AND PHILIP KASINITZ

Finding a good foothold in the labor market is a crucial test for the second generation in western Europe and the United States. In recent years, as large numbers of the children of immigrants have come of age and embarked on their careers, we can begin to see what place they will occupy as adults. Knowing whether they are finding satisfactory employment in the economic mainstream is a significant first indicator of whether their working lives will be on par with those of their majority peers or whether they will remain a group apart from the broader society.

This question surfaces regularly in media and public debates. In Europe, commentators have expressed growing alarm that an alleged lack of integration of children of immigrants is fueling anti-immigrant sentiment, particularly toward Muslim communities. In the United States, scholars have expressed concern over the potential for "downward assimilation" (Haller, Portes, and Lynch 2011; Alba, Kasinitz, and Waters 2011). Worry about second-generation entry into an underclass has largely focused on the children of Spanish-speaking immigrants. On both sides of the Atlantic, we see increased anxiety over whether the children of immigrants are becoming more isolated from the mainstream and are having more difficulty entering the labor market. Popular discourse often links this worry to criminal behavior and welfare dependence, evidence to the contrary notwithstanding (Bean and Stevens 2003).

Yet, though similar concerns over immigrant integration are raised on both sides of the Atlantic, they take quite different approaches to addressing these issues, reflecting the different ways in which national and local contexts shape second-generation transitions.

The overwhelming majority of first-generation immigrant parents are legally authorized to live in western European countries and have access to many of the same welfare state provisions as natives. These countries also usually have explicit integration policies for immigrants and their children. Other policies, such as apprenticeship programs, facilitate the transition into the labor force for all young people, including the children of immigrants. In the United States, by contrast, a sizable minority of immigrants are in the country without legal authorization and have few social rights—though, paradoxically, those in the country legally can easily naturalize and the U.S. Constitution affords full citizenship rights to their U.S.-born children. Because federal legislation bars first-generation immigrants from access to most welfare benefits for five years and requires them to show that they will not be a burden on the state to become naturalized, first-generation immigrants must generally enter the labor force merely to survive. Furthermore, the poor—including the worst-off immigrants and their children—face a sharper degree of material deprivation than in western Europe. Without much of a welfare state cushion, remaining outside the labor force is simply not an option for most first-generation immigrants, and their children rarely grow up in households where such assistance is a major source of income.

As difficult and uncomfortable as living with a weak safety net is, it could have the effect of integrating immigrants in the United States. Because the immigrant parents generally have extensive work experience, albeit often in low-wage jobs, they can provide their children with connections to and knowledge about local labor markets. In western Europe, by contrast, because first-generation labor market participation is far lower and social welfare benefits compensate for being outside the labor force, the children of immigrants often grow up in communities where the parents have relatively little knowledge about how to find jobs. Ironically, the claim that immigrants and their children rely too heavily on welfare is a common theme in anti-immigrant rhetoric even in the United States, despite its higher immigrant labor force participation rate and less extensive welfare state.

BECOMING A GROWN-UP: GOING TO WORK

The transition from education to the labor force is, of course, a crucial step toward becoming an adult. Its timing and the way it lines up with other coming-of-age milestones varies markedly by class, ethnicity, region, and gender within any one society as well as over time (Furstenberg 2008; Mouw 2003; Kogan and Müller 2003; Shavit and Müller 1998; Staff and Mortimer 2008). Comparing the European data from the TIES project with the IIMMLA and ISGMNY data from the United States gives us an opportunity to examine how labor market integration operates among various second-generation groups in various urban settings and in various nations. The variation in the experience of the children of immigrants across these different institutional settings offers us new insights into what works—and what does not work—when it comes to integrating the second generation.

The cities examined in the three surveys all differ and have different labor force dynamics. To simplify some of this variation, we look only at the largest cities in six of the TIES countries—Paris, Stockholm, Vienna, Berlin, Brussels, and Amsterdam—and at the two largest U.S. cities—Los Angeles (using the IIMMLA data) and New York (using ISGMNY data). All of these cities have significant immigrant and second-generation populations. In most cases, the second generation makes up a much larger share of the local population than is true for the country as a whole. Vienna, for example, is home to approximately one-third of the entire Turkish-origin population in Austria (Herzog-Punzenberger 2003). All are what might be termed world cities, in that they play significant roles in the global economy and are centers of communications and the sites of corporate headquarters. They are also all centers of cultural activities and, to varying degrees, of higher education. All of the European cities are also national capitals or, in the case of Brussels, an international capital. Most have disproportionately high white-collar and professional labor forces compared with the countries in which they are located. Thus, they are in many ways atypical of their national contexts. Conclusions based on these cities should not be generalized to the nations as a whole.

What would previous research lead us to expect second-generation labor force entry to look like in these cities? In the U.S. context, Gans's notion of second-generation decline and Portes and colleagues' theory of segmented assimilation suggest that the transition to the labor force will often be problematic (Gans 1992; Portes, Fernandez-Kelly, and Haller 2005; Portes and Rumbaut 2001; Portes and Zhou 1993). Although these models predict that some immigrant groups will integrate into the mainstream labor force with relatively little trouble, they also predict that others, particularly the children of poor and racially stigmatized labor migrants, will find themselves increasingly isolated from opportunities in the mainstream economy. At the same time, because they have become accustomed to the standards of the mainstream majority, many may be unwilling or unable to take the low-status, low-wage jobs their immigrant parents usually hold. As a result, some think that a significant portion of the second generation is experiencing downward assimilation or racialization into an urban underclass outside the mainstream economy (Telles and Ortiz 2008).

It has been suggested that this situation has strong parallels in Europe, where the context of reception may be even less hospitable for second-generation labor force incorporation (for a review, see Heath, Rothon, and Kilpi 2008). Indeed, even relatively well-educated members of the second generation may not be able to cash in on their human capital advantages at the same level as the children of natives (Heath and Cheung 2007). In addition, Alejandro Portes and Min Zhou suggest an intriguing alternative—the idea that some second-generation youth will experience upward mobility by staying within the sometimes lucrative ethnic niches and enclaves developed by the immigrant generation (Portes and Zhou 1993; see also Zhou and Bankston 1998). This, too, has echoes in Europe (Kloosterman and Rath 2001; Simon 2003).

Others have suggested that it is more common than these models would predict for the second generation to integrate relatively successfully into the labor force both in North America (Alba and Nee 2003; Smith 2008; Kasinitz et al. 2008; Attewell, Kasinitz, and Dunn 2010) and in Europe (Schneider and Crul 2010; Vermeulen 2010; Thomson and Crul 2007).

Although both views foresee variation within and across groups in terms of the degree of upward mobility in employment, they differ in terms of both which tendency will predominate in a given situation and what drives these patterns. In particular, it is critical—for policy as well as research—whether institutional mechanisms systematically bar significant parts of the second generation from decent jobs or perhaps any job, and, if so, which ones and how. Many analysts highlight how institutional variation in educational systems affects the transition to the labor market (Crul and Vermeulen 2003b) and the importance of the structure of labor market regulation and welfare state policies (Dolton, Asplund, and Barth 2009; Estevez-Abe, Iversen, and Soskice 2001; Kogan 2006) in Europe, as well as affirmative action and equal opportunity policies in the United States (Kasinitz et al. 2008).

In Berlin and Vienna, for example, a highly developed apprenticeship system links portions of the population directly with working-class jobs, in some cases quite well compensated (Müller and Gangl 2003). At the same time, the German and Austrian educational systems track students early in their schooling in a way that is quite closed once they designate an educational path, reducing mobility within the system. This system may make it harder to obtain university educations—and thus professional credentials—than in, for example, Brussels, Paris, or Amsterdam, where mobility between educational tracks is easier.

The differences in welfare arrangements in the United States and Europe have an obvious and important impact on their labor markets. The United States has been described as a residual welfare state (Titmuss 1958), in which most state benefits are limited to the citizens least able to compete in the labor market: the elderly, the disabled, and single mothers of young children (see also Esping-Andersen 1990). The European cities, particularly in Stockholm and arguably also in Paris, Berlin, and Amsterdam, have far more expansive welfare states with relatively generous unemployment benefits as well as pro-natalist policies that may make it possible for parents to spend more time out of the labor force (Gornick et al. 1998). Further complicating the comparisons is the outsider status of the immigrant parents and differences in their social embeddedness in the networks through which employment information often flows (Portes 2010; Behtoui 2008; Tilly and Tilly 1994; Granovetter 1973).

Other national differences also shape the second generation's transition from schooling to work. The age at which young people typically leave their parents' homes and the degree of state support for postsecondary education vary widely. The levels of female employment outside the home differ from country to country, reflecting different state policies as well as cultural differences. Different primary educational systems ranging from extensive very early state-funded full-time day care in France and Sweden to late school entrance and limited school hours in Germany and Austria also play a role in shaping the labor force participation of parents, particularly mothers (Crul and Vermeulen 2006). Although these differences are not explicitly about the children of immigrants, they shape the context in which the second generation comes of age. Furthermore, simple demography plays a role. The growth or decline of the native-origin labor force naturally shapes the number and types of positions available to the children of immigrants (Alba 2009; Myers 2008).

Finally, the levels of discrimination in the labor force and society that immigrants and their children face must also be taken into account. Being highly stigmatized is an obvious disadvantage, and we will suggest that value seems to be considerable in not being the most stigmatized minority in a given society.

Certain key differences between the cities should be kept in mind. New York and Los Angeles are not national capitals, and although New York has an almost European level of public-sector employment, the public sector is smaller in Los Angeles. Despite its central role in Germany's political and cultural life, Berlin has a relatively weak economy with high unemployment compared with other large German cities ("poor but sexy" is how Mayor Klaus Wowereit famously described it). Paris, by contrast, is a relatively well-off city, albeit in a somewhat poorer country. Despite the high level of youth unemployment in France in general, Paris has a relatively tight labor market. Stockholm has a considerably higher cost of living than the other cities (Eurostat 2010). Brussels and Amsterdam have quite high levels of ethnic segregation (Phalet 2007; Praag and Schoorl 2008).

We compare the labor market experience of the children of immigrants along three dimensions. First we ask what portion of the second generation is entering the labor force in the first place. To do so, we compare the proportion of the population that is not engaged in either education, employment, or training, the NEET rate (Quintini and Martin 2006, 8). This indicator points to the young people who have the strongest potential to create something like an underclass. We then look at the portion of the second-generation working populations in professional employment. Finally, we look at the wages earned by the second-generation groups. In each case, we examine the second-generation groups relative to each other, relative to similar groups in different cities, and relative to the mainstream comparison groups within their own cities, as well as gender differences within and across groups. In most comparisons, we look at a variety of second-generation groups, but at various points we focus on those groups in which much of the first generation was impoverished labor migrants: Turks in the European cities, Dominicans in New York City, and Mexicans in Los Angeles.

A central issue in these comparisons is the role of gender, which is explored in more depth in chapter 6. Although gender affects labor market entry and labor market status in many societies and among many groups, there are huge differences in the degree to which women in general and particularly the mothers of young children are expected to participate in the wage labor force. Some of these are cultural. Many immigrant groups to the United States and western Europe hail from places where the norms about gender roles are far more traditional than in the host nations to which they have come. This may be particularly important for traditional Muslim women. These women may face particular barriers from their ethnic communities regarding entry into the labor force (Read 2004), as well as discrimination from the larger society, particularly when their difference has been rendered highly visible by head scarves and other forms of distinctive dress.

The differences in where groups fit in the local ethnic "pecking order," such as where they stand in the terms of employer preferences, are important. Roger Waldinger's (1996) notion of a hiring queue—that employers generally prefer workers from certain groups who, as a consequence, can command higher salaries—plays a role here. In addition, it may be true that the bulk of discrimination in a given labor market may focus on particular groups, especially large groups that occupy a long-standing subordinate position. Groups such as African Americans (and perhaps long-standing Mexican Americans) in the United States, Turks in Germany, or Maghrébins in France play a particular role in the local imagination and may face particular barriers in terms of labor force entry. Other groups may actually benefit from not being the dominant minority group. However, the same group may be a stigmatized, racialized dominant minority group in one society but a relatively high-ranking group in another. Nancy Foner has argued, for example, that West Indians in New York occupy a relatively middle-level position in the local ethnic hierarchy and may benefit by being able to distance themselves from native African Americans. But in London, without a significant other black population, West Indian migrants of the late 1950s and early 1960s bore the brunt of nativism and antiblack racism (Foner 2005). Although the data presented in this comparison do not include Turks in the United States, this small and largely middle-class immigrant group is not particularly stigmatized—a dramatic contrast with western Europe.

METHODS

In each of the European cities, the second-generation groups are compared with a group of natives of native parentage. In the U.S. cities, the comparison group is native whites of native parents. In the U.S. cities, we also present data for African Americans and an Hispanic group with long tenure in the city—mainland-born Puerto Ricans in New York, third- and third-plus-generation Mexican Americans (native Mexicans in the graphs) in Los Angeles.

The first step in our comparisons is to ask whether the second generation is joining the labor force. To answer this question, the NEET rate provides a more expansive, and we feel more useful, measure than official unemployment rates because it includes only people who are not attending school or training programs full time or in the labor force. Given the age of the second-generation respondents in these surveys, the standard measures of unemployment and labor force participation can be misleading. Indeed, some of the most upwardly mobile respondents may appear to have extremely weak labor force attachment because they are still getting professional education and advanced training well into their late twenties. We find the NEET rate the most useful measure of isolation from the economic mainstream because it does not make the sometimes confusing distinction between those who are unemployed but still in the labor force and those not looking for work, a distinction that might be an artifact of different national unemployment policies. First introduced in the United Kingdom (Social Exclusion Unit 1999), the NEET rate has been used in educational research to examine employability, labor market marginalization, and social exclusion among young people (Quintini and Martin 2006; Robson 2008). There could be several reasons for being NEET. A person could choose to stay home as a homemaker or caretaker of young children (see chapter 6, this volume). A person could be trying to succeed in a field (such as the arts) without yet earning a living from it. A person could be looking for work but unable to find employment, be unable to work because of some disability, or simply be unwilling to work. Clearly not everyone who is counted as NEET is a member of a semipermanently unemployed underclass. Yet the existence of much higher NEET rates in certain groups and in certain cities clearly opens up this possibility.

In the second comparison, we defined professional occupations by using the occupational title of the current or most recent job (if available) from the ISCO-88 (International Standard Classification of Occupations) coding in TIES and transformed it into the Erikson-Goldthorpe-Portocarero (EGP) class scheme (Erikson and Goldthorpe 1992; Marshall 1998) using a modified version of the Ganzeboom and Treiman (1996) translation of ISCO-88 into EGP. Using EGP, we defined professional occupations as those occupations that fall into class category I and II. This definition includes higher-grade professionals, administrators and officials, managers in large industrial establishments, large proprietors, lower-grade professionals, administrators, and officials, higher-grade technicians, managers in small industrial establishments, and supervisors of nonmanual employees. Students and respondents who have never worked are excluded from the analysis of professional employment.

Income was measured differently in all three surveys. In TIES it was measured as average monthly income in euros after taxes, with euro-equivalencies in the case of Stockholm. This variable was recorded in income brackets and was then recoded into a continuous variable using midpoints and "top coding" based on the Pareto curve (see Hout 2004). The IIMMLA survey also originally recorded pretax income in brackets, representing average annual income in dollars. This variable was also recoded into a continuous variable using the same method as with TIES. In ISGMNY, pretax income was recorded as continuous annual income in dollars (for those respondents who preferred to answer in income brackets, the transformation using midpoints was performed). In the U.S. cities, this includes personal income from all sources, but in the European cities it includes only income from employment. The multivariate analyses in this chapter use the natural logarithm of these continuous income measures. Respondents with missing information on income were excluded from the analyses: this situation is particularly problematic in the IIMMLA data, in which 32 percent of the sample has missing information on this variable; in the TIES data, missing information on income for those in employment ranges from approximately 3 percent in Stockholm and Paris to 21 percent in Berlin. Only those respondents who were not studying and who reported having some sort of income in the relevant year were included in this part of the analysis.

We first ran simple comparisons (without controls) among the relevant second-generation and comparison groups for all three outcomes in each city. The ISGMNY data were weighted by INGRPWT, an adjustment to ensure the gender-age distributions within each group reflect a random sample. The TIES data also used a poststratification weight to adjust the age and sex distribution for each group and city in all cities except Paris, where a nonresponse weight was used instead. (The IIMMLA study did not have weights for this purpose.) Because we control for age and gender and analyze each city separately, it is unlikely that the different weighting schemes affect the results in any significant way. We then ran logistic regression models for the two binary outcomes (NEET and professional occupation) and linear regression models for income. Each of these analyses was performed separately by city and includes progressively more elaborate models. The first (model 0) includes only the group-gender categories (such as second-generation Turkish men, second-generation Turkish women, and so on), estimating raw differences in probability or (log of) income across the groups. The next model (model 1) includes controls for characteristics of the respondents' parents, whether the parents had been in the labor force during most of the time when the respondents were growing up as well as their parents' educational level. With these variables, we assess the degree of isolation from the mainstream economy in the immigrant generation and its impact on the second generation.

Model 1 also adds controls for the individual respondent's age and time in the labor force. Because the three surveys covered slightly different age groups, to maximize comparability we limited our samples to respondents between twenty and thirty-five years old. In the TIES data, time in the labor force corresponds to the age at which the respondents held their first job, truncated at age eighteen to avoid respondents reporting summer or part-time employment. Given the importance of parenthood to labor force participation, particularly for women, we control for whether respondents had children in the NEET and professional occupation analyses. In addition, we control for whether the respondents had grown up in the city in which they were surveyed, because all of these cities to some degree draw young people from other parts of their countries to begin careers or pursue higher education. This is particularly true among the native-origin comparison groups, who are often highly selected for the characteristics that might facilitate labor market success in cities like New York (see Kasinitz et al. 2008), Paris, Amsterdam, and Stockholm. Model 2 adds controls for the respondents' own level of education and whether the respondent had a professional occupation to the income regression.

We did not look at members of Asian groups in the New York and Los Angeles data or for Russian Jews in the New York data. We concentrated instead on the working-class labor migrants more comparable to the groups in the TIES samples. Thus, it should be remembered that the American data are for black and Latino immigrants, not for all immigrants. Had the Asian groups and the Russians been included, levels of professional employment among the second generation would have been considerably higher (see Kasinitz et al. 2008; Kasinitz, Matsumoto, and Zeltzer-Zubida 2011).

ENTERING THE LABOR FORCE

NEET rates are highest for the second-generation Turks in Brussels, Vienna, and Berlin (see table 5.1). This is to a large extent the result of the extremely high NEET rate among second-generation Turkish women in these cities. NEET rates for second-generation Turks are lower in Paris and much lower in Stockholm. The NEET rates in the two Latino groups in the U.S. cities, though high by U.S. standards, are also much lower than those found among second-generation Turks in the

TABLE 5.1   NEET Rates

		Male	Female
New York	Dominican second generation	19.6%	21.3%
Los Angeles	Mexican second generation	14.4	21.2
Brussels	Turkish second generation	27.7	43.2
Vienna	Turkish second generation	21.9	50.1
Berlin	Turkish second generation	21.4	46.6
Paris	Turkish second generation	14.2	22.5
Amsterdam	Turkish second generation	12.5	35.3
Stockholm	Turkish second generation	6.8	21.0

Source: Authors' calculations based on TIES survey 2007, 2008 (data not yet publicly available), ISGMNY (Mollenkopf, Kasinitz, and Waters 1999), and IIMMLA (Rumbaut et al. 2004).
Note: The TIES survey comprises eight separate national data sets, collected by Institute for Studies on Migrations (IEM), Comillas Pontifical University, Spain; Swiss Forum for Migration and Population Studies (SFM), Neuchâtel, Switzerland; Netherlands Interdisciplinary Demographic Institute (NIDI), The Hague, Netherlands; Austrian Academy of Sciences (ÖAW), Vienna, Austria; the European Research Centre on Migration and Ethnic Relations (ERCOMER), Katholieke Universiteit Leuven, Belgium; National Institute for Demographic Studies (INED), Paris, France; Institute for Migration Research and Intercultural Studies (IMIS), University of Osnabrück, Germany; Centre for Research in International Migration and Ethnic Relations (CEIFO), Stockholm University, Sweden. The TIES national surveys will be made publicly available by the national TIES partners individually, but were not yet available at the time of publication.

European cities, except in Paris and Stockholm. The ranking between cities may be partly explained by differences in the educational position of the second-generation groups across cities (see chapter 4, this volume). The second-generation Turks in Berlin and Vienna are overrepresented in the lower vocational tracks like Hauptschule and Realschule. From there they are supposed to move into apprenticeships, but many fail to do so (see chapter 10, this volume). Indeed, the apprenticeship system generally does not facilitate the transition to the labor market for the second-generation groups to the extent it does for native-origin youth. This is mainly because students have to find an apprenticeship place on their own. Many second-generation youth do not succeed in this, which puts them in a particularly weak position in a labor market that expects people to have had apprenticeship training.

The other city with very high NEET rates is Brussels. The labor market structure of the capital of Europe, with its emphasis on high-end jobs, is particularly problematic for people who do not have academic credentials, which disproportionately affects the second generation.

In Paris and Amsterdam, the NEET rates among men are relatively high compared with the NEET rate in Stockholm, despite very similar educational outcomes (see table 5.1). Previous analysis on the TIES data also shows that unemployment rates among second-generation Turkish men in Paris and Amsterdam are disproportionally high (Crul, Schneider, and Lelie 2012). In Paris, this is especially true for the initial transition into the labor market—something all young people in France often find difficult. The outcomes for the two cities in the United States reflect the generally high American labor force participation rates of both men and women (see also chapter 10, this volume). The weak welfare state limits benefits and forces both second-generation men and women into the labor market, much as it did their immigrant parents. Furthermore, being far more likely to have had employed parents, the American second generation may have better connections to the labor force. At the same time, competing in the labor force is much harder for members of the second generation with less education—and it is those with the least education who are most likely to be unemployed in both U.S. cities.

Thus, the overall differences between the cities for second-generation groups with similar socioeconomic backgrounds can largely be attributed to differences in educational credentials, a failing transition into the apprenticeship system, differences in the structure of the labor market, and national differences in welfare state structures. At the same time, the marked differences in the role of gender in the various cities—in particular the differences in the female NEET rate—require further exploration.

In Amsterdam, Brussels, Vienna, and Berlin, between 33 percent and 50 percent of all Turkish second-generation women in the samples are neither working nor pursuing education or further training. These very large numbers remain even when we control for background characteristics. Indeed, in Vienna and Berlin this could be seen as the normative situation for second-generation Turkish women. The gender gaps with men in many cities are enormous. In five cities—Berlin, Vienna, Brussels, Stockholm, and Amsterdam—the second-generation Turkish women are twice as often in the NEET category as men. Second-generation Turkish women have significantly higher NEET rates than both Turkish men and native-origin women in all the European cities. The gap cannot be attributed to lower education levels among second-generation Turkish women than among men (Crul, Schneider, and Lelie 2012). It is rather the result of lower participation of Turkish-origin women in the labor market. The relative isolation of these women from employment is one of the most striking findings in the TIES data. It seems that the women in the Turkish communities follow more traditional gender pathways.

Yet such cultural explanations can, at best, account for only part of the story. The NEET rates of Turkish women differ considerably across the cities. Second-generation Turkish women in Paris and Stockholm are far more likely to be working or in school than their counterparts in Berlin, Vienna, and Brussels. This almost certainly has less to do with differences in so-called Turkish characteristics than with differences in the structures and norms of the host society. For example, in Germany, Austria, and to some degree the Netherlands, the schedule of the educational system makes it particularly difficult for mothers of young children to be in the labor force full time, and the tax code in Germany provides strong incentives for married women to not work or to take marginal part-time employment. By contrast, in France and Sweden, widely available day care from a very young age and other incentives for a dual-breadwinner model mean mothers are often in the labor force. Ironically, in the United States, the lack of state support for child care may have an analogous effect, as mothers often have little choice but to work given the difficulty of supporting a family on one salary. These differences affect immigrants, the second generation, and those of native descent. Yet they will have more impact on groups with higher birth rates, which in most cases are the immigrants and, to some extent, their descendants (chapter 6 explains these differences for women in more detail).

When we compare the Turkish and Latino groups with other second-generation groups and native-origin comparison groups, many of the differences appear in sharp relief. In figures 5.1 through 5.12, bold percentages signify significant difference from the (white) comparison group at $p < .05$. In New York, we find that the second-generation Dominican group scores between the native white and the native black groups. Second-generation Dominicans are twice as likely to be in the NEET category as native whites, and, not surprisingly given their low educational levels, have the highest NEET rates of the three second-generation groups. Yet they are also considerably more likely to be working or in school than native African Americans are (see figure 5.1).

Indeed, in New York the native African American NEET rate is stunning and far higher than for any second-generation group. The gender gap for New York's Puerto Rican women is also particularly striking (14.3 percent for men versus 32.1 percent for women). As in Europe, having children is a strong predictor of being NEET in the U.S. cities, and higher birth rates may explain some, but not all, of this gender gap. Although the second generation shows some disadvantage relative to native whites, it is relatively advantaged compared to African Americans (italicized percentages signify significant difference from African Americans at $p < .05$). Not being the dominant minority group may actually facilitate integration

FIGURE 5.1   Weighted NEET Rates, New York

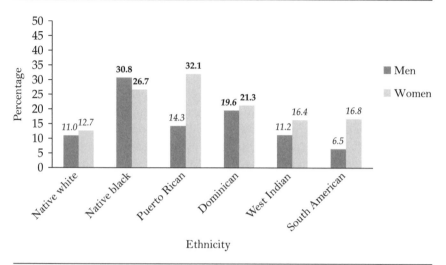

Source: Authors' calculations based on ISGMNY (Mollenkopf, Kasinitz, and Waters 1999).
Note: Bold numbers indicate a significant difference from native white. Italics indicate significant difference from native black.

into the mainstream or at least place them in a somewhat higher position in the hiring queue (see Waldinger 1996, 2007). Although the Dominican second generation most closely approximates the native minorities in New York, it seems to be doing better (see Kasinitz et al. 2008).

We see a similar but less dramatic pattern for second-generation Mexicans in Los Angeles (see figure 5.2). They too rank between the native white and native black groups and, as expected based on the socio-economic status (SES) of the parents, do somewhat worse than other Latin American second-generation respondents. Indeed, differences in the NEET rates between native white and second-generation men in Los Angeles are not significant. The real outliers in Los Angeles are the native (that is, third-plus generation) Mexican American women. This means that for Mexican American women, isolation from the labor force seems to increase with the family's time in the United States (see Telles and Ortiz 2008).

What immediately draws our attention in Vienna and Berlin are the very high NEET rates among second-generation Turkish women compared to native-origin women but also to women in the other second-generation group, former Yugoslavs (see figure 5.3). Although Turkish men also are in the back of the hiring queue in both Berlin and Vienna,

FIGURE 5.2   NEET Rates, Los Angeles

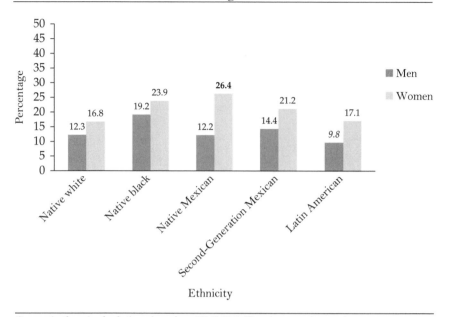

Ethnicity

Source: Authors' calculations based on IIMMLA (Rumbaut et al. 2004).
Note: Bold numbers indicate a significant difference from native white. Italics indicate significant difference from native black.

it is the differences in the Turkish female NEET rates that make the two German-speaking cities distinct. Previous research indicates that in other German cities unemployment rates among second-generation Turkish men and women are significantly higher than among other Germans, a gap not always reduced by increased education (see Worbs 2003; Kalter and Granato 2007; Schurer 2008).

It is interesting that in Berlin, although NEET rates for second-generation men are roughly comparable to those for their counterparts in Vienna, there is no significant difference between the native-origin comparison group men and second-generation Turkish men in the sample. This is, of course, due to the fact that in Berlin so many men of German descent are neither working nor in school.

In Brussels and Amsterdam, we can compare the Turkish second generation with another predominantly Muslim group, the Moroccan second generation (see figure 5.4). This comparison indicates that we should be cautious to attribute the high NEET rate among Turkish-origin women to Islam or traditional ideas about gender. In both of these cities,

FIGURE 5.3   Weighted NEET Rates, Vienna and Berlin

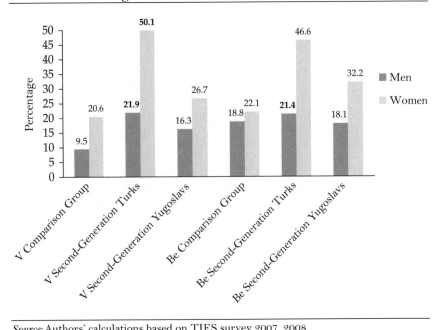

Source: Authors' calculations based on TIES survey 2007, 2008.
Note: Bold numbers indicate a significant difference from native-origin comparison group.
V = Vienna, Be = Berlin

FIGURE 5.4   Weighted NEET Rates, Amsterdam and Brussels

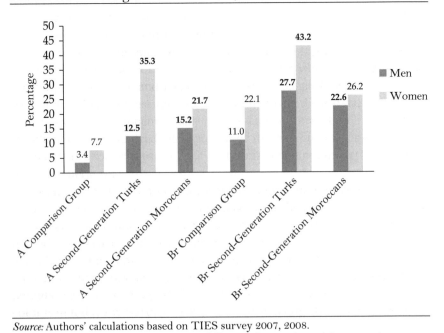

Source: Authors' calculations based on TIES survey 2007, 2008.
Note: Bold numbers indicate a significant difference from native-origin comparison group.
A = Amsterdam, Br = Brussels

TABLE 5.2   Predicted Probabilities of Being NEET

		Final Model, Percentage Probability	
		Male	Female
New York	Dominican second generation	19	21
	Native whites	21	20
Los Angeles	Mexican second generation	13	18
	Native whites	16	23
Vienna	Turkish second generation	23	43
	Comparison group	21	37
Berlin	Turkish second generation	31	66
	Comparison group	44	52
Paris	Turkish second generation	5	9
	Comparison group	3	4
Stockholm	Turkish second generation	8	32
	Comparison group	13	27
Amsterdam	Turkish second generation	17	44
	Comparison group	9	23
Brussels	Turkish second generation	29	54
	Comparison group	28	45

Source: Authors' calculations based on TIES survey 2007, 2008, ISGMNY (Mollenkopf, Kasinitz, and Waters 1999), and IIMMLA (Rumbaut et al. 2004).
Note: The following variables are controlled for in the table: age, has child, years in job, parents' education, parents' labor market participation, place respondent grew up, respondent's education.

the Moroccan-origin women seem considerably more akin to the native-origin comparison group than the Turks are (see Crul and Doomernik 2003). Puerto Rican women in New York and third- and third-plus-generation Mexican American women in Los Angeles, who are not Muslims, also have a high NEET rate similar to the Turkish-origin women in many of the European cities. Clearly, the situation of second-generation women merits a more in-depth analysis (see chapter 6, this volume).

In table 5.2, we introduce controls for age, education, whether the respondent grew up in the city in which they were interviewed, parents' education, parents' labor market participation while the respondent was growing up, and whether the respondent has a child. After we added these controls, we see that the differences between native and second-generation men generally disappear or are reversed (all regression tables are available in the online appendix).

Age is an important factor in New York, Vienna, Brussels, and Stockholm. In each of these cities, second-generation young people in their early twenties are far more likely to be out of work and school than those in their late twenties and early thirties. This suggests that the children of immigrants may take a few years longer to find a regular place in the labor market than their native-origin counterparts, but the differences may greatly be reduced over time.

The other important finding is that, in most cities, education and other background characteristics explain most of the huge differences in NEET rates between second-generation groups and native-origin respondents. Only second-generation Turkish men in Amsterdam are, after controlling for covariates, still significantly more often in the NEET category than young adults with native-born parents. This again shows the importance of differences in education levels between second-generation groups and the native-origin comparison group in explaining their different rates of labor market entry.

The control variables, however, do have different effects across cities. Parents' education level is an important factor in both of the U.S. cities, Brussels, and Berlin, although the effect is difficult to disentangle from that of the respondent's education. Parental background seems, as expected, to affect respondents' labor market participation in almost all the cities. The one exception is Stockholm. Although the data do not permit us to say why this is the case with any certainty, they clearly suggest that the highly inclusive Swedish welfare state plays a positive role in allowing the children of relatively disadvantaged immigrants to integrate into mainstream society.

In the U.S. cities, we also see that having grown up elsewhere in the United States and having come to New York or Los Angeles as young adults lowers the NEET rate and reduces differences between the groups. This is not surprising because in the United States, with its high inter-regional mobility, it is common for young adults to come to these cities specifically to pursue careers or education. Having migrated from elsewhere has a similar though smaller effect in Berlin. Having had parents in the labor force while the respondents were growing up also significantly reduces the differences between the second generation and native men in Vienna, Berlin, and Paris, suggesting that in those cities young people whose parents were outside the labor force have a harder time establishing their own careers. This highlights the potential dangers of long-term isolation from the labor force. Second-generation youth with parents out of the labor force are more likely to grow up in communities in which isolation from the labor force is the norm. This may have long-term effects on their own abilities to enter the labor force. Once again, however, Stockholm is an exception.

Last is where a group fits in the hiring queue. When Americans think of the problems of impoverished minority youth, they generally think of African Americans and Mexican Americans. Germans and Austrians generally think of Turks, to the point where the terms *immigrant youth, Muslims,* and *Turks* are at times used almost interchangeably. Indeed, in both German-speaking cities, the ex-Yugoslavs appear far less different from the comparison group than the Turks, suggesting that the ex-Yugoslavs are less racialized and occupy a different position in hiring queues. Similarly, the French tend to think of Algerians, Moroccans, and Tunisians (Silberman, Alba, and Fournier 2007). Without Maghrébins in the TIES sample, we cannot know how the Turkish and North African second generation stack up in Paris. However, it seems likely that the relative positions of the groups in the local ethnic pecking order is having some impact and may partially explain the relatively good labor market outcomes of second-generation Turks in Paris.

PROFESSIONAL OCCUPATIONS

Having a job is an important part of social integration. The type of job is also important, however. Having examined the question of labor force access, we now take up the question of whether second-generation youth are securing white-collar and professional jobs. The cities we study have different labor markets. As with the NEET rate, variation among the cities is considerable. Here the outcomes are much more closely linked to education levels. The relatively high percentages in professional occupations in Amsterdam, Paris, and Stockholm run parallel with the high number of second-generation Turks with higher education diplomas (see table 5.3). In fact, the percentages in Vienna and Berlin are somewhat surprising given the low percentages in higher education in these cities. In both New York and Los Angeles, second-generation women are more often in professional jobs. These outcomes indicate that obstacles for women seem to be fewer than for men in most U.S. second-generation groups but higher for second-generation Turkish women in Europe than for men. Even so, the gender differences in professional employment in Europe are generally far smaller than the differences in the NEET rates. Those second-generation Turkish women that succeed in education are often able to translate their credentials into a professional career. One striking exception is among Turkish second-generation women in Vienna, where the rate of professional employment stands at only 9.3 percent, versus 20.8 percent for Turkish-origin men. Controlling for age, whether they have a child, years in job, parents' education, parents' labor market participation, place they grew up, and

TABLE 5.3   Rates of Professional Occupation

		Male	Female
New York	Dominican second generation	27.5%	30.7%
Los Angeles	Mexican second generation	20.4	30.1
Berlin	Turkish second generation	14.4	15.8
Vienna	Turkish second generation	20.8	9.3
Brussels	Turkish second generation	21.1	24.4
Amsterdam	Turkish second generation	28.7	21.1
Paris	Turkish second generation	30.3	30.3
Stockholm	Turkish second generation	32.6	25.3

Source: Authors' calculations based on TIES survey 2007, 2008, ISGMNY (Mollenkopf, Kasinitz, and Waters 1999), and IIMMLA (Rumbaut et al. 2004).

respondents' education made little difference: Turkish-origin women in Vienna still have relatively low rates of professional occupations compared with their native-origin counterparts (see table 5.5). As we saw in the previous section, the NEET rates of second-generation Turkish women in Vienna are also the highest (see table 5.1).

Generally, the cities with the lowest NEET rates also have the highest rates of professional occupations, among both the second-generation and the native-origin groups. One surprising exception is Berlin, which has both a high NEET rate and a high rate of young professionals in the native-origin group (see table 5.4). It seems that although many young native-origin Berliners do not work (or go to school), those who do are very likely to work in white-collar jobs. The rates suggest a highly polarized labor force, or perhaps that being marginal in the labor market in

TABLE 5.4   Rates of Professional Occupation

		Male	Female
New York	Native whites	51.6%	55.1%
Los Angeles	Native whites	42.7	47.9
Vienna	Comparison group	28.1	41.6
Berlin	Comparison group	45.5	31.8
Paris	Comparison group	66.0	47.0
Stockholm	Comparison group	55.5	54.1
Amsterdam	Comparison group	53.3	65.9
Brussels	Comparison group	31.6	39.7

Source: Authors' calculations based on TIES survey 2007, 2008, ISGMNY (Mollenkopf, Kasinitz, and Waters 1999), and IIMMLA (Rumbaut et al. 2004).

FIGURE 5.5   Professional Occupations, New York

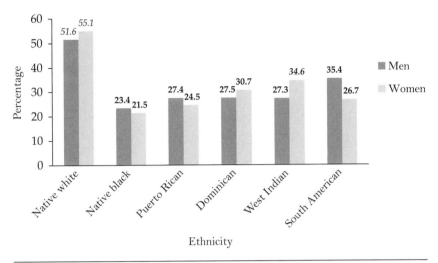

Ethnicity

Source: Authors' calculations based on ISGMNY (Mollenkopf, Kasinitz, and Waters 1999).
Note: Bold numbers indicate a significant difference from native white. Italics indicate significant difference from native black.

Berlin, with its long bohemian traditions, may in some ways be different than being marginal in the other cities. In any event, it seems clear that if, at first glance, the common high NEET rates suggest some similarities between German and immigrant-origin Berliners, the marked differences in the types of jobs they hold underline the real differences in their labor market experiences.

When we compare professional employment among second-generation Dominicans in New York with the other second-generation groups and the native white and black groups there, a pattern emerges that parallels the findings for the NEET rates. Dominicans are slightly more likely than native African Americans and Puerto Ricans, but less likely than other second-generation groups and much less likely than native whites, to be in white-collar employment (see figure 5.5). Gender differences are smaller in New York than in the European cities. Only among South Americans are men notably more likely than women to have professional occupations.

The second-generation Mexicans in Los Angeles were slightly less likely than African Americans to hold professional jobs and do less well than the native (third-generation or more) Mexicans (see figure 5.6). Latin Americans in Los Angeles stand out with a much higher percentage of

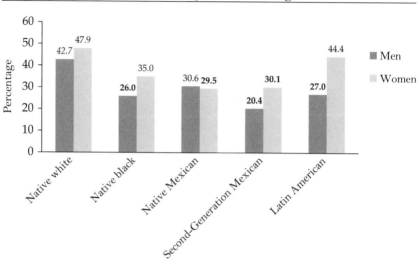

Source: Authors' calculations based on IIMMLA (Rumbaut et al. 2004).
Note: Bold numbers indicate a significant difference from native white. Italics indicate significant difference from native black.

professional occupations among women than men, with rates approaching those of native whites.

In Brussels, second-generation Turks have almost the same percentages of professional jobs as second-generation Moroccans (see figure 5.7). In Amsterdam, however, the difference between men and women among second-generation Moroccans is especially large. The rate of professional status among Moroccan-origin men is particularly low, lower than that of Turkish-origin men. Moroccan-origin women, in contrast, though still far less likely to hold professional jobs than native Dutch women, are two and a half times more likely to hold such jobs than Moroccan-origin men are. Indeed, Moroccan-origin women in Amsterdam are more likely to be professionals than members of any other second-generation group—men or women—in any of the European cities. This clearly points to the role of education among Moroccan-origin girls in Amsterdam—and the contrast in educational attainment among girls and boys there (for a fuller discussion of similar findings, see Crul and Doomernik 2003).

The differences between second-generation Turks and second-generation Yugoslavs are in line with the findings for the NEET rates (see figure 5.8). The second-generation Yugoslavs are precisely midway between the native-origin group and the Turkish second generation.

FIGURE 5.7   Professional Occupations, Amsterdam and Brussels

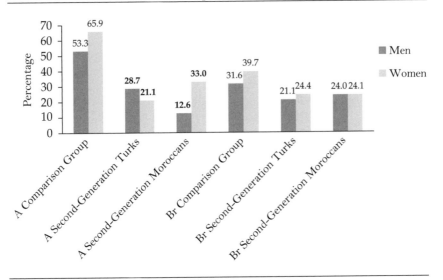

Source: Authors' calculations based on TIES survey 2007, 2008.
Note: Bold numbers indicate a significant difference from native-origin comparison group.
A = Amsterdam, Br = Brussels

FIGURE 5.8   Professional Occupations, Vienna and Berlin

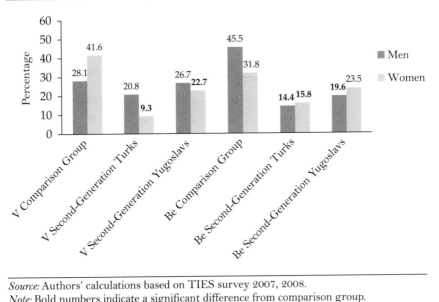

Source: Authors' calculations based on TIES survey 2007, 2008.
Note: Bold numbers indicate a significant difference from comparison group.
V = Vienna, Be = Berlin

TABLE 5.5   Rates of Professional Occupation After Controlling for Covariates

		Final Model, Percentage Probability	
		Male	Female
New York	Dominican second generation	22	28
	Native whites	28	23
Los Angeles	Mexican second generation	26	36
	Native whites	27	30
Vienna	Turkish second generation	58	29
	Comparison group	40	61
Berlin	Turkish second generation	43	45
	Comparison group	66	53
Paris	Turkish second generation	66	48
	Comparison group	63	62
Stockholm	Turkish second generation	64	58
	Comparison group	65	61
Amsterdam	Turkish second generation	53	57
	Comparison group	53	64
Brussels	Turkish second generation	66	74
	Comparison group	65	64

Source: Authors' calculations based on TIES survey 2007, 2008, ISGMNY (Mollenkopf, Kasinitz, and Waters 1999), and IIMMLA (Rumbaut et al. 2004).
Note: The following variables are controlled for in the table: age, has child, years in job, parents' education, parents' labor market participation, place respondent grew up, respondent's education.

In almost all cities, second-generation men are less likely to hold professional occupations than native-origin men. Yet, after controlling for background characteristics such as age, whether the respondent grew up in the survey city, parents' education, years in the labor market, parents' labor market participation while the respondent was growing up, whether the respondent has a child, and respondent's education, many differences between comparison groups and the second generation disappear (see table 5.5).

Age, having a child, parents' education, and where the respondents grew up are all significant explanations for the differences between the groups in the two U.S. cities. Having grown up outside the survey city is also significant in Berlin, with professionals in the comparison group more

TABLE 5.6   Average Monthly Income

		No Controls, Average	
		Male	Female
New York ($)	Dominican second generation	1731	1639
Los Angeles ($)	Mexican second generation	1658	1458
Vienna (€)	Turkish second generation	1281	954
Berlin (€)	Turkish second generation	1393	1163
Paris (€)	Turkish second generation	1987	1561
Stockholm (€)	Turkish second generation	1836	1467
Amsterdam (€)	Turkish second generation	1498	1137
Brussels (€)	Turkish second generation	1777	1381

Source: Authors' calculations based on TIES survey 2007, 2008, ISGMNY (Mollenkopf, Kasinitz, and Waters 1999), and IIMMLA (Rumbaut et al. 2004).

likely to have moved to Berlin than their second-generation counterparts. As with the NEET rate, the native-origin group in Berlin resembles the native whites in New York and Los Angeles in that many came to the city to pursue careers and higher education. They are thus highly selected for characteristics associated with professional employment. Age makes a difference in all the cities except Berlin, and time in the labor market is also significant in all the European cities. Not surprisingly, the respondents' parents' educational level is a significant predictor of professional employment in all the European cities except Brussels (where parents' labor market participation matters instead) and, tellingly, Stockholm. Indeed, as with the NEET rate, Stockholm stands out in that lower levels of parental education do not significantly reduce the chances of obtaining professional employment. This finding is consistent with previous research on the second generation in Sweden (Jonsson 2007; Heath, Rothon, and Kilpi 2008).

INCOME

It is more difficult to compare incomes across cities than our other two outcomes. In addition to the obvious currency differences across the Atlantic, and measurement differences across the surveys, differences across the European cities are considerable in average wage rates and the purchasing power of the euro.

The differences between the cities in the average monthly wages are not huge (see table 5.6). Those who are in the NEET category are not

FIGURE 5.9   Average (Weighted) Yearly Income, New York

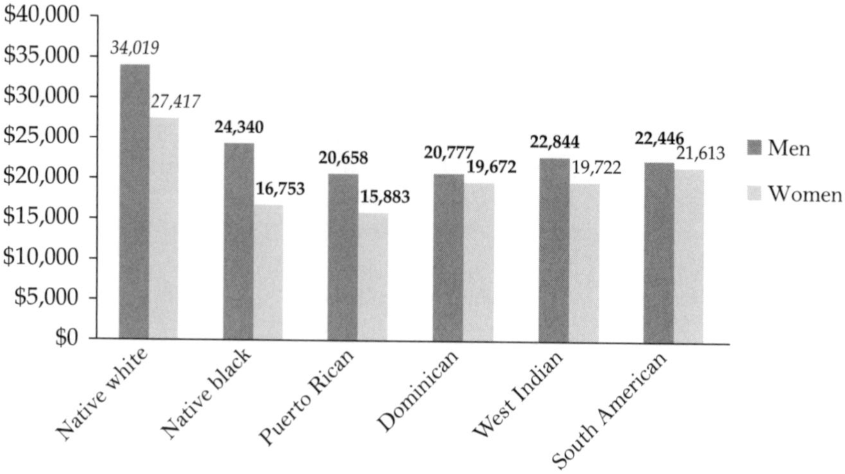

Source: Authors' calculations based on ISGMNY (Mollenkopf, Kasinitz, and Waters 1999).
Note: Bold numbers indicate a significant difference from native white. Italics indicate significant difference from native black.

included in the calculations. The numbers living on social benefits without income from wages at all obviously vary greatly across the cities. Income distributions in Europe are also generally more compressed than in the United States (see chapter 10, this volume).

When we compare the incomes of the second-generation Dominicans and Mexicans with other second-generation groups in New York and Los Angeles, the differences are actually very small, despite the substantial differences in the percentage holding professional jobs (see figures 5.9 and 5.10). In both cities, men earn more than women in most groups, with the notable exception of African Americans in Los Angeles, among whom men and women earn about the same. Indeed, African American women are roughly on par with native white women in Los Angeles.

In the European cities, differences between second-generation groups are substantial. In Brussels, second-generation Turks and Moroccans are almost equally likely to hold professional jobs, but the earnings of the second-generation Turks are much higher (see figure 5.12). In Vienna and Berlin, second-generation Yugoslavs come close to earning the same incomes as the native-origin comparison group (see figure 5.11). In only one case, second-generation Turks in Vienna, do second-generation men earn significantly less than comparison group men. Among second-generation

FIGURE 5.10   Average Yearly Income, Los Angeles

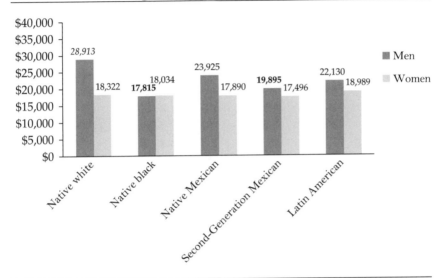

Source: Authors' calculations based on IIMMLA (Rumbaut et al. 2004).
Note: Bold numbers indicate a significant difference from native white. Italics indicate significant difference from native black.

FIGURE 5.11   Average Monthly Income, Vienna and Berlin

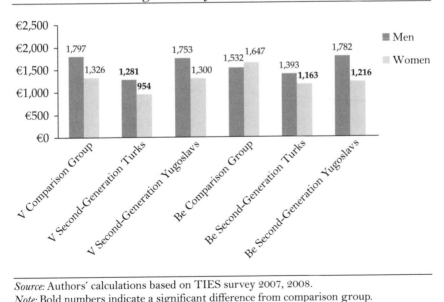

Source: Authors' calculations based on TIES survey 2007, 2008.
Note: Bold numbers indicate a significant difference from comparison group.
V = Vienna, Be = Berlin

FIGURE 5.12   Average Monthly Income, Amsterdam and Brussels

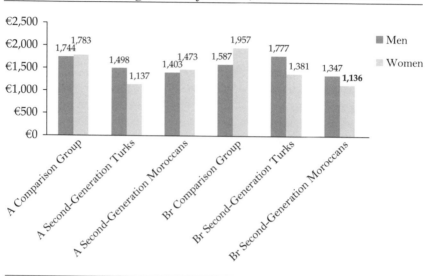

Source: Authors' calculations based on TIES survey 2007, 2008.
Note: Bold numbers indicate a significant difference from comparison group.
A = Amsterdam, Br = Brussels

Turks and Yugoslavs, men earn more than women across the board, and Turkish-origin women earn significantly less than native-origin women in Vienna and Berlin. In Brussels, Moroccan-origin women also earn significantly less than their native-origin counterparts, but Turkish-origin women do not.

Comparing the native (white) comparison group with second-generation Turks in the European cities, second-generation Dominicans in New York, and second-generation Mexicans in Los Angeles (table 5.7), we see that almost all the differences in income across these groups can be explained by the background variables included in our multivariate models. The only differences that remain after controlling for social background factors are among second-generation Turkish women and native women in Amsterdam, Berlin, and Vienna, where second-generation Turkish women have lower predicted incomes. Concerned that this might be the effect of having children (that is, that having children leads women to cut down their work hours and that Turkish-origin women are more likely to have children than native-origin women in these cities), we reran the income analyses but included a control for having a child. The results did not change substantially. Having a child had a significant effect on earnings only in

TABLE 5.7   Average Monthly Income After Controlling for Covariates

		Final Model, Predicted Average	
		Male	Female
New York ($)	Dominican second generation	1649	1362
	Native whites	1790	1412
Los Angeles ($)	Mexican second generation	1398	1075
	Native whites	1538	952
Vienna (€)	Turkish second generation	1437	973
	Comparison group	1652	1212
Berlin (€)	Turkish second generation	1224	963
	Comparison group	1224	1261
Paris (€)	Turkish second generation	2143	1686
	Comparison group	1556	1422
Stockholm (€)	Turkish second generation	1882	1480
	Comparison group	1845	1495
Amsterdam (€)	Turkish second generation	1720	1176
	Comparison group	1604	1556
Brussels (€)	Turkish second generation	1901	1556
	Comparison group	1703	1556

Source: Authors' calculations based on TIES survey 2007, 2008, ISGMNY (Mollenkopf, Kasinitz, and Waters 1999), and IIMMLA (Rumbaut et al. 2004).
Note: The following variables are controlled for in the right half of the table: age, years in job, parents' education, parents' labor market participation, place respondents grew up, respondents' education, professional occupation. Dollar amounts represent yearly income, euro amounts represent monthly income.

Amsterdam, but even there it did not change the remaining earnings gap between second-generation Turkish women and their comparison group counterparts that we see in the table. We cannot say with any certainty that discrimination is responsible for the lower incomes among Turkish-origin women in Amsterdam, Berlin, and Vienna, but the data suggest that this is a strong possibility.

As one might expect, the covariates that generally seem to make the most difference for income are age, time in the labor market, education, and professional occupation. All these are significant predictors in both the U.S. cities and Amsterdam. Surprisingly, professional occupation does not seem to matter in Brussels and Paris, and respondents' education level does not seem to make an independent difference in Vienna, Berlin, and Paris. Whatever the long-term benefits of higher education and professional status, in many of the European cities these attributes do not guarantee higher incomes, at least for people in their twenties and early thirties. Of course, this might be an artifact of the age of the TIES respondents. Even though they were not in education when income was measured, some of the best educated will still be getting further education and training. Their current low incomes may be a poor predictor of their eventual earning power.

Contrary to expectation, parents' labor market activity made no difference in the respondent's income except in Brussels and in New York. However, parents' education—often a proxy for class background—does matter in most cities. It was a significant predictor of income in Paris, Berlin, Brussels, Vienna, and New York. Having grown up outside the survey city, while a positive predictor of income in New York (as expected), is actually a negative predictor in Vienna. Just as international migration selects for certain characteristics, internal migration is also selective. In New York, it is clearly selecting for higher education and for being on a professional career trajectory, and the results are seen in the higher incomes. Why coming from other parts of Austria has the opposite effect for young Viennese is less clear.

CONCLUSION

The data presented in this chapter make a strong case for the importance of comparative work when assessing the progress of the second generation. In any one city or nation, it is easy to focus on the characteristics of the groups seen as problematic and to take the context of reception for granted. Comparing across cities and countries helps us understand how these group characteristics interact with different local and national contexts of reception, sometimes leading to sharply different outcomes.

On the whole, second-generation integration seems to be proceeding most successfully in Stockholm. Despite the relatively low labor force participation of their immigrant parents, Stockholm's second generation suffers little disadvantage relative to its native-origin peers. Parental background characteristics, such as low levels of education, have comparatively little effect on the second generation's life chances. Gender differences in labor force participation and entry into professional employment are also less pronounced in Stockholm than in the other cities, both for the comparison group and the second generation. The success of the second generation in joining the economic mainstream in Stockholm is a strong argument against the idea that generous welfare states discourage labor integration. Indeed, the results would seem to be a strong endorsement of the proposition that an active welfare state can and does compensate for many differences in parental background and greatly facilitates immigrant integration. Somewhat surprisingly, Paris, another city in which the state plays a significant role in the labor market, is also among the successful cities according to the data presented. This suggests a striking contrast to the usual image of alienated and socially marginalized immigrant and second-generation youth in the Paris suburbs. However, the lack of Maghrébins in the Paris TIES sample may leave a misleading impression. The relative success of the Turkish second generation in Paris may in fact be tied to their not being Maghrébins. The comparison confirms that nothing inherent about being Muslim or of Turkish origin produces the sorts of outcomes we see for Turkish-origin youth in the German-speaking cities.

On the whole, Berlin and Vienna are the least successful in terms of granting opportunities for advancement to the children of immigrants. Further research might explore why the well-developed apprenticeship systems in these cities do not seem to be working well for the second generation. At the same time, in Berlin a large portion of the native-origin comparison group is also having a hard time finding an employment niche. By most measures, Amsterdam and Brussels are positioned somewhere between these extremes. In the two U.S. cities, the second generation's incorporation into the labor force has also been less successful than in Stockholm, but generally more successful than in Berlin and Vienna. In both New York and Los Angeles, the second-generation groups generally occupy an intermediary position, doing less well than native whites but better than native African Americans on most measures.

In most cities, the central issue seems to be getting employment in the first place. The group differences in NEET rates are more dramatic and tell us more than the generally modest group differences in professional status and income. However, counter to the usual stereotypes about an urban underclass, the problem (if it is, in fact, a problem) of high NEET rates is most acute among women—and may have much to do with traditional family structures and child rearing. Indeed, being NEET is a quite different phenomenon for men and for women. For men, high NEET rates strongly suggest groups isolated from gainful employment and possibly meaningful social participation. The high rates for second-generation Turkish men in many European cities, like those for African Americans in the United States, suggest potential social isolation of the disadvantaged of the sort William Julius Wilson (1996) has suggested in the United States. At the same time, the much lower NEET rate for second-generation Turkish men in Stockholm is noteworthy.

Among women, however, a high NEET rate may indicate a second generation whose gender norms remain closer to those of their immigrant parents than of the native population. This is particularly true in Germany and Austria. That so many Turkish-origin women are engaged in neither the labor force nor education in these cities points to a major ongoing difference between the second generation and the comparison populations and may have implications for contact with the larger society and assimilation. But whether this continuing difference in gender roles, family forms, and lifestyles constitutes a real social problem is a matter of opinion. In any event, the situation among NEET women would seem less a matter of downward assimilation—to borrow Portes and Rumbaut's term—than a lack of assimilation and maintenance of traditional values and ties to the ethnic community. At least some U.S. observers have suggested that such ties can actually be an asset, giving second-generation youth access to the resources of their parents' ethnic enclave economies (Portes and Rumbaut 2001; Zhou and Bankston 1998).

At the same time, the high NEET rates for second-generation women are closely related to child rearing and are highest in those cities where labor force participation by the mothers of young children is low among native-origin women as well. Indeed, part of the difference between the native-origin comparison groups and the second generation is due to the latter's higher fertility in this age group. Yet while this explains differences in the likelihood of being in the labor force, it does not explain differences in income between Turkish and native-origin women, at least in the German-speaking cities where those differences are greatest.

Last is the importance of being (or not being) the dominant minority group within a labor market. In the United States, second-generation groups, far from forming an underclass, seem to occupy a position between native minorities and native whites. Studies suggest that employers often prefer them to African Americans (Kasinitz and Rosenberg 1996; Waldinger 1996). In those European cities where we have two second-generation groups in the TIES sample, it is usually the non-Turkish group that seems to occupy a similar, intermediate position. Moreover, Turks are best off in Paris—a city where they are clearly not the dominant minority. Exploring why the Turkish second generation does better in a city where another group is more strongly stigmatized would be a fascinating avenue for further research.

CHAPTER 6

IMMIGRANTS' DAUGHTERS AND THE LABOR MARKET

Thomas Soehl, Rosita Fibbi, and Constanza Vera-Larrucea

The previous chapter gave a broad analysis of labor market outcomes for the second generation. This one looks specifically at how the daughters of immigrants fare in the labor markets of different countries. Building on feminist critiques of the welfare state literature, we argue that welfare state arrangements play a critical role in whether and how these young women transition into the workforce. Although welfare state characteristics shape the labor force participation of women regardless of nativity or heritage, they have amplified effects for young women from immigrant families.

A major theme in the earlier chapters of this volume has been how institutional arrangements like those governing education and the transition from school to work are critical to the life chances of the second generation. For example, as chapter 2 shows, the ways in which particular systems sort and track pupils have a large influence on second-generation educational achievement (see also Kasinitz et al. 2008; Crul and Schneider 2009). This chapter follows that approach by looking at the gender dimension of policies and practices that shape the second-generation transition into labor market participation and family formation. This approach can be fruitfully subsumed under the term *welfare state regimes*.

A substantial literature has developed on how welfare states affect employment dynamics. Much less attention has been given to how different welfare state regimes affect population subgroups (Bambra 2007). First-generation outcomes have received some attention (Kogan 2006), but those of the second generation have until now received much less. This chapter contributes to filling this gap. We do this by analyzing the position of second-generation women in Germany, Switzerland, Sweden, and the United States. We thus follow the lead of feminist critics of the welfare state literature who point out that ways of providing welfare and ways welfare states shape labor markets both have substantial implications for gender relations and roles in many domains (O'Connor 1996; Sundström 1999).

WELFARE STATES, LABOR MARKETS, AND GENDER EQUALITY

The movement of women into the labor force is one of the most profound social changes of the twentieth century. Over recent decades, women in all advanced industrial economies have moved into the labor force, though their participation levels vary significantly across countries, from about 60 percent in Italy to almost 90 percent in Sweden. Entry into the labor market and diminished economic dependence on men are important elements in the empowerment of women. Feminist researchers have focused their analysis of welfare regimes on the extent to which they promote women's personal and public independence: they argue that we must supplement the traditional emphasis on decommodification with a concern for personal autonomy or insulation from dependence (O'Connor 1993). Women's right to economic, personal, and social autonomy is central in feminist debates of the welfare state. Eva Sundström defines gender regimes as "the ways in which political and institutional solutions affect and are affected by men's and women's actual possibilities to choose between paid and unpaid work, along with the ways in which both kinds of work are open up for entrance to social rights" (1999, 194).

Recent research provides empirical support for this view. According to Becky Pettit's and Jennifer Hook's (2005) analysis of the effect of having a child on female labor force participation across nineteen countries, social policies do substantially affect the overall labor force participation of women, as does the trade-off they face between family and work. For example, generous public provision of child care always increases female employment. Parental leave has more ambiguous results, with short parental leave provisions in Switzerland having positive effects but long ones in Germany tending to separate women from the labor force.

More generally, the question of how institutional arrangements and economic structures shape different outcomes is an important topic in welfare state analysis. Gøsta Esping-Andersen (1990) developed a typology to address this issue. He links the characteristics of welfare states to their performance in creating jobs, promoting certain economic sectors over others, and encouraging female labor force participation. He identifies three main welfare regimes: socialist, conservative, and liberal. Liberal and social democratic regimes are friendlier toward female labor force participation, and conservative models are biased against it. Esping-Andersen uses Sweden, Germany, and the United States as exemplars of these three types. Subsequent research has also classified Switzerland as a mixed conservative-liberal welfare state (Merrien and Bonoli 2000). Its welfare system has both conservative and liberal features: typical of conservative welfare states, it conditions access to benefits on employment status, but, at the same time, private organizations provide health care and pensions, and means testing is as widespread as in other liberal welfare states (Oesch 2008).

Liberal welfare states characteristically condition assistance on means testing. Eligibility for welfare provision depends on both personal or family situation and economic condition. Universal assistance is scarce, as are social-insurance schemes. Anglo Saxon countries typical take this approach. Their labor markets are generally flexible, making job changes and reentry comparatively easy. In most countries with these characteristics, the labor force has expanded rapidly in recent decades and female employment has risen sharply. Much of this growth was in the private service sector, including business and consumer services (Esping-Andersen 1990).

Social democratic regimes are oriented toward equality and decommodification (that is, insulating individuals from market forces) by providing universal social insurance. The emphasis is first on the individual and only then on the family. The idea is not to subsidize the family but rather to socialize the cost of parenthood. The social policies of such nations support women not only in their family roles but also in their roles as workers outside the household. Scandinavian countries take this approach with Sweden being the exemplar. Like the United States, Sweden experienced significant employment growth as well as increased female labor force participation. In contrast to the United States, where private services drove this development, government employment, especially in the welfare sector, was central to the labor force expansion in Sweden.

Conservative welfare regimes make the family, not the individual, the object of social services. Because social benefits are often tied to employment, those who are marginal to the labor market (often women) receive welfare benefits only indirectly, as dependents. Furthermore, social policies emphasize the motherhood role for women and provide fewer services like day care or whole day schooling. In effect, these policies reduce the available labor force and partly as a result, employment growth was sluggish and female labor force participation rose only slowly in these welfare states (Esping-Andersen 1990, chap. 8).

Taken together, the conservative welfare states assume the male breadwinner model—the man's position in the labor market provides not only wages but also the link to social benefits (Lewis 1992). These benefits in turn support women's position as a homemaker and do not encourage their participation in the labor market. However, this model, dominant until the 1960s, has been eroded by profound changes in family forms, the opening of education systems to women, the growth of the service economy, and women's new access to the labor market. Today, dual- and 1.5-earner models play an important role in the United States and most European countries (Lewis 2001). At the same time, countries have reacted differently to gender-based claims concerning family support, ranging from reliance on market mechanisms to support for the nuclear family to targeted support for the dual-earner family. Walter Korpi's study on such policy responses shows that Germany developed a general family support model, Sweden a dual-earner model, and Switzerland and the United States a market-oriented gender policy model (2000, 144).

This brief summary shows how the ways in which a welfare state provides benefits and structures labor markets has direct consequences on women's labor market position and how women make the trade-off between joining the labor force and establishing families. Welfare states shape different breadwinner models. Social democratic and liberal welfare states are more compatible with double breadwinner families, whereas conservative welfare countries are biased toward a single breadwinner in the family: conservative welfare states have the highest rates of part-time work among women (Pettit and Hook 2009).

WELFARE STATES AND IMMIGRANTS

Many observers contend that a strong welfare state with immigration is incompatible with ethnic diversity (Freeman 1986; Alesina and Glaeser 2004). Much less attention has been paid to the other direction—how welfare states' characteristics affect immigrant integration. To the extent that immigration scholars have considered this issue, they focus mostly on the first generation.

In a recent review symposium, Philip Kasinitz, John Mollenkopf, and Mary Waters speculate that the limited nature of the U.S. welfare state encourages men and women equally to enter the labor market. In contrast, European welfare states and more tightly regulated labor markets have "pushed the immigrant parents out of the labor force" (Alba et al. 2010, 355). Not only does this allow the majority to negatively stereotype immigrant groups as unproductive, it also means that members of the second generation are more likely to grow up in homes where at least the mother is not working. However, welfare benefits may work in their intended way by providing a temporary infusion of resources that allows people to overcome temporary disadvantage and regain economic independence. This might especially hold where welfare benefits could provide a temporary bridge until migrants figure out how to navigate their new context. Instead of having to develop day-to-day survival strategies, they could invest in long-term strategies of family mobility that promote socioeconomic incorporation (Bean, Stevens, and Van Hook 2003; Menjivar 1997).

At the same time, generous welfare states might also limit labor market options for immigrants. To the extent that generous welfare provisions go hand in hand with tightly regulated labor markets, fewer entry-level jobs are likely to be available (Esping-Andersen 1990). This will be especially consequential for those immigrants without specialized knowledge and educational credentials. Examining unemployment risks of immigrants, Irena Kogan (2006) finds that male immigrants are less disadvantaged in countries with flexible, less regulated labor markets, but the effect for women is not discernible. Immigrant women, however, are significantly disadvantaged relative to natives in Scandinavian countries with policies encouraging high female labor force participation.

Citizenship and integration policies provide another angle to this debate. Ruud Koopmans (2010) argues that strong multicultural policies together with a generous safety net create disincentives for labor force participation that hinder integration and lead to socioeconomic marginalization. Especially for a woman "letting . . . religious duties prevail over the local government's concern with employability has the likely consequence that she will remain a life-long dependent on social welfare benefits" (4). Following this argument, countries that condition naturalization on not relying on the social safety net provide stronger incentives for labor force participation. Those with multicultural policies, by contrast, will grant citizenship more easily, regardless of welfare dependence, thus removing incentives for immigrants to become economically independent.

Welfare States, Immigration, and Second-Generation Women

The welfare state context is only one aspect of the labor market integration of second-generation women. What sorts of labor markets and neighborhoods their parents entered, their class and human capital background, and the opportunities available to the mothers of our respondents are also critical determinants of the daughters' labor force participation, as pointed out in the previous chapter.

Table 6.1 summarizes the key social background and family indicators for our respondents, namely, fathers' education and mothers' labor force participation. The human capital of the Turkish-born parents varies substantially across countries. The first three rows show that Turkish-origin fathers in Germany had substantially lower educational credentials than those in Switzerland and Sweden: whereas 60 percent in Germany had a primary education or less, only about a third in Sweden or Switzerland did. Although different coding and interview schemes make comparison inexact, we see that the Mexican-born fathers of our IIMMLA respondents were on average more like the Turkish-born fathers in Sweden and Switzerland than those in Germany. (We coded the IIMMLA data to put those with no more than six years of education into the lowest education category. Using eight years as a cut-off, the share would rise to 36 percent for Mexicans.)

Germany

The Turkish and former Yugoslavian second generation in Germany largely grew up in guest-worker families. During the economic boom in the 1960s, Germany, like several other European countries, recruited guest workers from rural and poor areas to fill labor shortages. The hope was that they would be there only temporarily and eventually return home. But when the government halted recruitment in the wake of the economic crisis in the early 1970s, a large share of the guest workers decided to stay. From then on, migration continued through family reunion. For female immigrants, this meant coming to Germany as dependent spouses and not as labor migrants. Because family reunion happened mostly after the economy slowed, these women also faced unfavorable labor markets.

They also encountered legal hurdles to employment. Through the 1970s, spouses of guest workers faced a three- to four-year waiting period before they could legally seek employment (Mushaben 2009). Furthermore, their legal status and right to residence was tied to that of their spouses. Until

TABLE 6.1   Family Background

| | Fathers' Education | | | | Mothers' Labor Force Participation |
	Primary or Less	Secondary or Vocational	Academic or Higher Vocational	Missing	
Turkish descent Germany	61%	20%	2%	17%	17%
Turkish descent Sweden	36	41	16	8	63
Turkish descent Switzerland	34	47	10	10	59
Ex-Yugoslavian descent Germany	2	73	7	18	43
Ex-Yugoslavian descent Switzerland	5	70	10	15	58
Mexican descent Los Angeles	30	40	5	25	58
Chinese descent Los Angeles	7	30	56	7	75
Dominican descent New York	22	42	11	26	75
West Indian descent New York	3	43	15	38	90
Comparison group:					
Germany	1	74	22	4	48
Sweden	0	50	50	0	88
Switzerland	3	55	32	9	61
Los Angeles	1	49	43	8	missing
New York	2	42	44	12	70

Source: Authors' compilation based on TIES survey 2007, 2008 (data not yet publicly available).
Note: The TIES survey comprises eight separate national data sets, collected by Institute for Studies on Migrations (IEM), Comillas Pontifical University, Spain; Swiss Forum for Migration and Population Studies (SFM), Neuchâtel, Switzerland; Netherlands Interdisciplinary Demographic Institute (NIDI), The Hague, Netherlands; Austrian Academy of Sciences (ÖAW), Vienna, Austria; the European Research Centre on Migration and Ethnic Relations (ERCOMER), Katholieke Universiteit Leuven, Belgium; National Institute for Demographic Studies (INED), Paris, France; Institute for Migration Research and Intercultural Studies (IMIS), University of Osnabrück, Germany; Centre for Research in International Migration and Ethnic Relations (CEIFO), Stockholm University, Sweden. The TIES national surveys will be made publicly available by the national TIES partners individually, but were not yet available at the time of publication.

the 1990s, women could lose their residency (and other benefits) if they got divorced before a certain number of years.

Although Germany later lifted many of these restrictions, it maintains a strict citizenship policy. Access to citizenship was not even a right for the German-born children of noncitizens until 2000. For the foreign born, long-term dependence on welfare benefits can still block access to secure resident status and citizenship. Many immigrant women in Germany thus faced a double dependency: their residence rights were tied to their role as spouses and they faced legal restrictions to employment and economic independence. Germany also conditioned membership rights at least partially on economic independence. These women thus faced formidable obstacles to employment.

Sweden

Turkish migration to Sweden started with the formal recruitment of workers in the 1960s. The mostly male migration had a different character than elsewhere in Europe because Sweden expected immigrants eventually to become citizens (Jordan 2006). In the 1970s, the wives and children of the Turkish workers arrived through family reunification. Later, refugees who had been minorities in Turkey added to Sweden's Turkish population. Many were of peasant origin and had little formal education (Westin 2003). Turkish families, especially those with agrarian backgrounds, largely adhere to traditional family roles with men as the sole providers.

Yet these immigrants encountered a welfare state strongly oriented to integrating women into the labor force. It benefits women as workers and not merely as wives or mothers (Engelke and Astrom 1992). A woman's work history, not her family status, entitles her to generous benefits and social services. These institutional factors affect all women, enabling them to combine work and childbearing. In fact, first-time mothers with and without immigrant backgrounds have high levels of income and employment stability (Andersson and Scott 2005). Thus the integration of immigrant women into the labor force has been encouraged by a welfare state actively supporting the working population regardless of gender or ethnic origin.

Switzerland

As in Germany, today's native-born Turkish and former Yugoslavian second generations in Switzerland are largely the offspring of the guest-worker families of the 1970s. Only a few of the parents were refugees. Immigrant women in Switzerland differ in their skills and their impetus for migration. Former Yugoslavians were often skilled, and both women and men arrived as workers. Turkish migration was mostly low skilled, however, and many women came to Switzerland during family reunion rather than as workers. In contrast to Germany, Turkish migrants make up only a small part of the foreign-born population, and former Yugoslavians a larger share—5 versus 18 percent respectively (Burri Sharani et al. 2010). By the end of 2007, approximately 72,000 Turkish citizens and roughly 45,000 naturalized Swiss citizens of Turkish origin (Haab et al. 2010) lived in Switzerland, about 117,000 in all, versus some 290,000 former Yugoslavians.[1]

Switzerland has a strict citizenship policy solely based on jus sanguinis. Ongoing discussions have reaffirmed this principle. Access to citizenship is highly politicized. Each individual naturalization act is a political decision rather than an administrative matter. Swiss-born children of immigrants have no right to Swiss citizenship. Long-term dependence on welfare benefits can block access to secure resident status and citizenship; moreover, labor market participation along with proficiency in the local language may be considered a prerequisite for naturalization. In spite of this strict policy, large numbers of the Swiss-born second generation from Turkey and former Yugoslavia managed to acquire Swiss citizenship in the last decade, as did many of their parents.

Overall, the Swiss welfare state hinders female labor market participation by not encouraging women to work. Better qualified women from Swiss backgrounds often meet this challenge through part-time work in the service sector (Branger 2009), an option not always available to lower-skilled and lower-earning immigrant women.

United States (Los Angeles)

Given the enormous variation in background and legal status of migrants in the United States, it is almost impossible to sketch out the full range of labor market experiences of the mothers of the new second generation. Nevertheless, even painted in broad strokes, important contrasts emerge: compared with Europe, many women are labor migrants. Immigrant female labor force participation is a bit lower than the native (approximately 70 percent), but still high (about 60 percent). It is interesting that there is no difference in labor force participation between legal and undocumented migrant women (Fortuny, Capps, and Passel 2007, 51). But having children does have a disproportional effect. Although about 10 percent of native women with a child drop out of the labor force, about twice as many legal immigrants do, and about three times as many undocumented women do (52). This could reflect a trade-off between wages and child-care costs. If wages are so low that earnings do not or only marginally cover child-care expenses, women obviously have little incentive to seek employment. In this instance, the lack of public support for the cost of raising children, especially affordable day care, could dampen female labor force participation. This is especially true of undocumented female migrants, who likely rank at the bottom of the wage distribution.

Thus, although female migrants overall have a comparably high attachment to the labor force, the growing number without legal status may face difficult trade-offs between family and employment. For the second generation, this means not only having no working mother to provide a role model but also growing up in households that have to rely on only one income.

However, many of the U.S. second generation face fewer obstacles than their mothers did. English fluency, better educational credentials, and legal status translate into significantly higher earnings, shifting the balance in favor of working, even for those who have children. The situation might be different for the foreign-born but U.S.-raised 1.5 generation, for whom legal status and the associated disadvantages pose significant hurdles.

Different Contexts Pose Different Challenges

Not only do women in these different countries make different choices about working in the face of different institutional arrangements, they come from different family backgrounds. The first step in our analysis is to examine how second-generation female labor force participation compares with that of women from native-born backgrounds. We also look at the breadwinner arrangements for those who formed their own households and examine how parental background and family formation affect the labor force participation of second-generation women.

The institutional arrangements of the different welfare state regimes discussed do not discriminate according to immigrant or native background per se. That German social policy is biased against female labor force participation does not in itself explain any differences between the Turkish second generation and native Germans. Yet these policies interact with such characteristics as educational background, social class, family structures, or legal status in ways that have disproportionate impacts across groups. We argue that these institutional mechanisms in some cases have disproportional effects on those with migrant parents.

For example, children of Turkish background in Germany are heavily overrepresented in the vocational schooling tracks. This is because those with working-class parents, whether immigrant or native, tend to be sorted into nonacademic tracks (Crul and Vermeulen 2003b). The distributional pattern thus reflects the German schooling system's disproportionate negative effect on Turkish students with respect to their working-class background, not their ethnicity or migration status.

In going back to the case of labor force participation, we see that if second-generation women time childbearing earlier than their native counterparts, then social policies that make it hard for women to combine family and work can have a disproportionally negative effect on the second generation. Also, in contexts like Germany where social policies and societal expectations do not incentivize women's labor force participation, family precedent (for example, mothers' labor force participation) may play a more important role. In these cases low labor force participation among the first generation will lead to low employment rates among second-generation women. In contrast, in Sweden and the United States, where social policies encourage women to work and society generally expects them to do so, family background will be a less important factor.

ANALYSIS

We draw here on TIES data from the German, Swedish, and Swiss cases as well as IIMMLA and ISGMNY for the U.S. cases. In the European surveys, we analyze Turkish and former Yugoslavian second-generation respondents. In the United States, we look at second-generation Mexicans, other South Americans, as well as Koreans, Chinese, Vietnamese, and Filipinos in the Los Angeles survey (IIMMLA) and the Dominican, Russian-Jewish, and West Indian second generations in New York (ISGMNY). In every case, those with native-born parents make up the comparison group, and we used only the native white cases in the U.S. surveys. Although respondents are drawn from urban settings that may not be nationally representative, we do evaluate both second-generation and control groups in the same labor market. Thus the city basis of these surveys is not necessarily a disadvantage.

Labor Force Participation and Breadwinner Arrangements

The first three columns of table 6.2 summarize three main labor market outcomes for the women we are analyzing. We distinguish between unemployment and dropping out of the labor force because these positions could arguably represent different processes. Also, given the youth of our sample, the lengths of different educational trajectories could mask differences in labor force participation; we therefore dropped all full-time students from the analysis.

The German-Turkish second-generation women have substantially lower (by a factor of two) labor force participation than young women born to native parents. Respondents with former Yugoslavian origins were somewhat more likely to be out of the labor force than those with German parents, but the difference is less dramatic. Comparing those holding a job, we see that the former Yugoslavian second generation is on par with women born to native parents. Only slightly more than half of the second-generation Turkish women (excluding full-time students), versus three-quarters of the other groups, held a job at the time of the interview. Unemployment is actually lower for both Turkish and former Yugoslavian women than for their German counterparts.

As expected, female labor force participation among those with native parents is quite high in Sweden. Almost 83 percent were working. Although the Turkish second-generation female participation rate is about 8 percentage points lower, the corresponding 74 percent employment rate is still high and on par with that of German women. Unlike in Germany, where dropping out of the labor force accounts for the majority of the difference in employment between immigrant and native rates, Turkish second-generation women in Sweden are only slightly more likely to drop out of the labor force. However, difficulties in finding a job seem to play a significant role—the Turkish second-generation women in Stockholm have an unemployment rate of 8 percent, about twice as high as the reference group.

In Switzerland, as table 6.2 shows, former Yugoslavian second-generation women work at about the same rate as Swiss women, but Turkish women work at a slightly (and statistically nonsignificant) higher rate. Considering how many hold jobs, the former Yugoslavian second generation is on par with women of Swiss descent; the Turkish second generation does less well, but not significantly so. All in all, almost nine women in ten hold a job, regardless of their ancestry. However, when it comes to unemployment, the gap widens among origin groups. The rate for second-generation women is several times higher than for their Swiss counterparts and ten times higher for women of Turkish descent.

In the United States, at first sight New York and Los Angeles seem to differ somewhat. However, the data were collected at two quite different times—the New York survey in 1999–2000 and Los Angeles survey in 2004—and the labor market information questions differ slightly. The

TABLE 6.2   Women, the Labor Force, and Breadwinner Arrangements

| | All Women in Sample | | | Breadwinner Arrangements | | | |
	Not in Labor Force	Has Job	Unemployed	Male	One and a Half	Dual	Other
Germany							
German descent	18.8%	73.7%	7.5%	23.3%	11.8%	62.9%	2.0%
Turkish descent	39.0	56.5	4.6	41.8	6.8	47.8	3.6
Ex-Yugoslavian descent	21.7	74.6	3.6	26.3	10.8	61.8	1.1
Sweden							
Swedish descent	13.4	82.9	3.7	12.3	13.6	61.7	11.9
Turkish descent	17.6	74.3	8.1	33.3	12.3	45.6	8.8
Switzerland							
Swiss descent	10.5	88.3	0.6	17.2	34.4	44.1	4.3
Turkish descent	9.7	83.0	6.3	22.5	33.8	28.2	15.5
Ex-Yugoslavian descent	9.2	88.6	2.2	11.8	42.4	37.6	8.2

(Table continues on p. 142.)

TABLE 6.2   *Continued*

	All Women in Sample			Breadwinner Arrangements			
	Not in Labor Force	Has Job	Unemployed	Male	One and a Half	Dual	Other
Los Angeles*							
Native white	18.8	77.4	3.8	25.5	20.6	43.1	10.8
Mexican	13.8	78.9	7.3	30.7	12.6	45.1	11.6
Korean	16.6	74.5	8.9	37.0	17.8	39.7	5.5
Chinese	10.5	80.9	8.6	29.6	11.1	55.6	3.7
Vietnamese	7.5	84.9	7.5	21.8	16.4	50.9	10.9
Filipino	11.6	83.2	5.2	23.2	15.9	52.4	8.5
New York							
Native white	7.7	85.5	6.8	17.1	12.2	52.4	18.3
Dominican	9.4	74.0	16.6	23.2	10.7	50.9	15.2
West Indian	7.1	78.1	14.2	16.7	5.6	57.4	20.4
Chinese	5.6	86.0	7.9	13.3	6.7	63.3	16.7
Russian–Jewish	5.5	85.5	9.1	14.6	12.2	48.8	24.4

Source: Authors' compilation based on IIMMLA (Rumbaut et al. 2004); TIES survey 2007, 2008.
*Multiple answers were possible in IIMMLA data.

labor markets and comparison groups are also somewhat different. Especially in New York City, about 30 percent of the native white comparison group grew up outside the city and moved there specifically for work—setting a high bar in terms of labor force participation. Nevertheless, looking at each city's patterns, except for women whose parents came from the Dominican Republic, we see that second-generation women are no more and in some cases are less likely to be out of the labor force than the comparison group with white native-born parents. However, unemployment is higher for them. In Los Angeles, except for Koreans, all second-generation women were more likely to hold a job even though their unemployment rates were significantly higher. Similarly, unemployment among Dominican and West Indian women is more than double than that of native white women in New York, though in this case they are also less likely to hold a job.

We developed a typology to summarize the breadwinner arrangements in couples that allows for six theoretical combinations of the partner's economic activity and women's labor force participation. (Because the TIES survey asked women respondents only about their spouse's work status, the typology concerns only their household arrangements.) The second panel in table 6.2 summarizes the most frequent combinations: male breadwinner (the man works but the woman does not); dual breadwinner (both spouses work full time); one-and-a-half breadwinner (the man works full time and the woman works part time). Due to small cell sizes, we grouped all other arrangements together, including either the woman as the only breadwinner or neither spouse working. In cases with large enough sample sizes, we provide more detail.

The dual-breadwinner pattern is the common family arrangement in Germany for cohabiting and married women born to German and former Yugoslavian parents (almost two couples in three). However, this pattern is found only among half of Turkish-descent women, and a similar share are economically dependent on their spouse (male breadwinner model). The proportion of couples practicing the one-and-a-half arrangement is small.

The diffusion of the dual-breadwinner model in Sweden is similar to that in Germany for women with native parents. Among Turkish-descent women, the male breadwinner model is more common than among those with native parents, though less frequent than in Germany. The one-and-a-half arrangement is about equally frequent in both groups. Woman who are sole breadwinners (category other) make up a much larger share in all groups compared with Germany.

In the Swiss case, a striking 33 percent of all women in unions across all groups (even more among those with a former Yugoslavian background) work part time in one-and-a-half earner households—significantly higher than any other case. This suggests that the high labor force participation of women in Switzerland reflects part-time work. The Turkish women grouped under other have two distinct patterns: the highest percentage of women sole breadwinners compared with other origin groups but also the highest share of households without any breadwinners. Compared with Germany and Sweden, male breadwinner arrangements are less frequent among Turkish respondents.

The dual-breadwinner model is characteristic of a plurality of respondents' unions in both U.S. cases. Dual-breadwinner arrangements are mostly as or more frequent among women of immigrant descent than in the native white comparison group; exceptions include Koreans in Los Angeles and the Russian-Jewish and Dominican second generations in New York City, though the differences are only around 4 percentage points, too small to permit substantive interpretation. However, Chinese second-generation women in both cities are 10 percentage points more likely to live in dual-earner households. Especially in New York City, a large share of women live in households with other breadwinner arrangements, mainly women as the sole or main breadwinner.

Overall, we can see that no single model of household earnings is dominant among the young women in our urban samples: dual-earner couples comes closest as the modal category for all groups, with the exception of the one-and-a-half model in Switzerland. Male breadwinner models are more frequent among most second-generation groups relative to comparison groups with native parents; however, only for Turkish second-generation women in Sweden and Germany, Koreans in Los Angeles, and Dominicans in New York City is the difference with the comparison group more than 5 percentage points.

MULTIVARIATE ANALYSIS OF FEMALE LABOR FORCE PARTICIPATION

We now turn to multivariate analysis. For each sample, we present three models of female employment. The first includes age and education as well as group membership (the reference group is omitted). The second controls additionally for cohabiting or marriage and having a child. The third adds additional controls for family background, specifically, mother's employment status while the respondent grew up and father's educational background.

Germany

As table 6.2 shows, female employment among those born to German parents is about 18 percentage points higher than for Turkish second-generation women. Even controlling for age and education, the difference is statistically significant and only marginally smaller (see table 6.3). Introducing the respondent's family situation substantially reduced the group coefficient, and the difference between the comparison group and the Turkish second generation is only statistically significant at the 10 percent level. In other words, controlling for motherhood status and cohabiting accounts for about one-third of the difference. Having a child also has a large negative effect—the difference in predicted probability is about 50 percentage points. Controlling for parenthood, cohabitation, or marriage is positively associated with holding a job (the difference in predicted probabilities is about 6 percentage points).[2] The third model shows that mother's employment status and father's education account for a substantial part of the variation across groups. Adding these controls further substantially reduces the group coefficient and the between-group difference is no longer statistically significant. Holding other variables constant, we find that a woman whose mother worked when she was growing up is herself 18 percentage points more likely to work.

Sweden

Compared with Germany, not only is female labor force participation high in Sweden, the gap between the Turkish second generation and the reference group is also decidedly narrower. Looking at the first line across models in table 6.4, however, we see that this difference remains fairly constant even after all controls. Turkish origin is high and statistically significant in all three models. Although the coefficient for having a child is negative and significant at the 10 percent level in model 2, indicating that childbearing decreases employment, the magnitude is much smaller than in Germany and it does not account for much of the difference between groups. Contrary to the German case, the family background variables have no influence on the probability of holding a job.

Switzerland

Table 6.2 showed that female employment among the Turkish second generation is about 5 percentage points less than among those born to Swiss parents; this gap is due mainly to the second generation's higher unemployment rates and not so much to lower labor force participation. Women of

TABLE 6.3   Logistic Regression Models, Probability of German Women Having a Job

	I			II			III		
	Coefficient	SE		Coefficient	SE		Coefficient	SE	
Turkish descent	-0.68	0.22	***	-0.38	0.23	*	0.15	0.40	
Ex-Yugoslavian descent	-0.18	0.24		0.03	0.25		0.06	0.28	
Age	-0.03	0.02		0.06	0.02	**	0.06	0.03	**
Education (medium)	2.02	0.27	***	2.05	0.29	***	2.15	0.34	***
Education (high)	2.85	0.38	***	2.57	0.40	***	2.35	0.45	***
Cohabiting				0.31	0.27		0.68	0.31	**
Has a child				-2.18	0.29	***	-2.49	0.33	***
Mother had job							1.03	0.25	***
Father's education (secondary)							-0.07	0.39	
Father's education (high)							1.30	0.62	**
Constant	0.01	0.58		-1.90	0.67		-2.70	0.88	
N	675			675			589		

Source: Authors' compilation based on TIES survey 2007, 2008.
*$p < 0.1$; **$p < 0.05$; ***$p < 0.01$

TABLE 6.4   Logistic Regression Models, Probability of Swedish Women Having a Job

	I		II		III	
	Coefficient	SE	Coefficient	SE	Coefficient	SE
Turkish descent	-.75	.31 **	-.68	.31 **	-.65	.39 *
Age	.11	.03 ***	.14	.04 ***	.13	.04 **
Education (medium)	.44	.76	.26	.78	.09	.95
Education (high)	-.20	.76	-.54	.79	-.64	.97
Cohabiting			.13	.36	.16	.38
Has a child			-.70	.42 *	-.61	.44
Mother worked					.15	.37
Father's education (medium)					-.18	.43
Father's education (high)					.07	.52
Constant	-1.72	1.14	-2.18	1.20 *	-1.99	1.39
N	252		252		237	

Source: Authors' compilation based on TIES survey 2007, 2008.
*$p < 0.1$; **$p < 0.05$; ***$p < 0.01$

former Yugoslavian descent work about as often as Swiss-descent women, at a high participation rate. Labor force participation—be it full time or part time—does not differ significantly across groups. Individual factors such as age and education do shape participation: the higher the age, the less likely labor market participation is; the more education, the higher the probability of being economically active (see table 6.5). Family formation variables also strongly shape labor force participation, also diminishing the impact of individual factors: to be sure, the presence of a child most affects the probability of working, though less so than in Germany. The predicted child penalty is about 19 percentage points. Switzerland has the lowest rate of childbearing of any of the TIES countries, be the women of Turkish (21 percent), former Yugoslavian (25 percent), or native (19 percent) descent. Of the family background variables, only father's education affects the probability of holding a job. Mother's employment status when the respondent was in her teens does not seem to matter.

United States

Only second-generation Koreans show a statistically significant difference in labor force participation in the IIMMLA data. Not surprisingly, this does not change with the introduction of control variables (see table 6.6). Having a child and cohabitation are both negatively associated with labor force participation but do not affect the differences between groups. The IIMMLA data do not provide information on mother's work status for those with native-born parents, thus we cannot replicate model 3. Father's education, however, is not significantly associated with the probability of holding a job. Dropping the white native-born category and using the Filipino second-generation as the omitted reference group allows us to include the mother's work experiences but does not affect the probability of respondents' holding a job.

Similar analysis of the New York City data, summarized in table 6.7, yields broadly consistent results, hinting at similar processes. Variables reflecting the parents' situation again do not matter for the probability of their daughter's holding a job. The negative coefficient for having a child is approximately the same in both cities, producing a 13 percentage point drop in the probability of holding a job. Looking at differences across groups, we see that Dominican respondents are the only ones less likely to work after we control for age and education. Adding family formation variables reduces the coefficient indicating the difference by about half until it is no longer statistically significant.

TABLE 6.5   Logistic Regression Models, Probability of Swiss Women Having a Job

	I			II			III		
	Coefficient	SE		Coefficient	SE		Coefficient	SE	
Turkish descent	-.54	.34		-.42	.36		-.28	.40	
Former Yugoslavian descent	-.15	.35		.14	.37		.24	.38	
Age	-.15	.03	***	-.06	.04	*	-.06	.04	*
Education (medium)	1.19	.39	***	.89	.42	**	.88	.43	**
Education (high)	2.30	.56	***	1.42	.61	**	1.28	.61	**
Cohabiting				.12	.37		.08	.37	
Has a child				-1.82	.39	***	-1.82	.39	***
Mother worked							.09	.30	
Father's education (medium)							-.12	.43	
Father's education (high)							1.09	.68	*
Constant	5.07	.82		3.52	.90		3.44	1.00	
N	595			595			595		

Source: Authors' compilation based on TIES survey 2007, 2008.
*p < 0.1; **p < 0.05; ***p < 0.01

TABLE 6.6　Logistic Regression Models, Probability of Women Having a Job, IIMMLA Data

	I			II			III a			III b		
	Coefficient	SE		Coefficient	SE		Coefficient	SE		Coefficient	SE	
Mexican	0.12	.22		.26	.22		.43	.27	*	.41	.29	
South American	0.06	.23		.15	.24		.24	.27		.21	.29	
Korean	−0.64	.25	**	−.66	.25	**	−.77	.26	***	−.81	.27	***
Chinese	−0.14	.27		−.26	.27		−.25	.29		−.28	.30	
Vietnamese	−0.20	.26		−.24	.26		−.29	.28		−.31	.29	
Filipino	0.18	.27		.22	.27		.04	.28				
Age	0.02	.01	**	.01	.01		.02	.01	*	.04	.02	**
Education												
High school	0.76	.22	***	.79	.23	***	.53	.28	*	.46	.30	
Some college	1.36	.21	***	1.27	.21	***	.90	.26	***	.72	.28	***
Bachelor's degree or more	1.54	.22	***	1.42	.23	***	1.10	.28	***	.90	.30	***
Cohabiting				−.45	.15	***	−.55	.17	***	−.62	.19	***
Has child				−.52	.16	***	−.61	.18	***	−.69	.20	***
Mother working										.16	.17	
Father's education secondary							.14	.22		.15	.22	
Father's education higher							.37	.25		.39	.26	
Constant	0.61	.41		.14	.42		.08	.52		−.28	.56	
N	1506			1506			1283			1107		

Source: Authors' compilation based on IIMMLA (Rumbaut et al. 2004).
*p < 0.1; **p < 0.05; ***p < 0.01

TABLE 6.7   Logistic Regression Models, Probability of Women Having a Job, ISGMNY Data

	Coefficient	SE		Coefficient	SE		Coefficient	SE	
South American	-0.27	0.29		-0.10	0.30		-0.06	0.35	
Dominican Republic	-0.54	0.27	**	-0.26	0.28		-0.15	0.33	
West Indian	-0.36	0.29		-0.12	0.30		-0.06	0.37	
Chinese	-0.10	0.30		-0.15	0.30		-0.37	0.34	
Russian–Jewish	-0.18	0.35		-0.07	0.35		0.13	0.41	
Age	0.02	0.02		0.06	0.03	**	0.06	0.03	*
Education									
High school or GED	0.28	0.29		0.19	0.29		0.31	0.36	
Some college or technical	1.64	0.25	***	1.39	0.26	***	1.50	0.33	***
Bachelor's degree or more	1.74	0.30	***	1.30	0.32	***	1.41	0.39	***
Cohabiting				-0.01	0.21		-0.07	0.24	
Has child				-0.90	0.23	***	-0.94	0.28	***
Father's education secondary							0.12	0.27	
Father's education higher							-0.18	0.32	
Mother worked							-0.14	0.25	
Intercept	0.07	0.60		-0.55	0.64		-0.33	0.82	
N	1097			1094			862		

Source: Authors' compilation based on ISGMNY (Mollenkopf, Kasinitz, and Waters 1999).

$*p < 0.1; **p < 0.05; ***p < 0.01$

DISCUSSION

This chapter compares the labor market integration of second-generation women in four countries. Second-generation women seem to be working to a higher degree than their immigrant mothers in all four cases. Second-generation women in Sweden, Switzerland, and the United States do fairly well compared with overall rates of female labor force participation. In all countries but in Germany, they have high employment rates, in some cases even higher than those among women with native parents. The gap of about 10 percentage points between those with native parents and those with Turkish parents in Sweden remains and is statistically significant, but the overall level of female employment is quite high. In Germany, women with Turkish parents are much less likely to work, whether compared with natives or with Turkish women in other countries. These differences, of course, partly reflect differences in parental background, because the parents of our German-Turkish respondents have much less education on average than those in Switzerland and Sweden and even less than Mexican-born parents in the United States. Although Dominican, Mexican, and Turkish migrants occupy broadly similar labor market positions, the labor force participation of their daughters varies considerably. Especially in the United States, but also in Switzerland and Sweden, where the immigrant mothers were labor migrants, participating in the labor market even while raising children, their daughters are more likely to work, in contrast to Germany, where immigrant women had only a limited attachment to the labor market.

Despite the different family backgrounds and resources of the immigrant parents, the results of our analysis suggest that the institutional arrangements and policies grouped under the label *welfare state* also shape their daughters' labor market experiences in significant ways, particularly regarding family formation. Although having a child in the United States does dampen the likelihood of employment, the effect is small compared with Switzerland and especially Germany. Similarly, the Swedish welfare state, living up to its reputation, seems to minimize the trade-off between having children and working in a way that helps second-generation women, even though these women have children at younger ages than the reference group. At the other end, Germany, the exemplar of the conservative welfare regime, presents women with a steep trade-off between family and career. Women with native parents address this trade-off by delaying childbirth into their late twenties or early thirties.

But Turkish second-generation women, who often have children earlier, seem disproportionally affected. For them, having a child has a large negative effect on employment across all groups, though it is worse for the Turkish women; after controlling for all background factors, this accounts for about 33 percent of the difference in job holding between those with Turkish parents and those with native parents. The Swiss case presents an interesting mix of conservative and liberal welfare state elements. The motherhood penalty is relatively high, but whether mothers worked does not influence the daughters' employment. Overall, the labor force participation of second-generation women is high and the gap between them and women of native descent is small.

The interaction of family background differences and these policy settings is clear: in Switzerland and Germany, two countries with conservative features in their welfare systems, the family background factors matter for labor force participation, but these factors do not play much of a role in the United States and Sweden. Neither mother's job holding nor father's education seems to affect their daughter's labor force participation. Germany, by contrast, shows a clear intergenerational effect on both counts: father's educational background and mother's employment status both matter and account for a substantial part of the group differences. Switzerland again occupies an in-between position, with father's education but not mother's employment being a significant predictor of daughters' employment.

As a number of researchers have pointed out, the concept of assimilation does not apply exclusively to immigrants and their children. Rather, young people of every background face the challenge of assimilating into new contexts at each life stage, be it progressing through educational systems or entering the labor market (Bommes 2003). Viewed through that lens, how the institutional arrangements of welfare states shape female labor force participation is a powerful process that applies in principle to both those with immigrant and those with native parents. As our analysis and the more general comparative literature on welfare states show, these features yield systematic variations across countries.

In the United States, the state plays only a small role in mediating the forces of the market. For example, it provides few benefits and regulations for maternity or parental leave. Sweden, in contrast, actively absorbs the cost of parenthood and encourages female labor force participation through a wide spectrum of policies and benefits. Although these two cases at first seem to be at opposite ends of the spectrum, they both encourage female employment and seem to limit the influence of parental precedent for labor force participation. No matter what the parents' labor force situation, the context encourages their daughters to work. In contrast, conservative, family support welfare systems like that in Germany do not see working women and working mothers as the norm but discourage women from working, which reinforces the impact of family background.

In Germany, family background plays an important role in labor force participation for all women. A daughter's employment is significantly correlated with her mother's. In the context of an immigrant society, where groups have substantially different role models and expectations about how families will be organized, and where many mothers have been outside the labor force, this connection works against daughters and perpetuates between-group differences across generations. The Swiss case, with its mixed conservative-liberal features, produces some outcomes, particularly a high motherhood penalty, similar to those of Germany. However, Switzerland also resembles the liberal, market-oriented gender policies of the United States that induce high labor force participation among women across all groups. Our analysis thus supports the idea that institutional factors play a decisive role in explaining labor force participation rates among the women of the second generation—as well as among those born to native parents.

Our findings also lead us to question Ruud Koopmans's (2010) claim that multiculturalism is inconsistent with equality. By this hypothesis, Sweden, with its supposedly problematic mixture of generous welfare provision and multicultural policies, should be in trouble. Yet it seems to represent the best case in our analysis. Although falling somewhat short of the high bar set for female labor force participation in general, the country's second-generation women join the labor force in large numbers. The extent to which they still lag behind women with native-born parents reflects higher unemployment rather than failure to join the labor force. The trade-off hypothesis would see Germany, however, as a "good" case because it has fairly narrow multicultural policies and its welfare system is more family oriented. Yet Germany does poorly in our analysis, at least as far as Turkish second-generation women are concerned. Our analysis thus leads us to reject the notion that welfare states have a corrosive effect on the integration of the second generation. Rather than the overall level of welfare provision, the specific arrangements influencing breadwinner patterns—that either help working mothers balance work and family or discourage them from working at all—clearly shape how women encounter and respond to labor markets and how they balance family and career. The size of the welfare state is less important than the concrete policies and incentives it provides.

NOTES

1. See Auslaenderstatistik (http://www.bfm.admin.ch).
2. We also tested whether having a child has a similar effect across groups and could not detect any differences. A similar test for cohabiting shows a significant and positive effect for the German and former Yugoslavian subsamples but not for the Turkish respondents.

CHAPTER 7

NEIGHBORHOODS AND PERCEPTIONS OF DISORDER

VAN C. TRAN, SUSAN K. BROWN, AND JENS SCHNEIDER

The post-1960 influx of immigrants and the coming of age of their children have made the neighborhoods of the big immigrant-receiving cities in the United States and western Europe increasingly more diverse in ethnic terms (Logan and Zhang 2010). And yet, despite the growing presence of these immigrants, no systematic study has yet been made of the kinds of neighborhoods in which they grew up and mostly still reside. This gap is striking in light of the prominent role that neighborhood conditions and processes play in accounts both of immigrant assimilation and of larger patterns of urban inequality, specifically, within the research traditions of spatial assimilation, place stratification, and urban poverty. This chapter turns to this critically important but largely neglected topic by looking at the residential spaces and urban neighborhoods experienced by the second generation in Los Angeles, New York, and Berlin.

A robust literature has documented the pervasive racial segregation and stratification of American inner-city neighborhoods. From New York to Los Angeles, different ethnic and racial groups clearly occupy different urban spaces (Iceland 2009, 2007, 2004; Iceland and Nelson 2008; Logan, Stults, and Farley 2004; Anderson and Massey 2001; Massey and Denton 1993; Alba and Logan 1993). Although much attention has focused on how segregated African American neighborhoods exacerbate concentrated poverty and social problems (Anderson 2008, 1999, 1990; Venkatesh 2006, 2000; Wilson 2009, 1996, 1987; Massey and Denton 1993; Sampson 2008; Sharkey forthcoming), relatively little is known about how and where the post-1965 immigration fits into (and is also changing) the hierarchy of inner-city neighborhoods (but see Logan and Zhang 2010; Iceland 2009; Jargowsky 2009, 1997). Furthermore, we know next to nothing about the relative stratification of the new American immigrant ethnic mosaic, as good empirical data that go beyond the most basic racial-ethnic categories have not been available.

European scholarship does not use racial categories to analyze the spatial concentrations of different immigrant groups in European cities. Moreover, European countries have collected relatively little small area data on first-generation immigrants and their children. Finally, most western European countries have adopted welfare state and urban planning policies toward socially deprived neighborhoods that define them in terms of indicators of social problems or labor market exclusion, not ethnic ancestry or immigrant generation. Although many nonwhite and non-middle-class neighborhoods populated by growing numbers of immigrant families did of course emerge in their cities, they tend not to be dominated by one ethno-national-origin group in a way comparable to racial segregation in the United States. They often retain at least some working-class residents of native-born ancestry. Although European urban sociologists have examined the growing diversity of their neighborhoods, they have not yet done so through the perspective of their new natives, namely, the children born in them to immigrant parents (Crul and Schneider 2010). We know little about their experiences in these neighborhoods or whether they perceive them, as the larger society often does, as hot spots of social problems and social disorder.

Drawing on geocoded data from ISGMNY, IIMMLA, and TIES, this chapter begins to fill this knowledge gap. Our findings largely confirm the apparent differences across the Atlantic: to the extent that the U.S. second generation in Los Angeles and New York grows up in or near poor or black neighborhoods, these places feel disorderly and dangerous to them; in Berlin, however, growing up in the most heavily Turkish neighborhoods is also associated with the perception of disorder, but the connection is far weaker. It appears that growing up in "bad" or minority neighborhoods may exert a far more negative influence on second-generation trajectories in the United States than in Berlin.

We know a great deal about racial residential segregation in the United States but less about the spatial distributions of specific ethnic groups. The majority of American research on urban inequality continues to rely on the broadest racial-ethnic categories provided by the census—non-Hispanic whites, non-Hispanic blacks, non-Hispanic Asians, non-Hispanic others, and all Hispanics regardless of race (Alba and Logan 1993; Iceland 2009; Crowder, South, and Chavez 2006). Until the advent of migration-driven diversity, this made sense, because the original black-white dichotomy reflected the historical legacy of slavery, racial subordination, and racial segregation. In some parts of the country, the multigenerational presence of people whose ancestors came from Mexico or Puerto Rico caused observers to morph this biracial order into a black-white-Latino trichotomy.

Even this, however, no longer reflects the changing realities of urban life, because these broad categories hide intra-racial differences related to nativity. This is especially true in major immigrant gateway cities, such as Los Angeles, New York, Miami, and Chicago. New York's black population encompasses at least three major subgroups—African Americans who are descendants of slaves, West Indians descended from voluntary migrants, and more recent African immigrants whose great diversity reflects the fifty-four African countries from which they come. Similarly, the Hispanic-Latino category—which used to denote a predominant ethnic group depending on the geographical context (such as Mexicans in the Southwest or Puerto Ricans in the Northeast)—now encompasses a wide array of groups from Central and South America. Even though they share and partake in a pan-ethnic Latino culture and commonly speak a dialect of Spanish, Latinos are racially, culturally, politically, and socioeconomically diverse (Tienda and Mitchell 2006).

In Europe, researchers have used ethno-national-origin as the passe-partout category. They use labels analogous to the U.S. race category, such as Turks, Moroccans, or Russians, or sometimes people with migration backgrounds, which all tend to obliterate internal differentiation within the so-labeled groups—for example, between the first and subsequent generations, different education levels, migration motives, or legal statuses. Internal ethnic diversity (for example, non-Turkish-speaking Kurdish or Armenian minorities from Turkey) and the growing hybrid or bicultural backgrounds are easily overlooked when focusing only on ethno-national-origin groups. Ongoing immigration and cultural diversification have made neither this nor the widely used categories in the United States sufficient in light of the contemporary complexity of urban neighborhoods.

This chapter uses neighborhood segregation, neighborhood deprivation, and perceived social disorder to investigate the neighborhoods where the second generation grew up. In so doing, it provides a first comparison of U.S. and western European neighborhood contexts for the second generation. Whereas much previous research in this tradition has explored spatial assimilation and residential segregation in terms of either nativity or large ethno-racial categories (Iceland 2009; Alba and Logan 1993; Logan, Alba, and Zhang 2002; Wilkes and Iceland 2004; South, Crowder, and Pais 2008), here we examine multiple second-generation groups. Finally, the comparative approach permits us to examine neighborhood context not only for multiple immigrant groups within each cities but across cities in the United States and Germany. In this way, we begin to provide a more systematic description of neighborhood context for the second generation, exploring perceived levels of social disorder as well as traditional "objective" measures of racial composition and disadvantage.

THEORETICAL BACKGROUND

In this section, we briefly summarize the theoretical perspectives that our chapter seeks to build on. We begin with the literatures on spatial assimilation and place stratification, which have anchored much scholarly discussion on how immigration has transformed inner-city neighborhoods. We then briefly point to the lack of research on the neighborhood context where the new second-generation grew up, an empirical gap that our chapter hopes to address.

Spatial Assimilation and Place Stratification

The literature amply documents the racial stratification of American neighborhoods (Iceland 2009; South, Crowder, and Pais 2008; Logan and Zhang 2010; Jargowsky 1997). It finds, by and large, that American cities remain highly racially segregated (Timberlake and Iceland 2007). Whereas the first wave of research in this tradition focused on black-white segregation, more recent studies have considered the experience of Latinos and intra-Latino variations (South, Crowder, and Chavez 2005a, 2005b, 2005c). Relying on segregation indices, this literature has carefully documented the relative degrees of segregation between pairs of groups, including whites, blacks, Latinos, and Asians, as well as the hyper-segregation of blacks in many geographic areas (Massey and Denton 1989, 1993). Generally, blacks and whites are the most segregated from each other, with Latinos and Asians between; Asians are less segregated from whites and more from blacks, and Latinos are the other way around.

Research on the spatial assimilation of immigrants has explored how immigrant groups are distributed across space differently from native whites and how this difference may decline across immigrant generations for various groups (Brown 2007; Iceland and Nelson 2008; South, Crowder, and Pais 2008; Iceland 2009). The classic theory of spatial assimilation posits that socioeconomic gains among first- and second-generation immigrants translate into residential mobility over time and lead to closer proximity to native whites. This, in turn, facilitates informal friendships with native whites as well as membership in formal institutions such as churches and clubs (Alba and Nee 2003; Waters and Jiménez 2005).

Contemporary versions of this theory highlight the distinctive racial composition of the post-1965 immigrant groups (Rosenbaum and Friedman 2007). For example, John Iceland and Kyle Nelson (2008) document multiple forms of spatial assimilation occurring simultaneously for Hispanic groups. Specifically, native-born Hispanics are less segregated from Anglos than foreign-born Hispanics are, and black Hispanics are more segregated from Anglos than are white Hispanics of the same nativity status. This suggest that race and nativity both shape segregation patterns and residential attainment among Hispanics. More recently, Ann H. Kim and Michael J. White (2010) posit the theory of racialized spatial assimilation, which explicitly considers the racial composition of fifty-six ethnic groups drawn from the 2000 census data. They find that race and pan-ethnicity foster residential proximity among groups within the same pan-ethnic grouping, though the effect applies more to whites, blacks, and Latinos than to Asians.

Although they have extensively documented neighborhood racial hierarchies, scholars have been slower to explore the intra-racial variation in neighborhood context, even though this is becoming more important as the basic racial groups—and their neighborhoods—become more diverse (Maly 2005). A few recent studies have examined intra-Latino differences (Wen, Lauderdale, and Kandula 2009; South, Crowder, and Chavez 2005b, 2005c) and African American–West Indian differences (Crowder 1999). Similarly, a few studies looked at Asian subgroups (Pais et al. 2009; Zhou and Logan 1991; Wen, Lauderdale, and Kandula 2009). In their analysis of geocoded Panel Study of Income Dynamics (PSID) data, Jeremy Pais, Scott J. South, and Kyle Crowder (2009) show that Latino groups vary in propensity to exit neighborhoods with growing black populations, with Cubans reacting more negatively than Mexicans and Puerto Ricans to black populations. Analyzing 1980 census data, Michael White and Sharon Sassler found that "West Indians and Jamaicans have significantly higher neighborhood SES outcomes than African-Americans" (2000, 1006). Crowder's (1999) analysis of 1990 census data also documented that West Indians, though largely denied access to the white areas, tended to occupy higher income black areas than did native blacks.

American and European theorists both caution against applying American ways of understanding segregation to Europe (Alba 2005; Brubaker 1989; Drever 2004; van Kempen and Özüekren 1998). The United States clearly has more and larger native minority groups than western Europe does. The segregation of Turks and other immigrant groups from non-immigrant Germans in Berlin is considered low by European standards and is far lower than black-white levels typical of the United States, though the units of comparison are not equivalent (Musterd and De Winter 1998). Racial segregation in the United States long predates that of Europe and has historical underpinnings that Europe lacks. Similarly, Europe uses religion, citizenship, and ethno-national-origin to draw social boundaries, not race, which remains a taboo term. European national and local governments also play a larger role in determining access to housing and have larger supplies of public and social housing, with the result that U.S. neighborhoods are less mixed in socioeconomic terms (Drever 2004). Overall, scholars examining segregation in Germany have tentatively concluded that neighborhood poverty and ethnic concentrations—at least at their current levels—may not harm immigrants' prospects for integration, with the possible exception of children having to attend segregated schools (Drever 2004; Schönwälder 2007; but see Häussermann 2007).

Although much of this discussion also applies to Amsterdam, Vienna, and Stockholm, Berlin is a special case in Europe because of its division by two states between 1945 and 1989. The Berlin Wall was actually built the same year that Germany signed the Recruitment Agreement with Turkey—1961. The division between the former eastern and western parts is still marked, the former having few and the latter many immigrant residents of working-class and lower middle-class neighborhoods. Only 2 percent of the Turkish population lives in East Berlin (Kemper 1998), and most of the immigrant population in the eastern districts is of former Soviet or Vietnamese origin (Häussermann and Kapphan 2005).

As previous chapters have discussed, Turkish guest workers began settling in Berlin in the 1960s, when it was walled off from the rest of West Germany. Most large manufacturers had moved out, but government-subsidized plants still needed unskilled labor (Kemper 1998). When these male guest workers began to bring in their families, they found housing just where the Chicago School would have predicted: in declining white working-class neighborhoods and commercial zones of transition scheduled for renovation (Friedrichs and Alpheis 1991). Many of these districts abutted the Berlin Wall, making them less desirable both commercially and residentially for West Germans. In 1975, the period of maximum decay for these areas and also the cutoff point for active labor recruitment from Turkey, about 65 percent of the 87,900 Turks in Berlin lived in three aging areas (Özüekren and Ergoz-Karahan 2010, 363). Yet these districts were not exclusively Turkish; in the most concentrated district, only three blocks were more than half Turkish, inspiring one researcher to title a paper "The Myth of Turkish Ghettos" (Holzner 1982). The heterogeneous Turkish population included students as well as guest workers from various regions of Turkey (Özüekren and Ergoz-Karahan 2010). The 1980 military coup in Turkey had driven out a significant number of political activists, intellectuals, and Kurds, many of whom settled in Berlin.

The Berlin government nonetheless actively tried to deter the spatial concentration of Turks and other immigrant populations. It built many new social housing projects on the periphery of the city in the 1970s, which siphoned off some newcomers, although immigrants generally clustered in the less desirable public housing (Friedrichs and Alpheis 1991; Kemper 1998). The national government also enacted two types of quotas in 1975. One allowed cities to bar further settlement when the foreign population reached 12 percent (Drever 2004). The other capped the proportion of housing units that any large landlord could rent to foreigners at 10 percent, later raised to 15 percent (Arin 1991). Because many foreigners were exempt, these quotas worked poorly and were lifted by 1989 (Arin 1991; Drever 2004). Informally, however, German landlords continued to limit foreigners to retain their German tenants (Drever 2004). As a result, the segregation of foreigners probably peaked in the 1970s, although any decline thereafter was small (Friedrichs and Alpheis 1991; Kemper 1998). In the meantime, the absolute quality of housing occupied by immigrants and their offspring improved, though not relative to housing among ethnic Germans, which also improved greatly (Drever and Clark 2002). Moreover, despite gentrification in the old central-city districts with the heaviest Turkish concentrations, unemployment rates there remain some of the highest in the city (Häussermann and Kapphan 2005).

Neighborhood Context and the (New) Second Generation

From the recent emergence of ethnoburbs in the United States to the superdiverse neighborhoods in Europe, neighborhoods are central to theorizing about the immigrant experience (Waters and Jiménez 2005; Alba and Nee 2003; Portes and Rumbaut 2001; Massey and Denton 1985; Vertovec 2007). The theory of segmented assimilation, for example, emphasizes the role of neighborhood-level interactions with native minority peers and posits that second-generation youths with darker phenotypes growing up in poor inner-city neighborhoods may adopt an "oppositional culture" resulting in downward assimilation (Portes and Zhou 1993; Portes and Rumbaut 2001; Portes, Fernandez-Kelly, and Haller 2005, 2009). Interactions within the coethnic community are often facilitated by ethnic institutions tied to space and place, such as the Italian neighborhoods in the mid-twentieth century and the Chinatowns or Koreatowns of today (Zhou 2009; Whyte 1941).

Given the theoretical affinity between spatial studies of urban poverty and immigration incorporation, the lack of focus on the spatial contexts of the second generation is striking (Tran 2011). Neighborhoods clearly matter for socioeconomic outcomes (Furstenberg and Hughes 1997; Sampson, Morenoff, and Gannon-Rowley 2002; Tienda 1991; Sharkey forthcoming). The recent U.S. literature posits that concentrated economic disadvantage, social isolation, and high levels of violence have deleterious effects on neighborhood residents (for example, Massey and Denton 1993; Wilson 1987; Sampson 2008). An older social disorganization literature examines such behaviors as gang activity, crime, and the inability of residents to achieve common goals (Sampson 2009; Sampson, Morenoff, and Earls 1999; Shaw and McKay 1942).

The importance of neighborhood social organization or disorganization is echoed in the argument that the distribution of social capital in immigrant families and communities explains why some children of immigrants thrive even in poor neighborhoods (Coleman 1988; Dohan 2003; Zhou and Bankston 1998; Zhou 2009). Although a few older studies did look at second-generation adaptations (Whyte 1941; Suttles 1968; Small 2004), contemporary studies have mostly emphasized how family background and individual characteristics affect socioeconomic outcomes (Portes and Rumbaut 2001; Waldinger and Feliciano 2004; Waters 1999; Zhou and Bankston 1998). The few articles on neighborhood context suggest significant variation in neighborhood effects depending on community resources, such as the quality of the schools (Pong and Hao 2007; Kroneberg 2008).

Another underexplored question on both sides of the Atlantic is how objective measures of neighborhood segregation and disadvantage correlate with respondents' perceptions of their neighborhood environment. Individual perceptions of disorder are a key mechanism underlying how context affects individual outcomes (Harding 2010; Sharkey 2006; Sampson 2009; Sampson and Raudenbush 1999). Following Robert Sampson, we argue that "perceptions of disorder constitute a fundamental dimension of social inequality at the neighborhood level and perhaps beyond" (2009, 6). Along the same lines, John Hipp (2009) shows that perceptions of crime influence neighborhood satisfaction. Theoretically, we might expect second-generation and native youths who share the same social or geographical space to have different perceptions of their environments because their friendship and kinship ties differ, including how much unstructured leisure time they spend on the streets (Harding et al. 2010; Hipp 2010; Rountree and Land 1996). Social psychologists have argued that the experience of neighborhood effects is mediated not only by parents (in the case of children) but also by gender, class, and ethnicity (Furstenberg and Hughes 1997).

DATA AND METHODS

ISGMNY, IIMMLA, and TIES collected detailed information about where the respondents grew up. Here we use a series of questions about the neighborhoods where respondents reported living the longest between the ages of six and eighteen (that is, childhood neighborhood). The American surveys asked for the cross streets, name of the neighborhood, borough or county, city, and state of the respondents' childhood neighborhood. This information made it possible to geocode places of residence and identify the census tracts surrounding them. This, in turn, allowed us to match individual-level survey data with contextual data from the U.S. Census, relying on the Neighborhood Change Database from 1970 to 2000. This data set, jointly developed by GeoLytics and the Urban Institute, standardized census tract boundaries and data elements across four decennial censuses, allowing for effective comparison of census data over time (GeoLytics 2003). We used linear interpolation to estimate the tract-level characteristics for intervening years (Sharkey 2008; Brown 2007), thus matching contextual data to the exact years when the respondent was born (birth neighborhood), when the respondent was twelve (childhood neighborhood), and when the respondent was interviewed (adult neighborhood). For Berlin, TIES identified the exact place of residence at the time of the interview and gathered postcode information about the area. We also know the share of respondents still living with their parents or in the same area and whether this corresponds to the area where they lived at age sixteen. This was then matched with socioeconomic data from life-world oriented units (LORs) available from the Berlin Statistical Office.

We limited our U.S. analysis to Mexicans, Central Americans (Salvadorans and Guatemalans), Chinese, Filipinos, African Americans, and native whites in Los Angeles and to Dominicans, Chinese, South Americans (Colombians, Ecuadorans, and Peruvians), native blacks, and native whites in New York. This allows us to compare Chinese in both settings, as well as Dominicans with Mexicans and Central Americans, who all come from poor socioeconomic backgrounds. Finally, we compare Filipinos and South Americans because these ethnic groups arrived with higher levels of human capital among the first generation. Native blacks and whites provide baseline comparisons for the other groups. On the European side, the data permit us only to look at descendants of immigrants from Turkey and the former Yugoslavia in Berlin, comparing them with a group of ethnic German respondents with native-born parents. For the sake of simplicity, we label the Berlin groups as Turks (although about 20 percent of its members are Kurdish), former Yugoslavians (although Yugoslavia was only the parents' country of origin and no longer exists, being succeeded by states like Serbia and Croatia), and the comparison group (because European scholars prefer not to use a racial category such as native white).

Following previous research, we equate census tracts and postcodes with neighborhoods (Logan and Zhang 2010; White and Glick 2009; Crowder and South 2008; Sharkey 2008; Sampson and Sharkey 2008; Sampson, Sharkey, and Raudenbush 2008; Brown 2007; Logan, Alba, and Zhang 2002; Sampson, Morenoff, and Gannon-Rowley 2002; Alba and Logan 1993; Massey and Denton 1993). Data availability and compatibility also dictate this choice. We further restrict our analyses to respondents who grew up in Los Angeles or New York. This way, we are more confident that our measures of perceived social disorder are valid because our respondents spent a great deal of time in their neighborhoods and are familiar with their environments. On the European side, the Berlin postcode information derives from respondents' current residence, not any previous neighborhood in which they might have grown up. Although it would be ideal to have this latter information, it is not available. Among our 773 Berlin TIES respondents, however, 23 percent never left the parents' home and 80 percent of those who did continue to live in the same district.

FINDINGS

In this section, we will present three sets of empirical findings. First, we begin with descriptive results on neighborhood segregation by ethnic group across the three cities. Second, we outline how neighborhood social disorder varies by ethnic group and city context. Finally, we present multivariate results on how neighborhood disadvantage shapes perceptions of social disorder.

Neighborhood Segregation

Table 7.1 presents results on the demographic composition of respondents' neighborhoods by ethnic groups for Los Angeles, New York, and Berlin. Overall, second-generation groups' neighborhoods in New York include

TABLE 7.1 Demographic Characteristics of Childhood Neighborhoods

IIMMLA	Percentage Non-Hispanic Black	Percentage Non-Hispanic White	Percentage Hispanic	Percentage Non-Hispanic Asian	Percentage Immigrant
Mexican	9.0[wb]	29.8[w]	53.6[wb]	6.8[b]	34.5[wb]
N = 653	(15.5)	(25.5)	(26.6)	(7.3)	(15.9)
Central American	12.3[wb]	25.4[w]	52.6[wb]	8.9[wb]	41.2[wb]
N = 301	(20.5)	(24.7)	(26.1)	(9.4)	(18.2)
Chinese	2.8[b]	45.9[wb]	26.4[w]	23.5[wb]	31.9[wb]
N = 285	(6.3)	(26.7)	(21.7)	(17.2)	(15.9)
Filipino	5.8[wb]	44.5[wb]	32.8[wb]	16.2[wb]	29.9[wb]
N = 298	(7.0)	(23.5)	(20.3)	(12.5)	(16.2)
Non-Hispanic black	42.2[w]	25.1[w]	27.3[w]	5.2[w]	19.6[w]
N = 291	(33.4)	(27.7)	(19.8)	(6.6)	(13.0)
Non-Hispanic white	3.5[b]	70.6[b]	18.5[b]	7.1[b]	16.2[b]
N = 233	(6.2)	(17.0)	(14.0)	(6.3)	(10.0)

ISGMNY	Percentage Non-Hispanic Black	Percentage Non-Hispanic White	Percentage Hispanic	Percentage Non-Hispanic Asian	Percentage Immigrant
Dominican	21.3[wb]	30.1[wb]	41.6[wb]	6.4[wb]	35.2[wb]
N = 422	(24.6)	(28.3)	(25.5)	(8.6)	(17.7)
Chinese	8.4[b]	50.6[wb]	17.5[wb]	23.4[wb]	40.3[wb]
N = 564	(18.6)	(30.0)	(16.6)	(23.7)	(17.9)

South American, N = 377	13.0[b] (19.9)	41.9[wb] (26.7)	32.7[wb] (21.8)	11.7[wb] (10.9)	38.2[wb] (16.6)
Non-Hispanic black, N = 384	57.0[w] (33.2)	19.8[w] (28.2)	19.9[w] (19.7)	2.9[w] (4.2)	23.9[w] (16.1)
Non-Hispanic white, N = 257	12.1[b] (24.1)	71.7[b] (28.3)	10.3[b] (10.8)	5.1[b] (5.9)	24.1[b] (14.6)

TIES	Percentage German	Percentage Turk	Percentage Yugoslavian	Percentage Immigrant
Turk, N = 257	60.9[w] (14.5)	10.3[w] (7.5)	26.9[w] (14.6)	39.0[w] (14.5)
Yugoslavian, N = 202	70.7[w] (15.5)	6.1[w] (6.8)	20.9[w] (15.9)	29.3[w] (15.5)
Comparison group, N = 250	76.7 (14.3)	3.9 (5.5)	1.7 (15.8)	23.3 (14.3)

Source: Authors' compilation based on IIMMLA (Rumbaut et al. 2004); ISGMNY (Mollenkopf, Kasinitz, and Waters 1999); TIES 2007, 2008 (data not yet publicly available).

Notes: Standard deviations are in parentheses. The superscripts w and b indicate that the results are significantly different from those of non-Hispanic whites and non-Hispanic blacks, respectively, at the level of $p < .01$. Characteristics of census tracts are interpolated for respondents as of age twelve. Characteristics are given only for residents who grew up in Los Angeles and New York. The TIES survey comprises eight separate national data sets, collected by Institute for Studies on Migrations (IEM), Comillas Pontifical University, Spain; Swiss Forum for Migration and Population Studies (SFM), Neuchâtel, Switzerland; Netherlands Interdisciplinary Demographic Institute (NIDI), The Hague, Netherlands; Austrian Academy of Sciences (ÖAW), Vienna, Austria; the European Research Centre on Migration and Ethnic Relations (ERCOMER), Katholieke Universiteit Leuven, Belgium; National Institute for Demographic Studies (INED), Paris, France; Institute for Migration Research and Intercultural Studies (IMIS), University of Osnabrück, Germany; Centre for Research in International Migration and Ethnic Relations (CEIFO), Stockholm University, Sweden. The TIES national surveys will be made publicly available by the national TIES partners individually, but were not yet available at the time of publication.

more blacks and those in Los Angeles include more Latinos, reflecting the overall composition of these cities. In cities, whites, Chinese, and Filipinos mostly grew up in neighborhoods with the fewest blacks, suggesting that they are most socially distant from blacks. Chinese lived in neighborhoods that were, on average, less than 25 percent Chinese and up to 50 percent white. By contrast, the Latino groups lived among much higher concentrations of Latino coethnics but also in closer proximity to native blacks. In Los Angeles, the average Mexican respondent lived in a neighborhood that was 9 percent black, whereas Central and South Americans lived in neighborhoods that were 12 to 13 percent black. In New York, Dominicans were most likely to share their neighborhoods with blacks. However, in both cities, all second-generation groups are more likely to live near non-Hispanic whites than blacks. Native blacks are also more segregated from whites than any second-generation group. Not surprisingly, second-generation groups on average grew up in neighborhoods with higher percentages of foreign born than native-born groups did. These results reflect the prevalence of first-generation residents in immigrant neighborhoods, either by necessity due to the social support that coethnics provide or out of preference for such neighborhoods.

In Berlin, second-generation Turks and former Yugoslavs reported growing up in neighborhoods with far higher foreign-born populations than the comparison group did. These neighborhoods also had significantly lower concentrations of native Germans, who in turn live in areas where more than 75 percent are also native German. However, Turks and former Yugoslavs in Berlin also grew up in neighborhoods that were more than 60 percent white German. Not even the Chinese in the United States lived among such a ratio of whites, which indicates lower levels of ethnic segregation in Berlin.

Neighborhood Disadvantage by Ethnic Group

Table 7.2 presents the socioeconomic composition of respondents' neighborhoods by ethnic group. Variables include percentage female-headed households, percentage foreign born, poverty rate, and unemployment rate. For Berlin, our neighborhood characteristics variables include percentage households on social welfare, unemployment rates, percentage foreign born, and ethnic composition at the postcode level. The Chinese and Filipino second generation grew up in tracts where the levels of poverty, unemployment, and female-headed households were low in both cities, whereas Mexicans, Central Americans, Dominicans, and African Americans lived in the most disadvantaged tracts.

TABLE 7.2   Socioeconomic Characteristics of Childhood Neighborhoods

IIMMLA	Percentage Female-Headed Household	Percentage in Poverty	Percentage Unemployed
Mexican	9.1[wb]	18.8[w]	9.0[wb]
N = 653	(4.3)	(10.2)	(3.9)
Central American	9.7[wb]	22.1[wb]	9.8[w]
N = 301	(5.1)	(11.9)	(4.0)
Chinese	5.6[b]	10.3[wb]	5.2[b]
N = 285	(2.8)	(8.3)	(2.6)
Filipino	6.7[wb]	11.3[wb]	6.2[wb]
N = 298	(3.4)	(8.0)	(3.1)
Non-Hispanic black	12.6[w]	18.9[w]	10.0[w]
N = 291	(6.5)	(10.6)	(4.5)
Non-Hispanic white	5.8[b]	8.2[b]	5.3[b]
N = 233	(2.5)	(5.2)	(2.4)

ISGMNY	Percentage Female-Headed Household	Percentage in Poverty	Percentage Unemployed
Dominican	13.7[w]	26.6[w]	11.5[w]
N = 422	(9.7)	(13.6)	(5.1)
Chinese	5.6[b]	17.5[wb]	7.8[wb]
N = 564	(5.2)	(11.1)	(3.9)
South American	9.4[wb]	18.1[wb]	8.8[wb]
N = 377	(8.20)	(13.20)	(4.50)
Non-Hispanic black	16.0[w]	25.5[w]	11.8[w]
N = 384	(9.6)	(15.2)	(6.1)
Non-Hispanic white	5.2[b]	10.6[b]	6.3[b]
N = 257	(4.6)	(8.9)	(3.2)

TIES	Percentage Welfare Households	Percentage Unemployed (Long-Term)	Percentage Unemployed (Short-Term)
Turk	11.9[w]	2.5[w]	6.6[w]
N = 257	(4.4)	(0.8)	(2.4)
Yugoslavian	10	2.2	5.6
N = 202	(4.5)	(0.9)	(2.6)
Comparison group	9.6	2.1	5.4
N = 250	(4.5)	(0.9)	(2.6)

Source: Authors' compilation based on IIMMLA (Rumbaut et al. 2004); ISGMNY (Mollenkopf, Kasinitz, and Waters 1999); TIES 2007, 2008.
Notes: Standard deviations are in parentheses. The superscripts w and b indicate that the results are significantly different from those of non-Hispanic whites and non-Hispanic blacks, respectively, at the level of $p < .01$. Characteristics of census tracts are interpolated for respondents as of age twelve. Characteristics are given only for residents who grew up in Los Angeles and New York.

In Los Angeles, the average tract-level poverty rate was lowest for whites, Chinese, and Filipinos and was roughly two times higher for Central Americans, Mexicans, and African Americans. The unemployment rate always correlated strongly with the poverty rate but was highest for blacks. The prevalence of female-headed households was also lowest for whites and Chinese and highest for African Americans, Central Americans, and Mexicans. Overall, whites grew up in better neighborhoods than any other ethnic group, and these differences are statistically significant.

The average tract-level poverty rate growing up was also lowest for native whites in New York. In contrast, Chinese and South Americans grew up in tracts with substantial poverty, even though it was much higher for African Americans and Dominicans. The average tract-level unemployment rate was also lowest for native whites and Chinese, though it was also low for the other groups, even African Americans. The prevalence of female-headed households was lowest among whites and Chinese and almost three times higher among Dominicans and African Americans. Like their counterparts in Los Angeles, native whites in New York grew up in better neighborhoods than any other ethnic group.

In Berlin, native Germans also live in areas with the lowest indicators, but the levels for Turks and especially former Yugoslavians are not much higher. On average, Turks grew up in more disadvantaged neighborhoods. Differences between former Yugoslavians and the comparison group are not discernible, however. While Mexicans in Los Angeles and Dominicans in New York grew up in neighborhoods even more disadvantaged than those of African Americans, Turks in Berlin lived in neighborhoods similar to those of people of German ancestry.

Neighborhood Social Disorder

Table 7.3 presents respondents' perceptions of disorder in their childhood neighborhood by ethnic group for three measures of disorder and an overall disorder index. In the United States, New York respondents reported substantially higher levels of drug-dealing and crime in their neighborhoods than those in Los Angeles did. On the one hand, white and Chinese respondents were least likely to report that crime, drugs, and gangs were somewhat of or a big problem in their neighborhood while they grew up, corresponding to the better socioeconomic conditions reported. On the other hand, African Americans, Dominicans, Mexicans, and Central Americans were most likely to see these conditions as a problem, mirror-

TABLE 7.3   Perceived Neighborhood Social Disorder

IIMMLA	Drug-Dealing	Crime	Gang Activity	Mean Index Score (0 to 6 Scale)
Mexican	0.449	0.538	0.628	2.37
Central American	0.475	0.601	0.691	2.61
Chinese	0.137	0.337	0.319	0.88
Filipino	0.262	0.406	0.46	1.39
Non-Hispanic black	0.443	0.570	0.601	2.38
Non-Hispanic white	0.176	0.352	0.275	0.97

ISGMNY	Drug-Dealing	Crime		Mean Index Score (0 to 4 Scale)
Dominican	0.708	0.626		1.95
Chinese	0.339	0.601		1.15
South American	0.528	0.520		1.29
Non-Hispanic black	0.703	0.772		2.06
Non-Hispanic white	0.359	0.495		1.01

TIES	Vandalism	Crime	Garbage	Mean Index Score (1 to 5 Scale)
Turk	0.249	0.202	0.272	2.77
Yugoslavian	0.238	0.198	0.277	2.72
Comparison group	0.224	0.212	0.240	2.74

Source: Authors' compilation based on IIMMLA (Rumbaut et al. 2004); ISGMNY (Mollenkopf, Kasinitz, and Waters 1999); TIES 2007, 2008.
Note: For IIMMLA: 0 = Not a problem; 6 = Major problem. For ISGMNY: 0 = Not a problem; 4 = Major problem. For TIES: 1 = Not a problem; 5 = Major problem.

ing the relative disadvantages in their neighborhood environments. The three Berlin groups reported no significant differences in perceptions of neighborhood disorder.

In Los Angeles, fewer than 20 percent of white and Chinese respondents reported that drug-dealing and usage was a problem, whereas almost 50 percent of the African American, Mexican, and Central American respondents did. The same pattern exists with crime and gang activities— whites and Chinese were least likely to recall these being problems, followed by Filipinos, African Americans, Mexicans, and Central Americans.

Central Americans were the most likely to perceive disorder in their neighborhood on all three measures—drugs, crime, and gang activities. On the 7-point composite scale, Chinese and native whites scored the lowest and Central Americans, African Americans, and Mexicans the highest.

In New York, 33 percent of white and Chinese respondents reported that drug-dealing and usage was a problem in their neighborhood, versus more than 65 percent of Dominican and African American respondents. African Americans were most likely to report criminal activity as a problem, followed by Dominicans and Chinese. In contrast, South Americans and whites were least likely to perceive crimes in their neighborhoods. On the 5-point composite disorder scale, native whites and Chinese scored the lowest and Dominicans and African Americans the highest.

In Berlin, the groups once more showed no major differences: about 25 percent of Turkish and former Yugoslavian respondents reported that vandalism was a problem, versus 22 percent among the comparison group. Nor were there differences on criminal activity, though the comparison group was actually slightly more likely to perceive crime as a problem. About 25 percent of each ethnic group rated garbage on the street as a problem. Their native counterparts were least likely to see it as such.

How Neighborhood Disadvantage Shapes Perceptions of Social Disorder

We now turn to multivariate analyses of these perceived social disorder indices. Following the literature on ethnic-group advantage, we expect that native whites and Chinese, who grew up in higher-status neighborhoods, will report less disorder than Latino groups or African Americans. These perceptions of disorder should be associated with the family's socioeconomic status and with such individual characteristics as age, gender, and school performance, with girls and high achievers presumably more sheltered from neighborhood troublemaking. Neighborhood ethnic composition should also be positively related to perceptions of disorder. Higher concentrations of the foreign born, Hispanics, Asians, and blacks should be associated with higher perceptions of disorder, except that the prevalence of respondents' coethnics should not raise the perception of disorder. Last, poverty rates should also be strongly related to perceptions of disorder.

A multivariate analysis of the influence of neighborhood characteristics versus individual and family attributes on perceptions of drugs, crime, and gangs in respondents' neighborhoods in Los Angeles is presented in table 7A.1. Model 1 shows that African Americans, Central Americans, Mexicans, and Filipinos are all significantly more likely than native whites (the excluded group) to report disorder in their neighborhood, whereas the Chinese are not significantly different. Overall, respondents' ethnic-racial backgrounds account for 11 percent of the variation in perceptions of disorder. Model 2 controls for individual-level characteristics; although it reduces group differences for African Americans, Mexicans, and Central Americans, these differences remain significant. Differences for Filipinos actually increase slightly. Age and gender both predict perceptions of disorder, with older and female respondents being less likely to report having seen disorder in their childhood neighborhoods.

Family background (measured by parental education) is also a strong and significant predictor of disorder. Respondents with more educated parents report less disorder in their neighborhood, pointing to the role of social class in the parental generation in shaping the residential neighborhood locations in which the second generation grew up. In addition, those who grew up with both parents and earned better grades are less likely to have perceived neighborhood disorder. Together, ethnic-racial background and other individual-level characteristics explain 16 percent of the variation in perceptions of disorder (R-squared = .155). These findings confirm expectations about how family background and individual characteristics will influence perceptions of neighborhood disorder.

Model 3 adds neighborhood ethnic composition to the model. As predicted, higher shares of blacks, Hispanics, Asians, and the foreign born are all associated with more perceived disorder in the neighborhood growing up. In this context, however, the immigrant-origin groups no longer have statistically significantly different perceptions than native whites and the difference between African Americans and native whites is no longer significant. However, introducing the ethnic context increases the difference in perceptions between Chinese and native whites. As ethnic diversity rises, the Chinese become significantly less likely than whites to perceive disorder. This is in keeping with John Hipp's (2010) finding that whites are more likely than some others to perceive disorder. Altogether, model 3 explains 25 percent of the variance. But because respondents might be unlikely to perceive their own group as creating disorder, model 4 adds an interaction between the respondent's ethnicity and the person's group share in the tract. As expected, coethnic concentration has a negligible effect on perceptions of disorder for Mexicans, Central Americans, and the two Asian groups and significantly decreases perceptions of disorder among African Americans. Nonblacks are thus more likely than African Americans to associate the presence of blacks with disorder. Because these interactions do not add to the overall variance explained, the remaining models omit them.

Model 5 introduces one overall control for neighborhood poverty. This single variable accounts for 16 percent to 26 percent of the total, showing that, as predicted, poverty alone is already strongly associated with perceptions of disorder. After taking poverty into account, however, we find that Mexicans, Central Americans, Filipinos, and African Americans are still more likely than native whites to perceive disorder, but the control greatly diminishes the initial difference. Model 6 controls for both immigrant and ethnic-racial context and poverty level and demonstrates that poverty alone accounts for nearly half of the association between immigrant and ethnic-racial context and perceptions of neighborhood disorder. In this full model, the neighborhood Hispanic percentage is no longer associated with disorder perceptions and Asian percentage is associated with less disorder.

Similar analyses were performed with the New York data and are presented in table 7A.2. Model 1 again shows that all second-generation groups and African Americans are significantly more likely than native whites to perceive disorder and that group membership alone accounts for 8 percent of the overall variation. Controlling for demographic characteristics and social class backgrounds in model 2 removes the significant difference between Chinese and native whites: Dominicans, South Americans, and African Americans, however, are more likely to differ. As in Los Angeles, greater age and female gender are both strong negative predictors of perceptions of disorder. Because younger and male respondents spend more time outside their home and in the neighborhood, they are more likely to perceive disorder. Family background is also a strong predictor: respondents with more educated parents are less likely to perceive neighborhood disorder, as are those who grew up with both parents or had higher grades in school. In addition, the number of moves between the ages of six and eighteen is a significant predictor of disorder. Together, these individual characteristics explain 13 percent of the variation in perceptions of disorder.

Model 3 introduces further controls for neighborhood ethnic composition. The neighborhood proportions of non-Hispanic blacks, Hispanics, and Asians once again strongly predict perceptions of disorder, confirming the importance of neighborhood racial context in shaping perceptions (Sampson and Raudenbush 2004; Quillian and Pager 2001). In contrast to Los Angeles, however, a higher foreign-born population share in New York is associated with lower levels of perceived disorders, which might reflect the negative stereotyping of Mexicans in Los Angeles in contrast to the more positive views of Dominicans and Puerto Ricans in New York. However, African Americans and Dominicans are still significantly more likely than native whites to report that disorder characterized their neighborhoods growing up. Overall, this model explains 17 percent of the variance in perceived disorder. Model 4 adds ethnic origin interaction terms; coethnic concentration has a negligible impact for Hispanics, though having more coethnics significantly increases the perception of disorder for both African Americans and Chinese.

Moving beyond the ethno-racial context, the model controlling only for neighborhood poverty level (model 5) again shows that it is strongly associated with perceived disorder. Model 6 further controls for poverty but adds ethno-racial context along with all the other covariates. African Americans and Dominicans are still significantly more likely than native whites to perceive disorder, and living among greater proportions of blacks and Hispanics, along with higher poverty, remains positively associated with perceptions of disorder. Controlling for poverty actually explains away the initial negative impact of the foreign-born population on perceptions of disorder.

Table 7A.3 shows multivariate results for Berlin. Model 1 shows no ethnic differences in perceptions of disorder—a finding that persists even after controlling for individual and contextual covariates. In model 2, social background is a strong and positive predictor of perceived disorder, with respondents with more educated fathers being less likely to perceive disorder and mother's education having no discernible effect. To our surprise, neither age nor gender has statistically significant effects, which might reflect the higher level of actual individual safety in public spaces in Berlin. However, these individual-level characteristics explain less than 2 percent of the variation in perceptions of disorder. Model 3 controls for neighborhood ethnic composition. The proportion of Turks in the postcode strongly predicts perceived disorder, suggesting that the presence of Turks in a Berlin neighborhood sends the same kinds of signals (at least to the native comparison group) that concentrations of blacks do to whites in the U.S. neighborhoods. In contrast, neighborhood proportions of former Yugoslavians and the total foreign-born population have a negative, but not significant, impact. Adding these characteristics to the model increases its explanatory power to 3.5 percent of the variance, which is still quite small. Introducing interaction terms in model 4 has no statistically significant effect. Using only poverty levels (proportion on social welfare) in model 5 shows a positive relationship with perceived disorder, but at much lower levels than in the U.S. cases. Finally, the combined model 6 shows that poverty and immigrant concentration attenuate the effect of Turkish concentration, whereas former Yugoslavian concentrations have a significantly negative effect on disorder perceptions.

DISCUSSION AND CONCLUSION

This analysis leads us to a number of basic conclusions. First, Mexicans in Los Angeles and Dominicans in New York are more segregated from native whites than other second-generation groups and often find themselves growing up in neighborhoods with many African Americans, whereas Turks in Berlin grew up in areas that were not nearly as segregated. Second, Dominicans and Mexicans grew up in significantly more disadvantaged areas and Chinese (and of course native white) respondents in more advantaged neighborhoods. This was not the case for second-generation Turks in Berlin. On the one hand, these findings confirm the general picture of racial stratification across urban neighborhoods in the United States (Iceland 2009). On the other hand, they draw our attention to the significant ethnic stratification within the standard categories such as Asian or Latino. Filipinos grew up in only slightly less advantaged areas than Chinese but reported significantly more disorder. Similarly, the four Latino ethnic groups exhibited varying degrees of segregation and disadvantage compared with African Americans, pointing to the heterogeneity among Latinos (Tienda and Mitchell 2006). For example, the South Americans in New York grew up in residential environments more closely resembling those of Filipinos in Los Angeles than the other Latino groups in New York and Los Angeles: Dominicans, Mexicans, and Central Americans.

This pattern of ethnic neighborhood stratification closely maps onto respondents' perceptions about social disorder in the neighborhoods in which they grew up. In other words, so-called objective neighborhood characteristics have a strong, though imperfect, correlation with perceptions of neighborhood disorder. As Hipp (2010) has shown, highly localized neighborhood measurements can reveal some systematic bias in perceptions of disorder. Nonetheless, neighborhood poverty is a key predictor of perceptions of disorder, suggesting that problems with drugs, crime, and gang activity are more prevalent in poor neighborhoods and that is the way our respondents saw the situation if they lived in such areas. Respondents with educated parents are less likely to perceive disorder in their neighborhoods, suggesting that family background plays an important mediating role in how members of the second generation in the United States perceive their neighborhoods growing up, independent of objective levels of poverty and racial composition. In part, better educated parents live in better neighborhoods, but they may also shelter their children even when they grow up in poor neighborhoods.

Parental characteristics remain significant in all three cities. Specifically, first-generation social class background significantly shapes how members of the second generation experience their neighborhoods growing up by structuring how second-generation and native groups inherit advantages or disadvantages from their parents. Although more objective measures of actual social disorder would be useful to confirm subjective perceptions, they are not readily available. More important, we should explore subjective perceptions in their own right because they shape how second-generation respondents navigate their neighborhood environments, where they choose to spend their time, and how much time they spend in their neighborhoods (Tran 2011).

Finally, the transatlantic comparison points to important differences between the American and German contexts: the U.S. second-generation groups live in much more segregated and disadvantaged neighborhoods than native whites, whereas Berlin's second-generation groups live in more integrated neighborhoods that vary far less in their range of perceived disorder. Racial segregation plays a crucial role in shaping how and where the post-1965 second generation came of age in the United States. But it also suggests that urban neighborhoods as an ecological unit of analysis play a different role on the two continents, involving, for example, different prices of land in central and peripheral areas, different patterns of social and private housing tenure, and a different intensity of urban planning. Berlin simply does not have the physical space or great fluctuations in neighborhood trajectories to produce ethnically segregated neighborhoods comparable to those of the two American cities. This illustrates the inherent challenges of conducting comparative research, because the settings are so different in this respect. At the same time, the analysis makes clear that the kinds of neighborhood environments in which second-generation groups grew up have important implications for the quality of their educations, their labor market prospects, their engagement with civic and political life, and how the larger society sees them.

TABLE 7A.1 Ordinary Least Squares Regression of Neighborhood Social Disorder in Los Angeles

	Model 1	Model 2	Model 3	Model 4	Model 5	Model 6
Individual-level characteristics						
Race-ethnicity						
1.5, second-generation Mexican	1.398***	.811***	.062	-.081	.209+	.098
1.5, second-generation Central American	1.637***	1.113***	.079	-.087	.339*	.088
1.5, second-generation Chinese	-.090	-.078	-.356*	-.352+	-.219	-.312+
1.5, second-generation Filipino	.418*	.566**	.083	.083	.300+	.147
Third-plus-generation non–Hispanic black	1.404***	1.246***	.225	.606**	.561**	.283
Third-plus-generation non–Hispanic white (reference)						
Age	-.017**	-.001	.002	-.009	-.004	
Male	.440***	.427***	.439***	.410***	.415***	
Mother's education (reference is college graduate)						
Missing	.259	.165	-.166	.144	.141	
Less than high school		.625***	.360*	.351*	.392**	.343*
High school graduate or vocational education		.171	.095	.107	.042	.054
Some college		.048	.003	.010	-.001	-.004
Father's education (reference is college graduate)						
Missing		.571**	.412*	.418**	.370*	.367*
Less than high school		.535**	.357*	.360*	.292*	.297*

	(1)	(2)	(3)	(4)	(5)	(6)
High school graduate		.186	.100	.116	.067	.072
Some college		.211	.210	.214	.137	.168
Grew up with both parents		-.219*	-.218*	-.237*	-.177	-.193*
Grades in school		-.128*	-.100†	-.098†	-.116†	-.105†
Context of childhood neighborhood						
Percentage non-Hispanic black			.022***	.031***		.012***
Percentage Hispanic			.006†	.004		.003
Percentage Asian–Pacific Islander			-.017**	-.017*		-.010†
Non-Hispanic black × Percentage non-Hispanic black				-.016***		
Mexican or Central American × Percentage Hispanic				.003		
Chinese or Filipino × Percentage Asian–Pacific Islander				.002		
Percentage foreign born			.036***	.036***	.069***	.021***
Percentage below poverty line						.041***
Constant	.974***	1.458***	.389	.287	.760*	.459
N	2,060	2,060	2,060	2,060	2,060	2,060
R^2	.110	.155	.255	.260	.257	.270

Source: Authors' compilation based on IIMMLA (Rumbaut et al. 2004).
†$p < .10$; *$p < .05$; **$p < .01$; ***$p < .001$

TABLE 7A.2   Ordinary Least Squares Regression of Neighborhood Social Disorder in New York

	Model 1	Model 2	Model 3	Model 4	Model 5	Model 6
Individual-level characteristics						
Race-ethnicity (reference is non-Hispanic white)						
1.5, second-generation Dominican	.889***	.630***	.273*	.276*	.281**	.206+
1.5, second-generation Chinese	.183+	.009	-.011	-.133	-.143	-.094
1.5, second-generation South American	.403***	.217*	-.016	.059	.058	.015
Third-plus-generation non-Hispanic black	1.033***	.865***	.405***	.227	.535***	.395**
Age		-.033***	-.031***	-.032***	-.035***	-.033***
Male		.244***	.254***	.257***	.266***	.265***
Mother's education (reference is college graduate)						
Missing		-.005	-.059	-.049	-.062	-.077
Less than high school		.209*	.179+	.188+	.144	.142
High school graduate or vocational education		.088	.057	.061	.027	.025
Some college		.211+	.197+	.198+	.188+	.186+
Father's education (reference is college graduate)						
Missing		.210*	.170+	.171+	.128	.132
Less than high school		.344*	.259**	.255*	.234*	.228*

	(1)	(2)	(3)	(4)	(5)	(6)
High school graduate		.184+	.143	.141	.128	.122
Some college		.257*	.219+	.221+	.209+	.201+
Grew up with both parents		-.219**	-.177*	-.188**	-.171*	-.164*
Grades in school		-.028*	-.029*	.029*	-.027*	-.028*
Times moved between six and eighteen		.045***	.042***	.040**	.048***	.048***
Context of childhood neighborhood						
Percentage non-Hispanic black			.008***	.006***		.004**
Percentage Hispanic			.012***	.011***		.004*
Percentage Asian–Pacific Islander			.005*	-.007		-.001
Non-Hispanic black × Percentage non-Hispanic black				.013*		
Dominican or South American × Percentage Hispanic				.001		
Chinese × Percentage Asian–Pacific Islander				.005**		
Percentage foreign born			-.006**	-.005*		
Percentage below poverty line					.025***	.019***
Constant	1.035***	1.748***	1.602***	1.741***	1.567***	1.477***
N	2004	2004	2004	2004	2004	2004
R^2	.081	.129	.168	.173	.173	.186

Source: Authors' compilation based on ISGMNY (Mollenkopf, Kasinitz, and Waters 1999).

+p < .10; *p < .05; **p < .01; ***p < .001

TABLE 7A.3   Ordinary Least Squares Regression of Neighborhood Social Disorder in Berlin

	Model 1	Model 2	Model 3	Model 4	Model 5	Model 6
Individual-level characteristics						
Race-ethnicity						
Second-generation Turk	.039	.041	-.042	.011	-.017	-.038
Second-generation Yugoslavian	-.007	-.037	-.053	-.153	-.046	-.044
Third-plus comparison group (reference)						
Age		.004	.003	.003	.004	.003
Male		.093	.101+	.102+	.098+	.099+
Mother's education (reference is college graduate)						
Missing		-.169	-.137	-.137	-.162	-.139
Primary school graduate		-.252	-.232	-.244	-.247	-.223
Secondary school graduate		-.129	-.115	-.119	-.129	-.255
Father's education (reference is college graduate)						
Missing		.337*	.282+	.278+	.336*	.298*
Primary school graduate		.326*	.322*	.322*	.334*	.332*
Secondary school graduate		.271*	.257*	.255*	.257*	.255*
Parents married			.060	.063	.058	.062
Contextual-level variables						
Percentage Turk			.024**	.026*		.017+
Percentage Yugoslavian			-.045	-.062*		-.062*
Turk × Percentage Turk				-.004		
Yugoslavian × Percentage Yugoslavian				.049		
Percentage foreign born			-.002	-.002		-.002
Percentage on social welfare					.019**	.018+
Constant	2.736***	2.439***	2.466***	2.489***	2.248***	2.336***
N	709	709	709	709	709	709
R^2	.001	.015	.035	.038	.027	.039

Source: Authors' compilation based on TIES 2007, 2008.
+$p < .10$; *$p < .05$; **$p < .01$; ***$p < .001$

CHAPTER 8

CITIZENSHIP AND PARTICIPATION

BARBARA HERZOG-PUNZENBERGER, ROSITA FIBBI,
CONSTANZA VERA-LARRUCEA, LOUIS DESIPIO, AND JOHN MOLLENKOPF

The issue of citizenship is central to all other debates about the membership, belonging, and integration of immigrants and their children. Everyone who has citizenship from birth is inalienably entitled to full political, legal, and civic rights. Acquiring citizenship through naturalization requires a person to declare a formal allegiance to the granting nation, demonstrate an understanding of its constitutional principles and values and promise to uphold them, and, in some countries, abandon the previous allegiance. Not having citizenship, or worse, being ineligible for acquiring it, means remaining outside the circle of those with standing to shape the country's political affairs. Despite the intimation by some that immigrants to Europe do not need full electoral rights because they enjoy a Marshallian social citizenship (Marshall 1950), it is a truism that, at least under some circumstances, governments do respond to voters, including immigrant voters. The degree to which immigrants and their children hold and exercise citizenship is thus fundamental to their successful integration.

In reaction to the possibility that growing immigrant populations might ultimately undermine the superior political position of the native born, European debates are increasingly questioning whether newcomers should have these rights. Some European governments have made it easier for the children of immigrants to become citizens, for example, Germany in 2000 and or Greece in 2010. But others believe that raising the bar for achieving full membership is an appropriate way to promote social cohesion. The field has become so politicized that the European Union has even financed an observatory to collect and analyze data on citizenship.[1]

Although many in the United States take it for granted that legal immigrants should naturalize, widespread opposition has emerged to providing unauthorized immigrants with a "path toward citizenship." Critics argue that regularizing the status of the unauthorized extends a benefit to "lawbreakers" that those who seek permanent residence by the normal rules find difficult to obtain. A few conservative politicians have even advocated eliminating birthright citizenship for the U.S.-born children of unauthorized immigrants.

In Europe, many segments of the population worry that the movement of people across national borders calls into question the foundation of the modern nation-state. As detailed in earlier chapters, they see their nations as peopled by those who have shared historical, cultural, and political experiences for many generations and who also will have a common future within specific territorial borders. Migrants undermine this assumption by adding newcomers with allegiances to distant places. Although the United States was built on immigration and most Americans seem to consider the country so attractive that, with enough time, the great bulk of immigrants will naturalize, a significant minority never does. (The March 2009 Current Population Survey reports that one-seventh of the immigrants who had first entered the United States forty-five years earlier still had not naturalized.) Although the U.S. naturalization process sets relatively low barriers by international standards, the application process can still be daunting for some immigrants (DeSipio 2001). Because U.S. policymakers understand naturalization to be an individual decision, the government has no large-scale program to promote citizenship in immigrant communities or train immigrants for the application process, although it funds some community-based organizations and ethnic groups to try to fill this gap (federal spending for this purpose was $11 million in 2011). Although the United States accepts and expects naturalization more than Europe, it does little to actively promote this outcome.

Most empirical research on citizenship acquisition has focused on the individual determinants, with the often-replicated and unsurprising result that older, more educated, higher-income, host-language-speaking, longer-term residents are found to be more likely to naturalize (for a broader approach, see Bloemraad 2006). In fact, the decision to naturalize (or not) takes place in a family and community context, has major implications for the children in these families, and can generate different statuses for different family members. Both for institutional and life-cycle reasons, social scientists have paid relatively little attention to the children of immigrants. In the United States, birthright citizenship for the growing numbers of the second generation seems unproblematic. In western Europe, however, exclusionary jus sanguinis traditions, affiliations lingering from the colonial era, and the recent emergence of European Union (EU) citizenship have complicated the question of second-generation citizenship.

The emergence of a large second-generation cohort in western Europe and the United States, together with the availability of the TIES, ISGMNY, and IIMMLA data sets, now makes it possible to examine comprehensively the origins and consequences of citizenship for the second generation, taking into account not only individual factors but also the surrounding family, community, and national contexts. In the past, the discussion has largely focused on cross-national differences in legal regulations, institutions, and policies. We can now refine that discussion to see how they actually shape the lives of young individuals and how these young people in turn react, developing beliefs and engaging in civic and political action.

The investigation laid out in the following pages takes us far beyond the national models approach that contrasts the U.S. birthright citizenship approach with the more restrictive citizenship regimes of Europe to look at the great variation by group and city, to the conclusion that second-generation citizenship does not lag as much as would be expected in some of the European settings. Indeed, some attain higher levels of first-generation citizenship than is common in the United States, with important consequences for their second-generation children when compared with the many children in the United States who grow up with noncitizen or even undocumented parents. In the conclusion, we reflect further on the inadequacy of the broad national generalizations that have previously characterized this field.

RESEARCH QUESTIONS AND METHODOLOGY

Previous comparative thinking about citizenship has developed typologies based on the prevalence of jus soli, jus sanguinis, or jus domicili citizenship regimes: law of the soil, or birthright citizenship; law of the blood, or citizenship by descent from those defined as legitimate members of the polity; and law of residence, that living in a certain jurisdiction conveys rights to all who reside there (Brubaker 1992; Favell 1998). For a long time, such typologies were not linked to empirical outcomes like first-generation naturalization rates, let alone second-generation citizenship status. They either operated on an abstract, normative level (see Walzer 1983; Young 1990; Kymlicka 1996; Fraser and Honneth 2003; Parekh 2000) or condensed governmental regulations into indices, such as the Migrant Integration Policy Index (MIPEX; Niessen, Huddleston, and Citron 2007; Huddleston and Niessen 2011) and its forerunners (Waldrauch and Hofinger 1997).[2]

The empirical analysis of statistical evidence was typically confined to single-country studies seeking to explain differences across individuals or immigrant groups. They explained naturalization as a function of socio-economic, ethno-cultural, or regional factors (for the United States, DeSipio 1987; for Canada, Sweden, the Netherlands, Norway, and the United States, Bevelander and DeVoretz 2008). Naturalization was then sometimes related to economic outcomes across immigrant groups (Kogan 2003, 2006). Few studies took a detailed, cross-national, quantitative approach. Reinforced by the lack of comparable data (DeVoretz 2008), these single case studies left many important questions off the table. Ruud Koopmans (2010) was one of the first to undertake a comparative statistical analysis of labor market and housing market outcomes and criminality across national settings in an attempt to bring empirical patterns into a dialog with the legalistic and normative discourse on citizenship typologies. Initially, few studies also sought to understand the influence of supranational or transnational forces on the first and second generations, although such studies became more frequent over the last decade (for one attempt, see Østergaard-Nielsen 2009).

In Europe, TIES survey data enable us to look at single and dual nationality outcomes among the young adult second generation both as an outcome of and a contributor to other forms of civic and political engagement and identity. (The ISGMNY and IIMMLA studies did not measure dual nationality.) In keeping with the overall approach of this volume, we focus on descendants of Turkish immigrants in Europe, Mexican immigrants in Los Angeles, and Dominican immigrants in New York. In citizenship as in the other domains, we would expect these groups to face the greatest challenges of effective incorporation as well as the greatest risks of being alienated because of political exclusion.

For theoretical as well as practical reasons, we restrict our analysis to three German-speaking countries (Germany, Switzerland, and Austria), France, and Sweden. These cases are often thought to represent three different citizenship regimes: the republican (France), the multicultural

(Sweden), and the ethnic or primordial (German-speaking countries). Although analysts usually deem the German-speaking countries to share a citizenship regime, our data show markedly different rates of naturalization and dual citizenship across them. Although the United States is also thought to be characterized by an open, multicultural regime (though with little government intervention), the Dominicans in New York and Mexicans in Los Angeles face practical barriers in transitioning from immigrant to citizen. The low incomes and education levels of the parents, and their higher likelihood of having initially entered the United States without authorization, can make political incorporation challenging for their children, even though the latter have birthright citizenship.

Citizenship Typologies, Integration Philosophies, and Legal Regulations

France is thought to exemplify the republican model of an inclusive, assimilationist, and color-blind treatment of the second generation through the practice of jus soli. Indeed, France is said to have given birth to the modern idea of national citizenship during the French Revolution and imagines it to be a universalist political project allowing no distinction between foreigners and French nationals pertaining to rights and duties (Weil, Spire, and Bertossi 2010, 1–2). This strong conception of national identity is backed up by the pursuit of a largely monocultural philosophy of integration. The picture looks different, however, when we scrutinize how legal provisions actually treat third-country nationals, such as citizens of Turkey. Contrary to expectations, MIPEX actually gave republican France a slightly lower overall score (54) in 2010 than exclusionist Germany (60). In fact, France outperforms Germany only on one MIPEX factor, namely antidiscrimination, and just matches Germany on another, access to nationality (Huddleston and Niessen 2011).

A native-born child will be French at birth if at least one parent is French or born in France, or will become French automatically at age eighteen if neither parent is French or was born in France but the child has legally resided in France for at least five years and does not renounce French citizenship. France has long tolerated dual citizenship. Since 1973, maintaining a former citizenship has not been an impediment to becoming a French citizen for men or women (Weil, Spire, and Bertossi 2010). The question is rather whether the country of the previous citizenship allows dual nationality.

The literature considers the German-speaking countries to hold primordial, communitarian, or ethnic citizenship regimes. Nationality is a premium for successfully integrated immigrants that should not be granted easily. Legal discrimination against third-country nationals has been pervasive, and the law grants few rights for political participation or cultural recognition, especially in Austria (except for religious rights). The German-speaking countries receive the lowest MIPEX scores on anti-discrimination legislation, despite EU standards calling for the adoption of such measures. The predominance of jus sanguinis approaches to citizenship for second- and third-generation migrants exemplifies the differential exclusionist philosophy of integration in Germany, Austria, and Switzerland. Traditionally, these countries avoided dual citizenship.

After 1990, however, Austria, Germany, and Switzerland began to follow divergent strategies. Although Austria persisted with its restrictive stance towards dual nationality, Switzerland allowed naturalized foreigners to maintain dual citizenship after 1992. Austria facilitated naturalization for native-born children of non-nationals at age eighteen in 1999 conditional on having lived in Austria for four years. In 2006, native-born children of non-nationals became legally entitled to citizenship after six years of residence as long as they complied with general conditions of discretionary naturalization (Çinar 2010, 15).

Germany opted for conditional jus soli in 2000. If their parents have resided legally in Germany for eight years, German-born children of non-nationals can acquire German citizenship alongside the citizenship of their parents at birth. Between eighteen and twenty-three, they must choose which nationality to retain. In Switzerland, by contrast, it is not likely that any form of jus soli will be introduced, and voters have refused to provide it for the third generation. Switzerland also rejects any legal entitlement to naturalization (Fibbi 2011). The peculiar institution of Bürgerrecht—simultaneous legal citizenship affiliation at the municipal, cantonal, and national levels (Achermann et al. 2010, 1)—entails a triple naturalization procedure and gives municipalities a strong say.

Sweden exemplifies the multicultural approach to immigrant incorporation, though it is less frequently discussed than Great Britain or the Netherlands. Between 1964 and 1975, Sweden developed its own model toward guest workers (Hammar 2004, 11). In 1969, it established the National Immigration Authority as well as the Commission on Immigrants to research the situation of newcomers, settlers, first- and second-generation immigrants, and ethnic minorities and make policy recommendations. In 1975, all five political parties of the Riksdag unanimously adopted "The Principles of Sweden's Immigration and Minority Policy" and allowed legally resident noncitizens to vote in local and regional elections.

After the mid-1980s, however, conservative populists put pressure on the Swedish government to balance its liberal migration policy with elements restricting access to its welfare state (Tamas 2004, 35), Europe's most comprehensive (Esping-Andersen 1990). Still, populist pressure did not cause Sweden to limit access to citizenship, and MIPEX still gives it the top rating. At the same time, like Norway and Denmark, Sweden has not introduced jus soli. Access to nationality is a relatively weak MIPEX strand for Sweden, though it still performs better than the other European cases considered here. Sweden developed a de facto toleration of dual nationality through relaxed naturalization requirements and widening exemptions from renouncing one's original citizenship (Faist 2007, 103) and now legally accepts dual nationality (SFS 2001, 82). This reflects the reduced significance of national citizenship for residents of Sweden, a country that seeks to equalize the rights of citizens and foreigners (Lokrantz Bernitz 2010, 1).

The United States fits a broadly republican model with a multicultural twist. Legally resident immigrants may naturalize after five years (or three for immigrants who marry U.S. citizens or who are on active military duty). To do so, applicants must show a basic ability to read, write, and speak English and knowledge of American history and civics. The cost of applying for naturalization rose sharply a few years ago and it often takes several years to negotiate the process of applying, which includes completing a lengthy application form, filing the application, and waiting for an interview to be scheduled. This deters some immigrants, particularly those with less formal education.

The most defining difference with the European cases is that the United States grants citizenship at birth to all U.S.-born children of immigrants regardless of the parents' legal status. Although some conservative politicians have recently called for ending this practice, the jus soli recognition of citizenship is enshrined in the U.S. Constitution and would be difficult to change. Unlike the French republican tradition, which echoes the late nineteenth-century Americanization model, the current U.S. philosophy of integration does not call on immigrants to jettison their cultural heritage in favor of an Anglo-centric model but instead celebrates the contribution of new immigrant streams, whether from Cuba, Iran, El Salvador, or India. As Ewa Morawska (2001) argues, immigrants become Americans by establishing a made-in-America hyphenated or hybrid ethnicity. At the same time, given their relative poverty, share of undocumented immigrants, and darker skin colors, Mexican and Dominican immigrants have both often been negatively stereotyped.

ACCESS TO CITIZENSHIP

Although the second generation in the United States are citizens at birth, they often grow up in households where other members are not citizens, possibly including unauthorized parents or siblings. This can make it difficult for them to put their theoretical rights into actual practice. In Europe, different family members may also have different nationalities, though up until now this has received little or no attention. Scholars have begun to look at the impact of a country's legal framework on second-generation naturalization patterns (Honohan 2010; Vink and deGroot 2010).[3] Here, we are able to compare nationality outcomes for the same group across countries to reveal how the ensemble of citizenship policies—and the ways localities implement them—works out on the ground, in specific family terms.

The TIES survey asked second-generation respondents whether they had naturalized and, if they had not, whether they planned to do so. It also determined whether respondents had received citizenship at birth or later and also asked whether their parents had naturalized. The two U.S. surveys asked similar questions. For the Turkish second generation in Europe (age eighteen through age thirty-five), Dominicans in New York (eighteen through thirty-two), and Mexicans in Los Angeles (twenty through forty), table 8.1 shows the current naturalization rates of the second-generation respondents and their parents as well as the second-generation naturalization rates at birth. The table shows expected as well as unexpected patterns. Naturalization among the parents was indeed low in the German-speaking countries compared with the United States, but the highest rate was in Sweden, exceeding that of the United States substantially, and the lowest was in France, traditionally conceived as an effective country in drawing immigrants into its republican tradition. As expected, citizenship at birth was universal for the U.S. second generation and relatively low for the German-speaking countries. This time, however, France and Sweden were both in between, rather than being polar cases, as they were for the parents.

Quite remarkably, however, the vast majority of the second generation had become naturalized by the time of the survey in young adulthood. Even in Switzerland, the worst performer of the group, only 28 percent

TABLE 8.1   Nationality of Parents and Second Generation at Birth and Survey

	Turkish					Dominican	Mexican
	Austrian	Swiss	German	French	Swedish		
Parents naturalized at survey	66%	46%	38%	27%	83%	68%	68%
Respondents naturalized at birth	29	12	NA	53	57	100	100
Respondents naturalized at survey	88	72	84	96	99	100	100

Source: Authors' compilation based on TIES 2007, 2008 (data not yet publicly available) ISGMNY (Mollenkopf, Kasinitz, and Waters 1999) and IIMMLA (Rumbaut et al. 2004).

The TIES survey comprises eight separate national data sets, collected by Institute for Studies on Migrations (IEM), Comillas Pontifical University, Spain; Swiss Forum for Migration and Population Studies (SFM), Neuchâtel, Switzerland; Netherlands Interdisciplinary Demographic Institute (NIDI), The Hague, Netherlands; Austrian Academy of Sciences (ÖAW), Vienna, Austria; the European Research Centre on Migration and Ethnic Relations (ERCOMER), Katholieke Universiteit Leuven, Belgium; National Institute for Demographic Studies (INED), Paris, France; Institute for Migration Research and Intercultural Studies (IMIS), University of Osnabrück, Germany; Centre for Research in International Migration and Ethnic Relations (CEIFO), Stockholm University, Sweden. The TIES national surveys will be made publicly available by the national TIES partners individually, but were not yet available at the time of publication.

NA = not applicable

remained foreign nationals. The two other German-speaking countries had also absorbed even more, only 16 percent remaining Turkish nationals in Germany and 11 percent in Austria. It is remarkable that France and Sweden both achieved nearly universal citizenship for the second generation despite the fact that France has the most extensive jus soli system in Europe while Sweden never adopted this approach. Moreover, despite having a form of jus soli, Germany and Austria did not do as well. We can tentatively conclude both that actual citizenship practices for the second generation cannot be deduced directly from the national citizenship models and that different forms of jus soli across the countries have different outcomes. But why?

Forms of Jus Soli

The origins of the jus soli principle lie in the feudal tradition that individuals were subjects (Untertanen) of the lord of the land where they were born. Today, it is hard to imagine that individuals once had to adhere to their lord's religion or that their children were his property (Weil, Spire, and Bertossi 2010, 1). Jus soli therefore originally was not so different from the current jus sanguinis citizenship laws in that people were rooted in place. That said, because people are no longer rooted in place, jus soli is now a more inclusive legal framework for the second generation than the jus sanguinis emphasis on ethnic bonds. The concept of jus domicili, or right to legal status derived simply from legal permanent residence, as practiced in Sweden, is not often highlighted. Table 8.2 summarizes these different forms of jus soli and jus domicili for children born to non-naturalized parents.

Iseult Honohan (2010, 2) points out that jus soli can be combined with other elements to frame an inclusive citizenship regime, and jus soli varies in practice with respect to delay, discretion, and retrospective requirements, thus varying in terms of how liberal or inclusive they are.

The compelling case of Sweden shows that a society without jus soli can be even more inclusive than some jus soli countries regarding the children of immigrants (and especially their parents, whose status in turn affects that of their children). Sweden relies extensively on denizenship or jus domicili, granting rights to and requiring duties of those who have legally lived in the country for a certain period that are almost equal to those of full citizens. Sweden allows all children who have lived in the country more than five years to acquire Swedish citizenship independently (Lokrantz Bernitz 2010, 11–12).

TABLE 8.2   Naturalization Regulations for Children of Immigrants

	Jus Soli at Birth			Jus Soli After Birth		No Jus Soli	
	Pure Jus Soli	Retrospective Condition	Double Jus Soli	Retrospective Condition	Facilitated Naturalization	Jus Domicili for Minors	Ordinary Naturalization
Country	United States	Germany	France	France	Austria	Sweden	Switzerland
Requirements	Birth in the country	Birth in country and legal parental residence for eight or more years in country	Birth in country, parental birth in country	Birth in country and residence at age eighteen or after	Birth in country and residence at least six years during childhood	Unconditional after five years of legal residence	Conditional on residence, language proficiency, employment, law abiding

Source: Adapted from Honohan (2010, 6, table 1).

Do France and Sweden, with their high levels of second-generation naturalization, share a citizenship regime functionally equivalent to that of the United States, or do they implement different regimes in ways that yield the similar results? The MIPEX scores for France and Sweden regarding granting citizenship to native-born children of immigrants are in the middle, below what the United States would get on this dimension but above the German-speaking countries. Whereas the United States sends an absolutely clear message, "You—child of an immigrant—belong to us," the Europeans send a more ambiguous one, "Let's see where you will finally belong." This ambiguity not only reflects the consensus in mainstream society but may induce ambivalence among the young members of the second generation.

The German-speaking countries had the fewest among the second generation with survey country citizenship at birth, the United States the most, and France and Sweden in between, at about half.[4] Because all European countries regulate access to nationality with some degree of jus sanguinis, connecting the children's nationality with that of their parents, it is therefore important whether the immigrant parents had already naturalized at the time of their children's birth. Unfortunately, our surveys do not give us information on the exact timing of the parents' naturalization.

Naturalization of the Parents

As table 8.1 details, our surveys do tell us whether the parents had naturalized by the time we talked to our respondents. The huge variation is telling. Not only is the variation large, but the pattern is unexpected. Although Sweden has the highest share of naturalized parents (more than 80 percent), the other inclusive European country, France, has the lowest (about 25 percent). Two-thirds of the Austrian parents are naturalized, but fewer than half are in Germany and even fewer are in Switzerland. The Austrian figure may reflect a response to high legal discrimination against third-country nationals. The Swedish case represents the opposite condition: a high level of naturalization despite little legal discrimination. France is a particularly interesting case, because 96 percent of the children are citizens but only 27 percent of their immigrant parents are naturalized, a difference of 69 percentage points. The gains are much lower in the German-speaking countries: 46 points for Germany, 27 for Switzerland, and 22 for Austria. Sweden shows the least, but levels were already high for the parents. It is interesting that despite its reputation, the naturalization rate of the parents in the United States is lower than we might expect it to be, and the gain (32 points) puts it midway among the German-speaking countries.

In part, the low parental rates of naturalization in the United States reflect the situations of the Mexican and Dominican first generation in Los Angeles and New York, comparatively high rates of unauthorized entry and proximity to their home countries, factors that differentiate them from the Turkish immigrants to Europe.

The big differences within Europe raise many intriguing questions. Switzerland shows a comparatively low level of naturalization among the parents and little gain among their children, despite high levels of discrimination against third-country nationals, which should promote naturalization. Meanwhile, Sweden shows high levels of naturalization among the parents and children despite little legal discrimination. This supports the notion that people naturalize more because they identify with the survey countries rather than that naturalization conveys instrumental or pragmatic benefits. Despite the fact that naturalization conveys few additional material benefits in Sweden, many Turkish immigrants evidently want to become Swedish and be full members of this society. However, the French ideal of a civic nation rhetorically committed to equality and antiracism evidently does not lead the Turkish parents to behave the same way they do in Sweden. Quite the opposite. France displays almost as much legal discrimination against third-country nationals as Germany (Huddleston and Niessen 2011). France asserts a strong demand to assimilate, forget about one's previous culture, speak French, and not wear a head scarf. We might speculate that the low level of parental naturalization reflects their negative reaction to this set of demands. Yet jus soli helps France succeed with the second generation, with nearly all becoming citizens. Two of the German-speaking countries have relatively low rates among both the parents and children, yet Germany's new citizenship law seems to be reflected indirectly in higher levels for its second-generation young adults and their substantial gains over their parents.

CITIZENSHIP STATUS AND EDUCATIONAL ATTAINMENT

What difference does naturalization or dual citizenship make for the young adult second generation? This question of legal status has been on the U.S. research agenda for the last hundred years, but mostly for first-generation immigrants (for an overview of earlier research, see DeSipio 1987). The EU-funded research network International Migration, Integration, and Social Cohesion in Europe (IMISCOE) stated that little had been learned about the economic or political consequences of naturalization for the first generation in Europe (see also Kraler 2006, 63). The American and European comparative literature underscored the difficulty of drawing conclusions in the absence of panel data, because more successful immigrants are also more likely to naturalize (Aleinikoff and Klusmeyer 2000; Bevelander 1999; Bevelander and DeVoretz 2008; Bratsberg, Ragan, and Nasir 2002; Chiswick 1978; Kogan 2003; Herzog-Punzenberger 2007; Portes and Curtis 1987; Salentin and Wilkening 2003; Steinhardt, Straubhaar, and Wedemeier 2010). This research has produced mixed results: some authors (Chiswick 1978) find that acquiring citizenship yields better socioeconomic outcomes while others (Bratsberg, Ragan, and Nasir 2002) dismiss this as merely a selection effect. Few of these previous studies have considered the second generation.

Rosita Fibbi, Mathias Lerch, and Philippe Wanner (2007) analyzed Swiss census data from 2000 and found that differences in the legal treatment of first-generation immigrant groups affected the distribution of naturalization across their children. They note, however, that naturalized youth represent a positive selection in relation to all children of immigrants. Barbara Herzog-Punzenberger (2007, 244–45) analyzed Austrian census data from 2001 and found that young adults (twenty-five to thirty-four years of age) born in Austria who speak Turkish and hold Austrian citizenship are significantly more likely to hold white-collar positions than those holding a non-Austrian citizenship (see also, on Switzerland, Steinhardt, Straubhaar, and Wedemeier 2010; on Germany, Salentin and Wilkening 2003; on France, Fougère and Safi 2008).

Following up on these first steps, in our sample, naturalized second-generation young people were somewhat more likely to have university-educated parents in every case except the Dominican 1.5 generation in New York. This pattern both confirms previous findings and reflects the selective nature of the naturalization process. (The apparent negative selection in New York is puzzling and a bit troubling, though it parallels an even worse downward intergenerational mobility among Puerto Ricans, who hold citizenship from birth. The sample of Dominican 1.5-generation members is also relatively small.) Turning to the respondent's educational attainment, table 8.3 demonstrates the well-known pattern that those who have naturalized have higher levels of education than those who are still formally foreigners in their countries of birth, although the achievement levels among the naturalized groups vary considerably. We find similar results looking at the reciprocal conditions—those who are naturalized have lower unemployment rates.

These results suggest that naturalized and non-naturalized members of disadvantaged second-generation groups differ systematically. In

TABLE 8.3   Second Generation with University Education, by Citizenship

	Survey Country	Parental Country of Origin	Total Sample
Austria	20	6	18.5
Switzerland	15	9	13.7
Germany	7	5	7
France	44	–	44
Sweden	34	–	34
United States			
Dominican	62	38	
Mexican	56	44	

Source: Authors' compilation based on TIES 2007, 2008; ISGMNY (Mollenkopf, Kasinitz, and Waters); IIMMLA 2003 (Rumbaut et al. 2004).
Note: U.S. subjects are 1.5 rather than second generation.

countries with institutional arrangements leaving some of the second generation without citizenship in the countries where they have grown up, the naturalization process is selective on both sides. Young people decide whether to apply for citizenship—and run the risk of being turned down—and administrative authorities decide whether to accept their application. In Austria, Switzerland, Germany, and the United States, the naturalized youth of immigrant descent generally have more education and a more favorable labor market position. The intensity of the gap varies, however. Although selection bias makes the causal direction unclear, these correlations are consistent, confirming for second-generation youth what has been observed for first-generation immigrants, at least in some countries (Bevelander and DeVoretz 2008).

THE CIVIC AND POLITICAL WORLDS OF THE SECOND GENERATION

The central role of citizenship, of course, is to open access to political and electoral processes. In the United States, many studies have shown young adults to be less engaged in civic or electoral politics than older people (Verba and Nie 1972; Ramakrishnan 2005). Reflecting and reinforcing this pattern, political institutions that have traditionally reached out to new voters—like newly enfranchised immigrants—are in decline (DeSipio 2001; Joppke and Morawska 2003) and mostly play to older "prime voters." Consequently, we expect that the children of immigrants will show lower levels of political engagement than those with native backgrounds in the TIES, ISGMNY, and IIMMLA surveys.

The parents' immigration status can create additional barriers for the second generation even when they are citizens eligible to participate in electoral politics. Most important, many noncitizen parents cannot vote (or legally contribute to political campaigns) and therefore are highly unlikely to socialize their children into these practices. Even where the parents are citizens, or where legally resident noncitizens can vote in local elections, they are less able to socialize their children to their country's political norms. This reduces their children's resources for political engagement as they grow into adulthood relative to those with native-born parents (Tam Cho 1999). Finally, civic and political engagement also happens mainly when people are asked to participate, so the variation in local and regional mobilizing institutions across our research sites will also have an impact (Verba, Schlozman, and Brady 1995).

The immigrant parents who have naturalized are arguably more likely to train their children in the political worlds of the country of migration, although gaining the right to vote is only one of the motives to naturalize, and perhaps not the strongest. Those who have had the opportunity to naturalize but have not done so may be less inclined to participate, and parents who migrated under conditions that do not allow for naturalization simply cannot. We expect such parental backgrounds, particularly citizenship status, to manifest in clear differences in civic and political participation among their children.

Our three surveys measured political engagement in different ways, complicating our comparison. This reflects the European scholarly concern for nonconventional forms of political engagement, such as ethnic-religious nationalism and transnationalism, as the distinctive patterns of organizational activity, partisanship, and voting in the native population (Martiniello 2005). The question of cross-generation political incorporation has been studied far longer in the United States, and no evidence has been found that the second generation organizes in opposition to the dominant political culture. Scholars therefore tend to ask whether the second generation is on a path to more complete political engagement than their immigrant parents (DeSipio and Uhlaner 2007).

Second-Generation Voting

All the studies asked about voting. Our findings reinforce the message that the children of immigrants are becoming active members of their political communities (table 8.4). The variation in voting rates reflects signifi-

TABLE 8.4   Voting by Second-Generation Citizens

	Turkish	Comparison Group	Gap
European cities (last municipal election)			
Linz	32.6	39.4	−6.8
Vienna	25.9	39.2	−13.3
Paris	31.7	57.4	−25.7
Strasbourg	48.6	66.7	−18.1
Berlin	38.8	55.0	−16.2
Frankfurt	26.4	78.5	−52.1
Stockholm	64.3	76.6	−12.3
Basel	42.8	63.2	−20.4
Zurich	44.5	65.4	−20.9
		Native Whites	Gap
U.S. cities			
New York (1996 presidential election)			
Dominican			
Naturalized 1.5 generation	54.2	66.3	−12.1
Second generation	55.3	66.3	−11.0
Native black	72.0	66.3	5.7
Los Angeles (2003 gubernatorial recall)			
Mexican			
Naturalized 1.5 generation	61.5	73.2	−11.7
Second generation	57.7	73.2	−15.5
Third+ generation	59.8	73.2	−13.4
Black third+ generation	57.7	73.2	−15.5

Source: Authors' compilation based on TIES 2007, 2008; ISGMNY (Mollenkopf, Kasinitz, and Waters 1999); IIMMLA (Rumbaut et al. 2004).

cant cross-national and cross-city differences. Great caution must be taken in interpreting these figures for two reasons: first, the surveys looked at different elections (municipal elections in Europe, the 1996 presidential election in New York, and the 2003 California Gubernatorial Recall election in the Los Angeles region); second, respondents reported their voting behavior months after the elections, most likely overstating their actual turnout. Although rates are lower for the second generation than for the native (white) comparison groups, as expected, they are nonetheless substantial and generally show higher rates for those who have citizenship either at birth or early on.

Germany displays the biggest gap between the Turkish second generation and the majority comparison group. In Frankfurt, only 25 percent of the eligible Turkish second generation reported voting in the most recent municipal election, versus 75 percent of the comparison group. In Austria, however, both the second generation and the comparison groups participate at a low rate. Swedes, however, vote at high rates regardless of immigrant status, reflecting an open system that allows noncitizen adult residents of Sweden to vote in local and regional elections. In New York, 1.5- and second-generation Dominicans vote at lower rates than native whites and blacks. In Los Angeles, 1.5- and second-generation Mexican immigrants also vote at lower rates than whites but at comparable rates to third-generation Mexican Americans and blacks. Although many other individual and familial factors may shape these raw rates, such as age, education, income, parental citizenship, and the like, it appears that the negative stance toward citizenship for the parents (and sometimes also the children) in the German-speaking cities may have produced differentially lower rates of participation, at least compared with the more open systems of Sweden and the United States.

Patterns of Civic Engagement and Disengagement

Across the research sites, local organizations and community activities connect the second generation with their communities (see tables 8.5, 8.6, and 8.7). Generally, the second generation is more organizationally involved in Europe than in the United States, reflecting the relatively greater cohesion of the communities there. As noted, however, we cannot view Europe as a single political region. Organizational participation varies across countries and indeed across cities in a given country.

Across all sites, the second generation has lower levels of organizational engagement than the native parent population. Without performing multivariate analysis, we do not know whether these differences reflect characteristics unique to the children of immigrants, such as lower levels of citizenship or political socialization, or result from compositional differences (such as less education in the second-generation Turkish community). In Los Angeles, second-generation citizen respondents are more likely to belong to community organizations than non-naturalized Mexican immigrants are. Levels of political engagement for the second generation are comparable to those of third-plus-generation Mexican Americans and African Americans but somewhat lower than those of third-plus-generation whites.

These data should offer considerable comfort to those who worry that the second generation is developing oppositional political cultures or

TABLE 8.5　Community Organizational Membership and Civic Participation, Europe

	Sports Club		Youth Association		Religious Association		Turkish Association	Political Parties	
	Turks	Comparison Group	Turks	Comparison Group	Turks	Comparison Group	Turks	Turks	Comparison Group
Linz	59.7	61.1	22.3	34.2	8.7	4.7	19.4	6.8	4.3
Vienna	43.3	51.6	10.7	24.0	16.7	2.0	11.9	1.2	2.8
Paris	52.0	NA	32.2	33.9	1.2	2.3	11.3	2.8	4.0
Strasbourg	56.3	NA	30.6	38.4	9.1	7.9	26.2	4.4	2.8
Berlin	44.3	46.8	20.2	29.6	19.8	NA	NA	5.1	1.2
Frankfurt	NA	NA	28.0	38.3	14.0	NA	NA	2.4	4.7
Stockholm	42.5	61.4	18.6	32.0	5.1	6.7	16.8	4.5	1.6
Basel	56.3	72.2	35.7	37.6	9.9	8.6	17.4	2.4	5.6
Zurich	49.8	65.3	30.0	35.6	7.5	6.9	17.8	1.9	5.9

Source: Authors' compilation based on TIES 2007, 2008.
NA = not applicable

TABLE 8.6   Community Organizational Membership and Civic Participation, New York

	Church	Sports	Neighborhood-Tenant	Ethnic	Political
Dominican					
1.5 generation	27.5	20.0	11.9	11.9	7.4
Second generation	25.9	18.4	8.3	6.4	7.2

Source: Authors' compilation based on ISGMNY (Mollenkopf, Kasinitz, and Waters 1999).

that its political engagement might destabilize domestic politics. The share of European respondents belonging to Turkish associations (which are not inherently oppositional) is considerably lower than that belonging to other types of organizations. Only in Strasbourg did more than 20 percent of the respondents belong to a Turkish organization: 60 percent belong to sports clubs. In Los Angeles, 1.5- and second-generation Mexican immigrants are less likely to have protested in the last year than third-plus-generation whites and Mexican Americans. Participation in religious organizations was significantly higher in the United States than in Europe but was higher in Berlin, Frankfurt, and Vienna than elsewhere, reinforcing the finding in chapter 9 that religion is an impor-

TABLE 8.7   Community Organizational Membership and Civic Participation, Los Angeles

	Member of Community Organization	Asked to Support Candidate or Party in Last Twelve Months	Protested in Last Twelve Months
Mexican			
Non-naturalized 1.5 generation	7.6	13.9	11.5
Naturalized 1.5 generation	18.2	30.0	9.5
Second generation	16.6	33.0	15.6
Mexican third-plus generation	20.0	32.2	17.5
Non-Hispanic white third-plus generation	27.1	43.4	16.5
Non-Hispanic black third-plus generation	18.0	29.5	14.4

Source: Authors' compilation based on IIMMLA (Rumbaut et al. 2004).

tant element of Turkish identity in the countries where they are most stigmatized.

Participation in ethnic associations is low in all the cases, especially in the United States, though the two sides of the Atlantic have quite different civic opportunity structures, with much greater formal recognition of (and government support for) ethnic associations in Europe. Sweden and the Netherlands, for example, support ethnic associations as a key tool for integration. Ethnic organizations in New York also may be able to tap into more state support than in Los Angeles.

Although these indicators of political and civic participation are limited (and do not allow for exact comparison), they show that the children of immigrants are beginning to participate in the political lives of the countries in which they live. The heterogeneity across European settings, together with the considerable between-city differences, suggests that local institutional contexts and citizenship regimes may play an important role. An engaged citizen is not simply someone who has decided to be active but someone who has responded to incentives to participate. Immigrant societies like Sweden and the United States are evidently better at providing these incentives than Austria or Germany.

CONCLUDING THOUGHTS

This chapter has helped fill in some of the missing links between the individual and national levels in citizenship research, for once backgrounding group characteristics. The most general and most important result of this exercise is that, holding group position constant (that is, comparing the Turkish second generation in Europe with the most similar U.S. groups), the relationships between citizenship patterns and socioeconomic, civic, political, and transnational outcomes vary significantly across urban settings and sometimes depart from the national models prevailing in earlier citizenship typologies.

To date, scholarship has focused on the first generation, not the second, yet the second generation will forge the future patterns of immigrant civic and political incorporation. Our surveys provide a wealth of information not previously considered by scholars, including information on nationality at birth and in young adulthood and parental nationality, to explore this variation. We have investigated how citizenship statuses are connected to individual behaviors, legal and regulatory frameworks (as measured, for example, by MIPEX), and larger philosophies of integration and nationhood.

On the first level, we are not surprised to find that the second-generation groups participate less than native-born comparison groups, that the non-naturalized participate less than those who have naturalized, or that naturalization has been less likely in the German-speaking countries than in France and Sweden. It was a bit of a surprise, however, to find that despite the guarantee of birthright citizenship to the second generation in the United States, many first-generation parents and 1.5-generation children have not become citizens, indeed far fewer than the second generation in Sweden, which lacks jus soli. It was also surprising that first-generation parents have different naturalization patterns than their children, with France having less parental naturalization than all other countries, even the German-speaking ones, but almost universal naturalization of immigrant children. In the field of political participation, Sweden has the highest voting rate, whereas second-generation citizens in the German-speaking countries, especially Germany and Austria, have not been motivated to vote. This suggests that national policies toward promoting civic and political engagement (or the lack of them), as well as the attitudes among native populations toward immigrant minorities, may contribute substantially to patterns of second-generation civic and political participation.

Our findings often depart from the logic of legal regulations and the grand citizenship typologies built upon them. For example, the same share of the second generation holds dual nationality in France and Germany even though France has long been open to the practice and Germany has removed German citizenship from 40,000 naturalized Turks who sought to reassert their Turkish nationality. We tentatively conclude that the legal frameworks for naturalization may not be as important as identification with the receiving society (or feeling rejected by it), which flows from larger philosophies of integration and is sensitive to local inter-group relations. Logic would suggest that France, which sets up many more legal impediments for the non-naturalized than Sweden does, should have higher naturalization among first-generation parents seeking to get around these impediments, yet the opposite is true. Parental naturalization in Sweden may thus be a positive response to Sweden's minority policies, founded on the values of equality and freedom of (cultural) choice, in contrast to the monocultural assimilationist policies of France. Sweden also allows denizens to vote in local and regional elections, which may foster the relatively high participation rates of the naturalized second generation in local elections.

In transatlantic perspective, the U.S. commitment for birthright citizenship to all children of immigrants is a fundamental institutional difference. At the same time, Sweden's normative and legal orientation toward denizenship may produce similar or even superior results, certainly when compared with European countries with more exclusionist orientations, as can be seen in the German-speaking countries. Moreover, birthright citizenship in the United States may have led second-generation researchers not to pay enough attention to the influence of parental lack of citizenship. The Los Angeles case suggests that the undocumented status of the parents can have a significant negative impact on the prospects of their citizen children (Bean et al. 2010). The possibly radical conclusion may be that the strong jus soli system of the United States does not yield consistently superior second-generation results compared with Europe but rather puts it somewhere in the middle of the distribution—better than the exclusionary regimes of the German-speaking countries, but perhaps not as good as results in Sweden.

Finally, despite the controversies that have arisen over the threat that some observers believe immigration poses for the integrity of their national political cultures, we find that members of the second generation are gradually but fundamentally committing themselves to becoming active participants in the countries in which they have grown up. Their progress may be hampered by many factors—low levels of education and wages of their parents, legal discrimination against those who are not naturalized, being shunted into the less desirable schools and jobs, facing prejudice or lack of acceptance from native-born populations—yet they are nonetheless showing progress toward full integration and participation even in the most difficult circumstances, such as Germany or Switzerland. This is far and away the most important conclusion to be drawn.

NOTES

1. See the European Union Democracy Observatory (http://eudo-citizenship.eu.
2. The 2011 MIPEX index reviews government policies in seven areas: immigrant access to the labor market, sponsorship or entry by family members, granting of legal permanent residence, education, opportunities for political participation, ease of naturalization, and adoption of antidiscrimination laws (http://www.mipex.eu).
3. See the European Union Democracy Observatory on Citizenship (http://www.eudo-citizenship.eu).
4. Many French respondents have mixed parentage, mostly French mothers and Turkish fathers, which may explain why more than half have French citizenship at birth.

CHAPTER 9

BELONGING

JENS SCHNEIDER, LEO CHÁVEZ, LOUIS DESIPIO, AND MARY WATERS

Feelings of belonging or of being at home are difficult to grasp in surveys because how one feels about one's identity depends so much on the context. The enactment of identity and identities is situational, depending on who one is interacting with, when, and where. At the same time, people forge identities within a set of institutional arrangements, for example, citizenship and naturalization regimes or school systems or the labor market, that make it easier or more difficult to self-identify with specific identity categories. As Fredrik Barth (1969, 15) has argued, it is not the "cultural stuff" that determines the boundary between insiders and outsiders, but rather the underlying social processes.

Identity labeling consists of three interactive processes: the self-ascription of the individual, the *habitus of the category* (or the group itself), and the outside world's perspective on the nongroup members. How contested the ascription of an identity label may be depends on consensus across these three perspectives. There are, of course, many empirical examples for cases in which the identities felt by individuals or groups diverge from social categorizations mainstream society uses to describe them, which demonstrates that labeling is generally not based on actually observable behaviors or similar seemingly objective attributes (Devereux 1978; Balibar and Wallerstein 1991). But at the same time, identities are also connected to, or closely intertwined with, distinct cultural and social practices, which may have symbolic, interactional (or situational), and discursive dimensions.

The second generation sits between forces that often pull them in different directions: their immigrant parents, their wider family and community networks, their friends, their schools, and the wider society into which they were born or moved as a child. The second generation is influenced by peers of different cultural backgrounds, by teachers, and by the mass media. The history of the receiving nation places positive or negative associations on different identities and therefore their relative attractiveness. For example, the break-up of Yugoslavia opened the identity options available to migrants living in Berlin or Vienna. In the United States, the large number of poorly educated, low-wage Mexican immigrants (both documented and undocumented) has shaped the public perception of Mexicans and anti-Mexican prejudices in a way that has made a Mexican American identity much more problematic. So the question is how children of immigrants cope with the challenge of reconciling these contending pulls and pushes. How do they manage to feel at home and, more important, can they feel part of the society into which they were born or socialized yet not alienate themselves from the cultural and social context, or the wider ethnic community, of their parents?

This chapter examines these questions among the young adult children of Mexican and Chinese or Taiwanese immigrants in Los Angeles; of Chinese and Dominican immigrants in New York City; and of the Turkish and formerly Yugoslavian immigrants in Berlin, Germany, and Vienna, Austria. We have chosen in each site to focus on two groups that seem to be located at different ends of a continuum of structural participation. In educational terms, the Chinese second generation in Los Angeles and New York is extraordinarily successful, and Mexicans in Los Angeles and Dominicans in New York have relatively low educational outcomes. In Europe, the Turkish second generation represents the lower end of educational outcomes, and public discourse frequently mentions Turks when referring to integration problems. The children of immigrants from former Yugoslavia come closest to the educational success of the Chinese in the United States. However, as in the other chapters, we particularly examine the Turks and Mexicans because they are the largest immigrant groups in Europe and the United States and their identities and feelings of belonging are important to understanding the second generation cross-nationally.

The following sections examine the questions in our three surveys that probe how the second generations feel about *here* and *there*. Because, as noted, surveys have a hard time capturing identity, we supplement the analysis of survey questions with qualitative data from in-depth interviews. We address the following issues:

- What labels do the second generations use to identify themselves among the categories presented to them in the surveys?

- What is the role and practice of different languages in the lives of the second generation?

- What role does religion play in second-generation self-definitions and everyday life, and how does it relate to religious practices and beliefs in the wider society?

- What transnational connections does the second generation maintain with their parents' country of origin?

We want to begin with how members of the second generation see themselves in terms of broadly used categories, as shallow as they can sometimes be. Language is probably the most visible cultural trait marking the difference between an immigrant community and the majority society—even though, obviously, language skills reflect individual abilities in the first place. Language use can demonstrate belonging, mark a difference, be used to avoid trouble, show loyalty, ease communication, demonstrate cultural intimacy, and much more (Herzfeld 1997). Among the second generation, there are often (at least) two languages framing childhood and youth socialization, and the parental language is the first one learned. That is, children of immigrants generally learn the dominant language of their country as their second language, either on the street or when they enter school. As the children of immigrants (whether 1.5 or second generation) have spent (most of) their childhood and youth socialization in the United States or Austria or Germany, we can expect them to be fluent in English and German. Yet the degree to which they can read, speak, and write the language of their parents' country of origin will vary considerably and can have an important effect on their sense of belonging in the host societies.

Religion, like language, is an important symbolic marker for attachment and belonging to a particular culture. But it differs from language in that religious practice means participating in collectively shared rituals at a physical place, for example a church or a mosque. At the same time, belief has a universal character, the personal relation to (some) God can express itself in different ways and change over time or under specific circumstances. Abandoning or changing one's religious belief is a social practice directly related to a specific societal and historical context. Religion, moreover, has a strong potential to serve as a bridge between immigrants and the native population, creating shared spaces, but it can also be a boundary that reinforces other differences between immigrant and native cultures or across immigrant cultures.

Transnational relations refer to social practices that connect members of the second generation to their parents' country of origin. In the past, difficulties in transportation and communication made maintaining such relations more difficult, though transnationalism was nonetheless common. Today, the potential exists for even greater transnational activity, because travel costs are low and channels of communication ubiquitous. Equally important, ethnic and home-country-focused institutions have emerged to facilitate transnational engagement with the country of origin. By contrast, however, Ellen Fensterseifer Woortmann (2001, 214) describes the complete absence of the premigration history and family links to the home country in the narratives of the descendants of German immigrants to southern Brazil in the first half of the twentieth century. Sarah Mahler (2001) analyzed how deeply the availability of mobile phones has changed the character and quality of the home country relations of Salvadorian immigrants in the United States.

This chapter contributes to a rapidly growing body of literature focusing on identity issues among immigrants and their children. The by-far-larger part of this literature consists of qualitative or even ethnographic research that is difficult to compare with the kind of large-scale surveys presented in this book, but even more so when these surveys are multisited, such as TIES. One of the most influential concepts used in quantitative work has been John Berry's well-known model of the four acculturation attitudes of integration, separation, marginalization, and assimilation (Berry 1997; see also chapter 3, this volume). In one of the largest recent quantitative studies in the field, the International Comparative Study of Ethnocultural Youth (ICSEY) in thirteen western countries executed by John Berry and his colleagues Jean Phinney, David Sam, and Paul Vedder, defining one's place and position in society is constructed along the two axes of Berry's model (preserving the ethnic culture versus adopting to the national culture), leading to a matrix of four acculturation profiles: an ethnic and a national profile, an integration profile (being strong on both axes), and a so-called diffuse profile that includes incoherent and unclassifiable responses (2006, 102). Not only has the Berry model in itself been very influential and frequently used in surveys on identity and acculturation, but even when not directly referring to the model most surveys have tended to operate with dichotomized models of ethnic versus national identity, or ethnic retention versus host culture adoption (compare Ersanilli 2010; Ersanilli and Koopmans 2009).

In our view, this is a major shortcoming in two directions. First, dichotomization reduces the fuzziness and hybridity described as characteristic for national, ethnic, and cultural identities (compare Modood and Werbner 1997). It is probably no coincidence that the diffuse profile in the ICSEY survey is at the same time the one with the largest N in quite some ethnocultural groups—among them the Turks in Germany (Berry et al. 2006, 109). Second, the almost exclusive focus on national culture—for limits of space we do not discuss here the wide criticism of the concept of a national culture as a variable in analysis (compare Schinkel 2007)—does not allow analysis of contextual situations beyond the standard categorizations of nation-states and their integration models (for example, Brubaker 1992; Koopmans 2010).

This chapter thus aims to contribute to the literature not only through this unique possibility of transatlantic comparison across three major surveys but also by giving the statistical figures a reading that, on the one hand, attempts to avoid the oversimplifications of dichotomization and, on the other, introduces a spatial category—the city—that is much better for contextualization than the nation-state. We therefore begin our analyses with a description of the four local contexts and brief sketches of each of the second-generation groups.

BERLIN

Berlin harbors the oldest and largest Turkish community in western Europe, which is also the largest immigrant group on the continent. Immigrants from the former Yugoslavia and their descendants also make up a sizable share of the migrant population in Berlin, forming the second-largest group originating from the influx of labor migrants between the late 1950s and the early 1970s.

Despite earlier waves of mass migration to Germany, for example, of Poles to the Ruhr area in the second half of the nineteenth century and ethnic Germans from eastern Europe and Russia after World War II, the guest-worker migration was a historically new experience, met with

widespread fears and little political and administrative preparation or pro-
fessionalism. It is an ongoing experiment in the sense not only that the
current second generation is a new one but that the concept of the second
generation until recently had no discursive place because Germany did not
consider itself a country of immigration. In addition, native Germans see
Turkish immigrants as a culturally distant group. They view their Islamic
religion, in particular, as distancing them.

More than 90 percent of Turkish and former Yugoslavian-descent
respondents to the TIES survey, as well as the comparison group with
native-born parents, grew up in Berlin. Determining the size of the
Turkish population is difficult not only because the group is ethnically
diverse but also because official records only register Turkish nationals—
first- or later-generation people of Turkish origin who do not have German
citizenship. Berlin's Turkish population is estimated at around 200,000,
including naturalized persons of Turkish origin, either foreign born or
native born, and Turkish nationals, whether documented or undocumented
(Greve and Orhan 2008, 13; Statistisches Bundesamt 2007). This amounts
to about 6 percent of the city's population. Close to half are second and
subsequent generations in Germany and thus do not have a personal
migration experience. The Turkish-origin population of Germany is estimated at 2.5 million (Statistisches Bundesamt 2011), accounting for about
58 percent of the Turkish population in western Europe (Abadan-Unat
2011, 244; Bade et al. 2007).

Among the other groups of labor migrants in the 1960s, the second-
largest came from what was then known as the Socialist Federal Republic
of Yugoslavia. Because Yugoslavia no longer exists, we refer to the area as
the former Yugoslavia. Yugoslavia was a multiethnic, multireligious, and
multilingual country that broke apart in the 1990s and is now divided
into six independent states. The civil war in Bosnia drove out several
hundred thousand refugees, Germany being the main destination.
However, the community of persons of former Yugoslavian descent in
Berlin is much smaller than the Turkish community, at about 65,000 with
Bosnian, Serbian, or Croatian backgrounds. Two-thirds are foreign born
(Statistisches Bundesamt 2007, table 51). Yet, despite this sizable number,
they do not form one visible community. After Yugoslavia's dissolution,
the diaspora also experienced an ethnic split-up, creating three similarly
sized communities affiliated with the new republics of Serbia, Croatia,
and Bosnia. The former Yugoslavian second generation is also dispersed
across the city and more mobile than Turks with regard to residential
neighborhood. While the Turkish residential pattern reflects the old

division between East and West Berlin (on the Turkish trauma with German unification, see Çil 2010), many respondents with former Yugoslavian backgrounds live in eastern city districts today.

Because of the large size of its Turkish community, certain areas in Berlin have a visibly Turkish character and offer a wide range of Turkish-oriented services, including restaurants, grocery stores, travel agents, doctors, and lawyers, although in hardly any neighborhoods are more than 30 percent of the inhabitants Turkish. These neighborhoods are home to most of the second generation: 80 percent of the Turkish TIES respondents still live in the district where they grew up—even though 69 percent no longer live with their parents anymore. According to the TIES data, 54 percent of the Turkish respondents reported living in a neighborhood in which—according to their self-assessment—50 percent or more was Turkish, although official statistics suggest that this is an overestimate.[1]

VIENNA

The capital city of Austria is located at the eastern limit of western Europe. For many decades, the adjacent region was a major sending area for labor migrants and refugees. The high point of Austrian history was the Habsburg Empire of Austria-Hungary, which extended so far into southeastern Europe that it is quite common for the native white population to have Slavic or Balkan names. Vienna is therefore a particularly interesting place to study the children of immigrants from the former Yugoslavia. Yet the fear of Islam (and the Turks in particular) is more deeply rooted in Austria than elsewhere in Europe because the Islamic Ottoman Empire extended almost to Vienna's city limits in the seventeenth century and the stopping of its advance was inscribed into the national and European historical self-imagination. Finally, right-wing populism has also gained more electoral support in Austria than in Germany, placing the questions of immigration and integration at the center of public debate.

As in Berlin, more than 90 percent of Turkish and former Yugoslavian descent TIES respondents grew up in Vienna. Only 75 percent of the native comparison group grew up in Vienna, however, with the remainder coming from villages and towns surrounding Vienna and from other parts of Austria.

Vienna's Turkish community is estimated at 74,000, some 4 percent of the population. The second and subsequent generations make up about half of the city's Turkish population (Statistisches Jahrbuch der Stadt

Wien 2011, 69). Austria's Turkish community is estimated at about 260,000 (Statistik Austria 2010, 107). Guest workers from the former Yugoslavia and their descendants are now the largest immigrant group in Austria and Vienna, at about 170,000 in Vienna, Serbs being the main group (Statistik Austria 2010, 107). They are less dispersed than in Berlin, mostly living in immigrant neighborhoods close to Turkish immigrants and their children. They are generally younger than in Berlin and fewer live independently from their parents. The residential concentration of Turks appears lower, only 31 percent reporting living in a mainly Turkish neighborhood.

LOS ANGELES

The IIMMLA survey in Los Angeles included many immigrant populations, but here we focus only on those of Chinese and Mexican descent, comparing them with native whites and native blacks. Chinese and Mexicans have a long history in California and greater Los Angeles. California was part of Mexico until 1848, when it was annexed by the United States, and Mexican migration to the United States was not subject to the same national-origin quotas adopted for the rest of the world in 1921 and 1924. The Chinese began arriving in California in 1850, shortly after the beginning of the Gold Rush, and soon established segregated Chinatowns in San Francisco, Los Angeles, Santa Ana (Orange County, within the larger Los Angeles metropolitan area), and other California cities. However, the adoption of the Chinese Exclusion Act in 1882 and later the Chinese revolution limited further Chinese migration to the United States until the reform of U.S. immigration laws in 1965 and the end of the Cultural Revolution in China. The contemporary migration from Mexico and China (from both Mainland China and Taiwan) is distinctive both for the large numbers of immigrants and for the public debate about the new wave of migration.

The Mexican and Chinese-Taiwanese communities in Los Angeles have different generational compositions, reflecting the timing of each group's arrival in the United States and California. Although only about a third of those of Mexican descent in Los Angeles were born in Mexico, a majority of the Chinese and Taiwanese were born abroad. Moreover, respondents to the IIMMLA survey report about 50 percent of those born in Mexico came to the United States without authorization, whereas only 14 percent of foreign-born Chinese-Taiwanese were unauthorized immigrants. More than a third of the Mexicans unauthorized at entry were still unauthorized immigrants at the time of the interview, versus 7 percent of the Chinese-Taiwanese.

NEW YORK

In the New York survey, we focus on the Chinese and Dominican second generations. Even though the parents of both groups had the least education of those studied, their second generations have markedly different outcomes. The Chinese show exceptional upward mobility, 65 percent having attained a BA or more. Dominicans are the least successful, only 18 percent earning that level of education.

New York has a quite diverse Chinese population. Before the 1960s, the vast majority of Chinese in New York were descended from migrants from South China who came to the West Coast of the United States as laborers and who later moved east seeking work and fleeing anti-Chinese violence. In addition to their wives, who came in large numbers only after the Chinese Exclusion Act was repealed in 1943, they were joined by refugees and stranded scholars and business people whose temporary stays in the United States became permanent during the Chinese revolution. Even after the liberalization of American immigration law in 1965 this population grew slowly until the People's Republic of China (PRC) and Taiwan both liberalized emigration in the 1970s and 1980s. They were joined by immigrants of Chinese descent from Malaysia, Singapore, Thailand, Vietnam, and Indonesia as well as the Caribbean and Central and South America. Our second-generation respondents' parents, while primarily from the PRC, Hong Kong, and Taiwan, also hail from across the Chinese global diaspora.

Although the median level of education of the parents of the second-generation Chinese respondents was similar to that of the other immigrant groups, these parents were more likely to be found at the two extremes. One-third of the Chinese in the parental age group in New York had a college degree, but more than one-third lacked a high school degree, some reporting only a few years of formal schooling. Given that family background, the Chinese second generation shows remarkable social mobility, with an educational attainment exceeding that of native whites who grew up in New York.

The initial zone of settlement for the Chinese first generation was the historic Chinatown of Lower Manhattan. This densely packed residential, commercial, and industrial neighborhood has seen its rents rise rapidly in recent years, so Chinese families have followed the subway lines out to the neighborhoods of southern Brooklyn and northern Queens. Chinese families settled there alongside whites, better-off Hispanics, and Russian Jews.

Dominicans are the New York area's largest national-origin group, approximately 640,000 living in the area in 2000. This reflects the long history of ties between New York and the Dominican Republic. The end of the decades-old repressive regime of dictator Rafael Trujillo in 1961 and the U.S. invasion in 1965 prompted an initial middle-class flight from political unrest and included critics of the regime, labor union organizers, and dissident students. The dismal state of the Dominican economy soon led to much broader waves of economic migration. The vast majority of economic immigrants coming since the late 1960s have had little education and few professional skills. The parents of the Dominicans in the New York study were the most disadvantaged immigrant group. They are the most likely to have no formal education and the least likely to have a college degree. Many second-generation Dominicans are dark skinned and thus subject to racial discrimination.

IDENTITY CHOICES IN SURVEYS

The United States, Germany, and Austria present different identity contexts to the second generation. The United States has a long history of hyphenated identities, but neither Germany nor Austria supports the idea (Çağlar 1997). To the contrary, both countries promote exclusive ethno-national labels. Only recently have such notions as Deutschtürken (German Turks) gained some presence in public discourse in Germany. The following response from a second-generation Turkish female politician in Berlin in the mid-1990s illustrates the linguistic difficulty of simultaneously adhering to two ethno-national reference frames (Schneider 2002, 18):

> Interviewer (I): Are you German or Turkish?
> Respondent (R): I think I'm both: I'm a German and I'm a Turk. I'm a German Turk.
>   I: Does it make a difference to say German Turk or Turko-German?
>   R: No, I'm no Turko-German [laughs]. I'm a German with a Turkish background.

As a consequence, anyone with non-German or non-Austrian family roots faces an ambiguous task in defining themselves as German or Austrian. The TIES respondents most frequently answered a question about how strongly they felt attached to the host country identity with an ambiguous response: "neither weakly nor strongly." This is especially true of the Turkish respondents. Although the feeling of belonging to the national society is positively associated with educational attainment, working, studying, or meeting people of other ethno-national backgrounds also increases second-generation identification with the society. The people reporting least identification with the host country tended to be unemployed or staying at home for other reasons.

City contexts also make a difference. In Vienna, the formerly Yugoslavian diaspora and its youth figure most prominently in public discourse. Possibly as a result, the former Yugoslavian respondents in Vienna are significantly more ambiguous about belonging to Austria than their counterparts in Berlin are to being German. A quarter feel ambiguous or indifferent (versus 18 percent in Berlin), and 18 percent report weak or no feelings (versus 8 percent in Berlin). The Turkish second generation, however, shows little difference between the cities, despite its larger presence in the German capital.

The wider society and much of the political discourse insinuate that it is not possible to be German and also Turkish. The following response illustrates the second generation's difficulty in opting for a label. It also shows that even when they recognize their cultural connections to Germany or Austria, they still see themselves mostly as others see them, as Turkish (Çil 2010, 21):

> R: When I am asked if I am German or Turk, I would always say I am Turk. Although what connects me to being Turkish is maybe 20 percent of myself. But that's the minority part, and I feel more attached to the minority than to the others.

It is interesting that those with the most ambiguous or indifferent feelings toward being German or Austrian in both cities are also most ambiguous or indifferent about being Turkish. Such a split is not possible for former Yugoslavians. Yugoslavian identity does not make sense in the wake of the ethnic split-up of the former republic into the Serbs, Croats, Bosnians, and other ethno-nationalities. Yet these ethnic labels still do not allow for a clear-cut linguistic or cultural distinction but map onto religious distinctions, Serbs being predominantly Christian Orthodox, Croats being Roman Catholics, and Bosnians being Muslims. Yet religion did not play an important role in the former socialist republic of Yugoslavia, and high levels of residential mobility and cross-religious or cross-group marriages prevent many former Yugoslavians from fitting neatly into one category, so many simply refuse to accept the new nationalisms. Twenty-five percent of former Yugoslavian second-generation respondents in Berlin, as well as almost 20 percent in Vienna, could not be categorized according to the definitional criteria of any of the ethnicities.

Unlike the Europeans, the New York second generation did not feel forced to choose between their parents' ethnic heritage and being a full American. Hyphenated identities were the norm in the city's multicultural milieu. Most moved fluidly back and forth between the racial and panethnic identities, as a thirty-year-old Chinese woman explains:

> I: Which is more common for you to identify with, Chinese or Asian?
> R: It depends. When you fill out the ethnic group it has Caucasian, Hispanic, Asian, so if they have Asian I check Asian, if they have Chinese, I check Chinese.

The New York survey asked not about national belonging but about panethnic or racial identity as well as attachment to the national origin of the parents, replicating the race and ancestry questions of the U.S. Census. The Chinese and Dominican respondents could identify with their parents' national origin, as Dominican or Chinese, or they could identify with a pan-ethnic racial or ethnic category such as Hispanic or Asian. The Chinese overwhelmingly identified as Chinese (95 percent), only a small percentage as Asian (5 percent). The Dominicans had much more diverse responses, only 15 percent identifying as Dominican, 34 percent as Hispanic, 12 percent as white, 12 percent as black, 5 percent as Latino, 5 percent as Spanish, and 7 percent not specifying.

The issue of belonging is perhaps more complex and layered for the Mexican second generation because Mexican-origin people have lived in Los Angeles and the Southwest for many generations. As a result of this history and their widespread presence, the descendants of Mexican immigrants in Los Angeles often hold the belief that they are at home. Nevertheless, anti-Mexican sentiments are widespread, which, as observed, makes Mexican American identification more problematic than it probably is among the Chinese-Taiwanese. So when the Los Angeles survey asked respondents whether the United States felt more like home or rather their parents' countries of origin, 95 percent of the Mexican and 99 percent of the Chinese-Taiwanese second generation reported that the United States feels more like home.

Despite this indication of integration, the often hyperbolically anti-immigrant climate compounds the process of normal transition from immigrant to citizen to native (Chávez 2008; Reed-Danahay and Brettell

2008; Yuval-Davis 2006). Anti-immigrant rhetoric often targets immigrant and U.S.-born Latinos equally. Attempts to fix the immigration problem by deporting illegal immigrants can amount to a racial profiling of all Latinos. The children of immigrants may internalize such policing practices in the form of social stigma and social rejection, leaving an indelible imprint on their identity. One nineteen-year-old, 1.5-generation, undocumented student explained it this way:

> I am an immigrant, immigrant Mexican. . . . You know you are not [American] because society keeps telling you that you're not. You don't have the opportunities that a Mexican American has, because you don't have the social security. So you have to make the decision. I don't fit in here. They don't want me in here. Then I fit there, with Mexicans. . . . I think if you have obstacles to integrating, one, they don't want you to integrate. Obviously, they have the obstacles for you not to integrate, so you get to the point where you know what, I don't want to integrate, whether you will eventually want me to integrate for any reason, I am no longer willing to integrate.

In the European cities and New York, local belonging often provides an alternative identity. In Berlin, Vienna, and New York, local attachments are closer to daily life experiences than any national referent. In fact, at least in Berlin and Vienna, the two second-generation groups demonstrate significantly higher levels of neighborhood involvement than the native white comparison group. In Berlin, 62 percent of the Turkish and former Yugoslavian second-generation respondents scored high on an index of neighborhood belonging and participation, versus 48 percent for the native comparison group. In Vienna, 61 percent identified with and participated in their neighborhoods, versus 47 percent for the comparison group.

The following response from the Berlin respondent quoted earlier (Schneider 2002, 17) indicates how the neighborhood can be the main reference frame for feelings of belonging and home for the Turkish second generation:

> I: Are you a Berliner?
> R: Of course, I would even go a step further: I'm a Neuköllner, I think, I talk like these old ladies from World War II, who always say "I'm a born Charlottenburger" and so on. I have been living pretty long in Neukölln, twenty-six or twenty-seven years. I've moved four times and never left Neukölln. So, at a certain point, I said, I'm a born Neuköllner.

This was also true in New York, where the second generation developed strong city and neighborhood attachments. Many young people identified as New Yorkers because they saw this as an inclusive identity that encompassed both natives and immigrants and differentiated them from a generic American identity that might be conceived as white and Midwestern and thus exclusionary. Especially after we reinterviewed some respondents following the terrorist attacks of September 11, 2001, we found a strong sense of patriotism as Americans and pride in residence in New York, a city most respondents were well aware had absorbed many waves of immigrants and their children over the centuries.

Local identities are also strong in the Los Angeles region with neighborhood, high school, sports team loyalties, and county among the geographies and institutions that individuals tap when seeking to place themselves in reference to others. These local identities, however, supplement rather than replace other sets of identities.

LANGUAGE SKILLS AND USE

Language use is another key factor in identity among the second generation. Each survey asked a series of questions about language skills and language use. In the presence of the parents or other (senior) family members, speaking the parental language can be a matter of respect and an indication of one's connection to the diasporic community. Because language is a carrier for concepts and particular meanings, it can help preserve a connection to the parental origins and culture.

In all four cities, the second generation is bilingual. The variation is generally not in how fluent the second generation is in English or German but rather how much they retain or prefer their parents' language.

Turkish is important to the second generation: fewer than 10 percent in each city were not raised in Turkish or consider their Turkish language skills to be weak. Yet more than 90 percent consider their German language skills also to be very good or excellent, and fewer than 3 percent were not exposed to German as children.

Berlin and Vienna do differ with regard to language use with different interlocutors. The second generation uses Turkish more often in everyday life in Vienna than in Berlin. In both cities, most Turkish second-generation respondents speak mainly Turkish with their parents, but in Berlin, respondents speak mainly German with their siblings (62 percent) and friends (73 percent) and partners (59 percent)—despite 90 percent of the partners also being of Turkish descent. In Vienna, 75 percent of the partners were born in Turkey, so Turkish is more common as the main language between spouses than in Berlin (53 percent versus 36 percent). This is even much more so among friends (Vienna, 91 percent; Berlin, 25 percent).

Although the former Yugoslavs are also fully bilingual, they are more likely than Turks to use German in both cities. They almost exclusively communicate in German not only with their friends and partners but also with their parents, especially their mothers. Respondents from former Yugoslavian backgrounds are much more likely than Turks to have a mixed circle of friends and a non–Yugoslavian partner (which requires German as the main common language).

Because the second generation in Los Angeles grew up in households with immigrant parents, both Mexican and Chinese-Taiwanese respondents predominantly spoke Spanish (92 percent) or Chinese (91 percent) at home. But both groups show tremendous linguistic adaptation. Of the second-generation respondents, 64 percent of the Mexicans and 74 percent of the Chinese prefer speaking English at home as young adults. Parents living in the household influenced language preference. Many Mexicans (70 percent) and Chinese-Taiwanese (82 percent) still lived in households with one or more parents; among those who did, 46 percent of the Mexican second generation preferred to speak English, versus 56 percent among those who did not live with parents. Similarly, 42 percent of Chinese-Taiwanese living with parents preferred English at home, versus 64 percent of those not living with parents.

Citizenship status is positively related to using English. Fewer adult children of either Mexican (32 percent) or Chinese-Taiwanese (37 percent) immigrant parents who entered the United States without authorization indicated that they preferred to speak English at home now, whereas those with legal immigrant parents were much more likely to do so (59 percent and 56 percent, respectively). However, many Mexicans (26 percent) and Chinese-Taiwanese (27 percent) with unauthorized parents still used English as well as Spanish or Chinese at home. That is, a majority of both groups prefer to speak English at home all or some of the time. Of the second-generation Mexican respondents, 90 percent preferred to be interviewed in English, suggesting the pervasiveness of the transition to English. In sum, we found little evidence that these children of immigrants remain linguistically isolated. To the contrary, they use English and are linguistically integrated into English.

As might be expected, education and income influence the social use of language. For example, 64 percent of Mexicans with thirteen or more years of schooling preferred to speak English at home, versus only 38 percent of those with twelve or fewer years. Chinese-Taiwanese exhibited a similar, but not statistically significant, trend, 56 percent to 44 percent. Similarly, 69 percent of Mexicans with personal incomes of $30,000 a year or more preferred English, versus 31 percent who preferred Spanish. Higher-income Chinese-Taiwanese (60 percent) also preferred English. Preference for English, along with education and income, also significantly influences the partner's ethnicity.

Evidence of linguistic assimilation in New York was also strong. Although all of our second-generation respondents were fluent in English, they varied somewhat in terms of the language they spoke at home growing up, their language preferences now, and how much knowledge they retained of their parents' language. Many more of our Dominican (37 percent) and Chinese (41 percent) respondents in New York than their counterparts in Los Angeles and the two European cities grew up speaking English at home. Now, however, the degree of preference for English at home, 42 percent of Dominicans still preferring Spanish and 33 percent of Chinese preferring Chinese, is not remarkably larger than in Los Angeles. Only a slim majority of the Chinese say they can speak Chinese well (56 percent), and far fewer can read it (8 percent) or write it (6 percent). Dominicans are far more likely to use Spanish as a language, some 91 percent among those born in New York speaking it well. Chinese is much more difficult to maintain. Most Chinese immigrants speak Cantonese or Fukienese, reflecting their parents' home provinces. Because written Chinese is not phonetic, even a child who grows up learning to speak to parents and grandparents requires a great deal of formal instruction to be literate. A common pattern is that parents would speak Chinese to their children but the children would respond in English. Children would only speak Chinese to grandparents who could not understand English, and once those grandparents died, the children quickly lost their abilities in Chinese.

Dominicans keep much higher levels of Spanish because of the same factors that promote the language in Los Angeles. The presence of Dominican, South American, Puerto Rican, and Mexican immigrants in New York provides a large pool of people who speak only Spanish, creating many opportunities to converse in Spanish in schools, workplaces, and public spaces. This population also means a vibrant radio and television market for Spanish-language programs. High levels of travel to and close connections with the Dominican Republic also help preserve Spanish-language fluency.

The three surveys asked in different ways similar questions of linguistic adaptation, and the results also show some variance across groups and cities. In general, however, members of the second generation neither have adaptation problems with regard to the language that is the vernacular in the society they were born into nor abandon their parents' language of origin as an expression of being and feeling part of that society. The specific skills in the parental language might be different—strongly dependent on the attitude of the parents towards the language issue in the education of their children and a number of other factors—but this does not affect, in principle, the symbolic value and meaning of that language for maintaining ties with the ethno-national-origins of the family.

RELIGION

Religion is probably the main dividing line between the Turkish second generation and their peers of native-born parentage. In Berlin, 65 percent of Turkish respondents report having a religion, versus fewer than 25 percent of the native comparison group. In Vienna, 88 percent of Turks are religiously observant Muslims (comparison group: 34 percent). Among religiously observant Turks, 90 percent in both cities have strong or very strong Muslim identities. For the second generation, being Muslim is closely related to being Turkish, but more so in Berlin than in Vienna. In Berlin, those not reporting a Muslim identity also report low Turkish identity: 75 percent of those who do not have a religious affiliation reported having weak or no Turkish feelings at all. In Vienna, more than 60 percent of the nonbelievers still expressed strong feelings of Turkishness. However, those with strong Turkish feelings generally also have strong Muslim identities in both cities—even when they state no religious affiliation. The contradiction between being German or Austrian and being a Muslim is apparently even stronger than the one between being German or Austrian and being Turkish. As one eighteen-year-old noted, "Looking at it from outside, I don't find it that easy to identify with being Muslim and being German at the same time. It is, in the end, a religion from another region. I know people who cannot bring these two things together, who say: I am not German because I cannot identify with what Germans identify with" (Arnfried Schenk, "It Comes from Inside," *Die Zeit,* no. 27, July 1, 2010)

The question of religion is more complicated for those of former Yugoslavian backgrounds. Yugoslavia had four distinct religious traditions: Catholic, Orthodox, Muslim, and Jewish. Catholicism dominates in Croatia and Slovenia; the Orthodox Church in Serbia, Montenegro, and Macedonia; and Islam in Kosovo and Bosnia-Herzegovina. But the ethno-national identities, as noted, are not always directly linked to specific religions. As a result, people from former Yugoslavian backgrounds are much less stereotyped along religious lines than Turks are—with the possible exception of religiously observant Bosnian Muslims (who are then mostly mistaken as Turks).

Turks in Berlin are clearly becoming secularized: almost 30 percent report that though they were raised in a religion, they no longer have any religious ties. Their religiosity differs markedly from that of Turks in other TIES cities in this respect. Only 11 percent of Frankfurt's Turkish second generation and 8 percent of Vienna's report this secularization, whereas in Amsterdam and Rotterdam no secularization trend could be observed, and the two French cities even show a slight growth in religiosity. In Berlin, the Turkish respondents seem to be divided between two quite polarized positions over religion. In the first, respondents identify more with being Turkish than with being German, have fewer non-Turkish friends, are more likely to marry a partner from Turkey, and live in poorer and more segregated neighborhoods. They also went to more segregated schools, have lower levels of education, and are less ambitious about pursuing further education. Almost all of these respondents are believers and many strictly follow Islam.

The second position is seen mainly among nonbelievers and those with a more liberal interpretation of Islam. These respondents are more likely to think that Turkish immigrants should do more to integrate into society and not follow the norms and customs of their Turkish origins when outside their homes. They think relations between Turks and Germans are moving in a positive direction and that diversity is good for the society and the economy in particular. This position is much closer to that of the comparison group—respondents with both parents being native-born—especially with regard to gender roles and gender equality.

Vienna presents a similar picture, though its secularization trend is less pronounced. However, the same kinds of differences between believers and nonbelievers can be observed. The believers live in poorer and "more Turkish" areas. Despite similar levels of education, they are more likely to be unemployed (19 percent versus 7 percent) or economically inactive (19 percent versus 0 percent). The nonbelievers express much stronger feelings for being Austrian (and Viennese) than the believers (71 percent versus 28 percent) and are more likely to marry a partner not born in Turkey. They have much more relaxed attitudes about sex before marriage and significantly less negative views about Jews. In both cities, the former Yugoslavian second generation mostly occupies the same intermediate position as its nonbelieving Turkish peers.

Mexican and Chinese-Taiwanese immigrants and their children in Los Angeles have somewhat different religious practices than native white and black Angelinos, who are likely to be Protestant. The Mexican population is largely Catholic, two of three in the Mexican second generation reporting that religion. Chinese-Taiwanese residents of the area are either Buddhist or have no religious preference. Approximately 10 percent of the Chinese-Taiwanese second generation in the Los Angeles region are Buddhist and 28 percent have no religious preference. Among the minority of second-generation Mexican and Chinese-Taiwanese Angelinos who are Protestant, about 65 percent view themselves as evangelicals, a rate somewhat higher than for the white population (54 percent) of Los Angeles but not as high as the black (76 percent).

The majority of Mexicans and Chinese-Taiwanese report that they practice the same religion as their parents. This is particularly true of Mexican-ancestry residents of the Los Angeles region. More than 80 percent of second-generation Mexicans continue to practice the same faith as their parents, as do nearly 65 percent of the Chinese-Taiwanese. Of the relative few who have converted, most have become Protestants, particularly evangelicals.

Native New Yorkers are far more Catholic and Jewish than native Angelinos or the country as a whole. Among native whites in New York, Catholics predominate with 46 percent, followed by Protestants at 16 percent and Jews at 12 percent, with 19 percent having no religion. Many of our Chinese respondents (56 percent) report they have no religion, and this figure is probably even higher for their parents. About 20 percent report Buddhist belief, 15 percent Protestant, and 5 percent Catholic. Many of their parents were Buddhist or did not have a religion in Communist China, and many young people become more religious and convert to Christianity in the United States. The minority of Chinese who were Christian were among the most active Christians in our sample, 59 percent reporting that they attended religious services once a week or more. These converts have often joined pan-Asian, campus-based, and often evangelical Christian ministries. Such a high level of religiosity is sometimes a source of tension with the converts' more secular parents (Chai Kim 2004). Although Buddhism is not common in the United States, it also does not place many demands on its adherents. Even practicing Buddhists generally describe a minimal relation to a formal religion that does not have much effect on their lives.

Only 16 percent of Dominicans report no religion; 72 percent were raised Catholic and another 9 percent Protestant. Although a few young adults had switched from Catholic to Protestant, or had switched from

Christian to no religion, the vast majority (91 percent) reported that they still held the same religion as the one in which they were raised. Christian Dominicans were not as active in their churches as the Chinese, 46 percent reporting that they attended church once a week or more.

Religion did not play a large role in most respondents' lives. It certainly did not provide a sense of identity or a source of discrimination in the way that being Muslim does in the United States or western Europe. Indeed, as Nancy Foner and Richard Alba (2008) have argued, many second-generation Chinese become more religious than their parents because being religious can be seen as part of assimilation to a very religious country.

Thus the possible role of religion as either a bridge or a barrier between native and immigrant cultures also marks an important difference between the United States and Europe. In the United States, most immigrants are Catholic or Protestant and the host society not only already practices these but also embraces the religiosity of the newcomers, whatever it may be. Indeed, many members of the second generation change religions, a phenomenon not observed in the German and Austrian TIES data. In Europe, the host society is far more secular, so having any religion is already a mark of difference for immigrants and their children. For the predominantly Islamic descendants of migrants in the European survey, the boundary is even brighter (Alba 2005) because the established religious institutions of the host society cannot perform the same bridging function as churches do in the United States.

TRANSNATIONALISM

The literature on immigrant transnationalism has focused on how immigrants and their children are connected to the country of origin (Basch, Schiller, and Blanc 1994; Levitt and Schiller 2004; Levitt and Waters 2006). Although evidence is now abundant that transnational connections play an important role for many first-generation immigrants, the facts are much less clear for their children. All three surveys therefore asked similar questions about transnational connections, including the frequency of visits to the parents' country of origin and remittances to family there. As table 9.1 shows, most of the respondents in New York, Los Angeles, Berlin, and Vienna have indeed visited the home country of their parents, but this rate varies considerably by group and city. Proximity to the parental countries matters in New York: Dominicans are more likely to visit their parents' home than Chinese. In Los Angeles, proximity matters less, with Mexicans and Chinese about equally likely to have visited their parents' homeland. The frequency of visits in both cities is determined

TABLE 9.1   Transnational Aspects

	Berlin		Vienna		New York		Los Angeles	
	Turks	Former Yugo	Turks	Former Yugo	Chinese	Dominican	Chinese/ Taiwanese	Mexican
Visited parents' home country in past five years	67%	50%	80%	74%	62%	89%	69%	72%
Visited parents' home country occasionally	75	89	83	48	82	46	59	65
Remitted money to parents' home country in past five years	11	10	11	18	14	34	16	39
Watch television, only or mostly survey country channels	59	92	37	65			32*	22*
Watch television, only or mostly parents' home country channels	12	1	30	10			24**	50**
Use Internet for information about parents' home country	15	10	23	21			NA	NA
Birth country of partner or spouse is same as parents'	21	12	79	53			44	47
Birth country of partner or spouse is Germany, Austria, or United States	79	85	21	41			50	37
Origin of partner's parents is Turkey, Former Yugoslavia, Hispanic-Latino, Asian–Pacific Islander	87	32	92	78			84	83

Source: Authors' calculations based on data from the IIMMLA (Rumbaut et al. 2004), ISGMNY (Mollenkopf, Kasinitz, and Waters 1999), and TIES survey (data not yet publicly available).

NA = not applicable

*Listen to Chinese or Spanish television or radio

**Listen more than once a week

Note: The TIES survey comprises eight separate national data sets, collected by Institute for Studies on Migrations (IEM), Comillas Pontifical University, Spain; Swiss Forum for Migration and Population Studies (SFM), Neuchâtel, Switzerland; Netherlands Interdisciplinary Demographic Institute (NIDI), The Hague, Netherlands; Austrian Academy of Sciences (ÖAW), Vienna, Austria; the European Research Centre on Migration and Ethnic Relations (ERCOMER), Katholieke Universiteit Leuven, Belgium; National Institute for Demographic Studies (INED), Paris, France; Institute for Migration Research and Intercultural Studies (IMIS), University of Osnabrück, Germany; Centre for Research in International Migration and Ethnic Relations (CEIFO), Stockholm University, Sweden. The TIES national surveys will be made publicly available by the national TIES partners individually, but were not yet available at the time of publication.

by proximity, with Dominicans and Mexicans more likely to visit frequently (more than three to five times) than Chinese.

Looking at the patterns of visits to Turkey or the successor states of Yugoslavia reveals differences within the same groups across the European cities. Turkish and former Yugoslavian respondents in Vienna are significantly more likely to have visited their parents' country of origin than their peers in Berlin. The former Yugoslavia is geographically and historically closer to Vienna than Berlin, but the level of visits from the Berlin respondents to former Yugoslavia is still surprisingly low: only half visited the country at all in the past five years. Geography is also unlikely to be the main reason that the Turkish second generation in Berlin travels less often than their Viennese peers. The other items in the table confirm that the Viennese Turkish second generation has higher levels of connectedness to Turkey. They are more likely to watch Turkish television, to use the Internet for information about Turkey, and to have a partner born in Turkey.

Remittances to family in the country of origin are also a major transnational activity for the first generation. In all four cities, however, remittances sent by the second generation are modest for both groups in Europe and the Chinese in New York and Los Angeles. Only 10 to 16 percent have ever sent money to the home country of the parents and, if they did, they did so infrequently and sent only small sums of money. The remittance patterns are different for second-generation Dominicans in New York and Mexicans in Los Angeles—in both countries remittances are major sources of income. Approximately 33 percent of the respondents remitted money, but the second generation is far less likely to do so than their parents or even the 1.5 generation.

A similar picture emerges in terms of the consumption of Turkish and Serbo-Croatian, Spanish, and Chinese media, specifically television. All second-generation groups have large majorities who mainly or exclusively watch English-German language channels—even though Spanish, Turkish, or Chinese channels are easily accessible. The Turkish respondents in Vienna are again most likely to watch Turkish television (almost one-third only or mainly Turkish channels), and they more frequently use Turkey-oriented websites.

In Los Angeles, the children of Mexican immigrants often tuned into the widely available Spanish-language television or radio, about half doing so at least once a week. However, these respondents also consumed English-language television and radio. In contrast to the TIES survey, the IIMMLA survey asked about radio as well as television, the former being ubiquitous and probably more listened to by respondents than television. Los Angeles is one of the major production sites for Spanish-language music in the world, with much crossover appeal to English-speaking and bilingual radio stations. Music is an area of major cultural hybridity in Los Angeles. In New York, about 83 percent of our Dominican respondents reported watching or listening to Spanish-language programming frequently, often, they told us, when a grandmother or parent was watching with them. Reflecting their more limited language skills and the lesser amount of programming available, the Chinese reported lower levels of consumption of Chinese-language programming, about 41 percent.

Transnational activities tend to be associated with a few key factors. Income, for example, has an obvious effect on the possibility to travel and is related also to age, gender, and employment. Remittances in Europe are significantly related to these variables but also to the motivating factor of whether the parents had moved back to their homelands. A person's legal status also makes a difference. Citizenship affords a freedom of movement that probably explains why second-generation Mexican respondents in Los Angeles are more likely than the 1.5 generation to have accompanied their parents for an extended stay in Mexico. Transnational activities are also significantly related to two cultural variables. Logistic regressions on the IIMMLA, TIES, and ISGMNY data revealed that preference for, and an extended practice of, the language of origin of the parents in all second-generation groups in the four cities is significantly related to the intensity of the transnational engagement of individuals. In the TIES analysis, religiosity also made a significant difference in the intensity of the transnational engagement.

The direction of this relationship remains an open question, however. Do people prefer to speak Spanish or Turkish because they maintain close relationships to the country of origin of their parents, or are the stronger preference and better skills the result of intensified relations and frequent travel? Analyses of the TIES data, measuring the relationship between transnational activities and cultural practices with feelings of belonging, indicate that these practices are related to the sense of ethnic belonging. It is likely that there is a strong element of reactive identification here, but developing intense relations to *there* does not contradict being firmly rooted *here*.

Conclusions

The second generations in these four cities share a generational experience that distinguishes them from the majority population. They grow up under comparable conditions, especially with regard to the low educational and socioeconomic backgrounds of the parents, and in societal settings that—despite their being native born and raised—consider them to be aliens, though the Mexican-ancestry population of the Southwest may be a partial exception. They are the object of competing discourses about whether their strategies of identification, of finding a place and developing a sense of belonging, are predetermined by external institutions in ways that may conflict with their feelings, at least to some degree, or whether they have real agency in the matter. In all four settings, they minimally face a family-diasporic narrative pulling against a wider societal narrative, with both demanding certain minimum degrees of loyalty. In identity terms, it is a basic characteristic of the second generation that they must reconcile these two loyalties in one way or another.

How they do so depends in part on the extent to which the larger society makes it problematic to have two loyalties. This is a major difference between the dominant integration schemes of Europe and the United States. In the latter, being born in the country, or not, marks a major difference, whereas being of immigrant descent does not contradict being American. As chapter 8 has shown, naturalization rates in the first generation are not higher in the United States than in most European countries (at least for the groups analyzed here). In this sense, the United States does not draw a bright line between the native-born children of immigrants and nonimmigrants (which does not preclude the possibility of constructing different degrees of Americanism or subjecting the second generation to racial othering schemes). The U.S. second generation can easily become hyphenated Americans and develop pan-ethnic identities that offer resources for civic and political organizing.

In Europe, by contrast, being native-born children of foreign-born parents provides far less protection from othering discourses, because European countries do draw a strong line between immigrant and native descent. The second generation poses a particular challenge to European integration rhetoric, and Europe constantly applies claims of foreignness and not adapting to the second or even third generations. For example, in every soccer match between the national teams of Germany and Turkey both teams feature outstanding second-generation German-Turkish players, such as Hamit Altintop for Turkey and Mesut Özil for Germany. Both players were born in the city of Gelsenkirchen in the Ruhr area and have been professional soccer players in the German premier league for many years. Altintop's decision to play for the Turkish team put him at odds with the metaphysical relevance attached to the nation as a main reference frame for belonging—and to the national team as one of its main symbols. This applies, by the way, also to Turkish national discourse: German media tend to present Altintop as an example of failed integration, and the Turkish media has repeatedly accused Özil of being a traitor to his people. The level and intensity at which one must negotiate one's belonging to society seems quite different in Europe than in the United States. As the TIES survey shows, self-definitions of national belonging in most European countries have a strong ethnic element that constitutes a major impediment for an unquestioned belonging of the second generation to the nation: the children of Turkish or Yugoslavian parents would normally not consider themselves ethnically German or Austrian.

It could also be argued that New York and Los Angeles have different approaches to this issue. Los Angeles may be closer to Europe in seeing the rise of new immigrant groups as a cultural and economic threat. There, being an Anglo Protestant is still central to membership in the American mainstream (Chávez 1991, 2006, 2008). The long historical presence of Mexicans in the Southwest, the American conquest of the Southwest through war, and the threat of a so-called reconquest by Mexicans through immigration and biological reproduction all reinforce this perspective. New York, by contrast, has a robust and continuing belief that new immigrant groups will inherit leadership positions and institutions from previous immigrant groups and that this succession is an inevitable and good part of the city's dynamism (Kasinitz et al. 2008). New Yorkers would not be surprised if today's newcomers were to become tomorrow's establishment, though they might not go out of their way to make it happen. These different ideologies and contexts, along with the very real discrimination nonwhite young people face, will certainly influence their sense of belonging to the American nation.

In the areas of cultural integration examined here, the young adult children of Mexicans and Chinese, of Turkish and former Yugoslavian backgrounds, are shifting from the world of their parents to the world of the country they were born into. This does not mean that they are not bicultural or bilingual but only that they are fully engaged in the cultural life in the United States, Austria, and Germany, though they may have joined it at difference paces. There is no evidence of self-marginalized outsiders. Nor is there any evidence of a failure to learn English or German. Instead, all four analyzed criteria indicate that these young people are responding to the cultural and social influences around them as they also change the cultural makeup of their societies through their ability to mix their parents' culture with it. With the important exception of the role of religion and religiosity in respondents' daily lives, this observation is also valid for Berlin and Vienna, even though it might seem less obvious. The second generations in Europe do not show a markedly different profile of host culture adoption versus ethnic retention than those in the United States. And with regard to religion, the odd one out among all the groups analyzed in this chapter is, in fact, the European native whites and their very low levels of religiosity—in relation not only to their age peers of immigrant descent but also to their parents or grandparents.

Immigrants and their children pose different types of challenges to all host societies. Despite many obstacles, challenges, and problems, this chapter has found that second-generation groups have gone a long way to embrace their countries. As described here, members of the second generation are neither melting (in the near future) into the mainstream, nor are they aliens who need particular integration incentives. Because the second generation is native to our American and European cities, they do not see themselves, nor should they be seen, as outsiders (Schinkel 2007; Crul and Schneider 2010, 1251). The second generation is an integral part of the mosaic of society. None of the analyzed groups in any of the settings can be considered isolated from the mainstream or living in some kind of parallel society, a finding that goes counter to public, political, polemical, and media discourses that are common in the three countries analyzed here.

Analytically, the more interesting question is what long-term effects the large-scale presence of this new second generation will have on its societies. In all four urban settings examined, the second generation is not simply dissolving into the mainstream but instead remaking it (Alba and Nee 2003) by creating and occupying new social spaces and bringing in new (or reinforcing existing) cultural elements, such as languages and religious beliefs. By sheer demographic force, the second generation will change the faces of our cities—altering, for example, their linguistic and religious landscapes as well as cultural practices related to food, music, socializing, community organization, and so on.

Increased cultural diversification and creativity in all kinds of directions not only makes these cities of the world more interesting places to be but creates more room and acceptance for people to preserve cultural influences from their families. To be multilingual and to demonstrate intercultural competencies is becoming a must for careers in many industries. This suggests that we should consider the second generation a vanguard for cultural creativity, the administration of diversity, and commercial competitiveness in Europe and North America. Large segments of the second generation seem well prepared for this—indeed often more so than their peers with native-born parents. The increased diversity of the young people in these cities not only yields constant cross-group encounters but is producing a third culture that hybridizes or synthesizes the various ethnicities or ethno-national backgrounds, including that of the native born. This trend may ultimately dissolve the originally dominant meaning of categories like native white or the autochthonous, especially as juxtaposed with such ethnic categories as Chinese or Mexican or Dominican or Turkish or Yugoslav on the one hand and American or Austrian or German on the other.

Finally, this transatlantic comparison teaches us something new about how research perspectives are embedded in the idiosyncrasies of their respective societies—especially with regard to identity. The two American surveys did not even think to ask about feelings of national belonging (with the exception of the question for feeling at home in Los Angeles), even though many members of the U.S. second generation may not feel entirely American. Instead, they asked many questions about racial and ethnic identity. European researchers, by contrast, placed a great deal of stress on the supposed problem of nonidentification with the host society. The real problem in Europe is more likely to be the mainstream's lack of imagination about how people can hold multiple forms of belonging. Despite these continental blinders, however, members of the second generation on both sides of the Atlantic are facing, and largely surmounting, the challenges to their full membership.

NOTE

1.   See Statistik Berlin-Brandenburg (http://www.statistik-berlin.de).

PART III

TRANSATLANTIC COMPARISON

CHAPTER 10

CHALLENGES AND OPPORTUNITIES

MAURICE CRUL AND JOHN MOLLENKOPF

O ver the last fifty years, the major cities in western Europe and the
United States have developed many ways of integrating immigrants
and their children into their social, economic, and political fabric. This
creates an opportunity to compare outcomes for similarly positioned
groups of immigrant descent facing a variety of national and local integration policies and practices across roughly similar urban contexts. This
concluding chapter focuses on Turkish second-generation youth in six
large capital cities in Europe (Amsterdam, Berlin, Brussels, Paris, Stockholm, and Vienna) compared with Dominican second-generation youngsters in New York and their Mexican second-generation peers in Los
Angeles, the two largest cities in the United States. Our conclusion draws
on the previous thematic chapters as well as some additional analysis of
the TIES, ISGMNY, and IIMMLA surveys.

This comparison examines only those whose parents entered these
cities at great comparative disadvantage. Their experiences do not represent the modal or typical outcomes for the immigrant second generation,
but only the outcomes achieved under the most difficult circumstances.
This way, we can see how each urban and national setting has faced its
toughest test: providing advancement for young people from the most

disadvantaged immigrant ethnic group. Although their experience obviously does not represent that of the entire second generation, it is particularly meaningful because social scientists would predict it to be the most problematic.

As noted, the great majority of Turkish, Dominican, and Mexican parents were labor migrants with little education. Although almost all of the first-generation Turkish fathers initially worked, a great many now do not. Turkish mothers were least likely to work all along. And though the Dominican and Mexican parents have higher and longer levels of labor force participation, they remain overwhelmingly in low-wage, low-skilled jobs. On both sides of the Atlantic, the parents' low levels of education, income, and host language ability, together with religious differences in western Europe, make their children candidates for forming an ethnic underclass in the sense of being a marginalized, isolated, or separate group from the larger society. Whether they do in fact form such a group reveals much about the barriers and opportunities they face, the strategies that they and their parents have forged in response to them, and how various public policy environments affect their prospects. The final result is a good indication of how well the assimilation or integration process is working.

Although Dominicans and Mexicans came to New York and Los Angeles as voluntary labor migrants, western European governments specifically recruited Turkish contract workers (usually males) from the most undeveloped parts of Turkey in the 1950s and 1960s to do dirty, dangerous, or difficult jobs in European factory settings. They were thus probably somewhat more negatively selected than Dominican or Mexican migrants, though they too were among the least educated or skilled in their home countries. Deindustrialization, jobs offshored to low-wage countries, the oil crises of the late 1970s, the ending of guest-worker programs, and the more general closing down of immigration into western Europe pushed many Turkish guest-worker fathers out of work and into various kinds of social support. Their wives, who arrived later through family reunification, always had low levels of labor force participation.

Although the Dominican and Mexican parents also worked in low-skill, low-wage jobs, they migrated under their own steam, were not tied to specific jobs in specific places, and generally remain in the labor force today. Dominican and Mexican women tended to arrive at more or less the same time as men and were much more likely than their counterparts in Europe to work. Indeed, the Turkish second generation in Europe mainly grew up in traditional households with two legally resident parents. The Dominican and Mexican parents often did not migrate as a family unit and some were not initially authorized to live in the United States. Their family situations were more likely to be characterized by divorce or single motherhood than those of Turks. Finally, in recent decades, Turkey's economy has arguably grown more quickly than that of Mexico or the Dominican Republic, and that growth has driven business formation in the Turkish communities in western European cities. (Gross domestic product per capita is about the same in Mexico as Turkey but is significantly lower in the Dominican Republic, which is also much smaller than the other two countries.)

The Turkish, Dominican, and Mexican first generation not only arrived in different work and family circumstances but also settled into quite different receiving contexts, even though all were in large cities. In the western European cities, they entered neighborhoods and jobs from which white industrial workers were exiting, often living in public or subsidized housing. Turks often did manual labor beside other guest workers from southern Europe and North Africa, forming the biggest of several immigrant minority groups.

In New York and Los Angeles, by contrast, manufacturing employment had already declined significantly by the 1970s and 1980s. Dominican and Mexican immigrants therefore mainly entered sectors like construction, landscaping, and retail sales, where they encountered not only other Spanish-speaking and Asian immigrant groups but also African Americans, Puerto Ricans, and multigenerational Mexican Americans. Although European countries limited further immigration from Turkey to family reunification or formation, Latino immigrants continue to enter New York and Los Angeles in large numbers, heightening competition at the bottom of the labor market. Finally, Latino immigrants to New York and Los Angeles settled fairly close to poor Puerto Rican and African American neighborhoods but were not typically able to enter the public or socially supported housing stock.

These differences in the background situation of the first-generation parents have a number of potentially contradictory consequences for their children. In western Europe, Turkish communities have been stereotyped as having low skills, poor educational outcomes, low labor force participation, and dependence on social welfare. At the same time, family life is strong, the community is well organized, and solidarity is high. As a result, their children do not grow up in destitution, but the parents have a hard time linking them to jobs. By contrast, the parents of the Dominican children in New York and Mexican children in Los Angeles have to work to survive and are less likely than the larger native minority groups—African Americans, Puerto Ricans, and Chicanos—to be on welfare or live in the most negatively stereotyped neighborhoods, but their material circumstances are sometimes worse than those of their Turkish counterparts in Europe.

EUROPEAN AND U.S. OUTCOMES: PRIMARY DIFFERENCES

The previous chapters have drawn many complex comparisons across ethnic groups, cities, and national settings. These comparisons do not yield one consistent pattern. Indeed, the outcomes seem to differ depending on the domain under consideration. Cities rank somewhat differently on educational outcomes than they do on identity formation or social relationships. The differences among the western European cities often are larger than those between European and American cities. This makes it challenging to draw overall conclusions about differences between Europe and the United States.

In general, our results suggest that U.S. cities are more open toward newcomers and their children in terms of belonging and identity formation. Although the western European cities vary on this point, it is problematic to be a Muslim in any of them. This makes it hard for young people of Turkish origin to identity strongly as German, French, or Swedish. It is far easier for Dominican Americans or Mexican Americans to identity as American, in part because hyphenated identities are taken for granted. The United States also expresses this concretely by granting citizenship to all who are born in the United States, regardless of the status of their parents. No European nation does this. At the same time, with the exception of Switzerland, the overwhelming majority of Turkish Europeans ultimately do become citizens and the naturalization rate of their parents is not markedly less than those of their counterparts in the United States.

The socioeconomic picture is more diffuse. In every city we studied, many young people from the most disadvantaged immigrant backgrounds made progress against all odds. Indeed, many of these second-generation youngsters now hold professional positions. However, a good many also work in service occupations (though mostly in rising sectors rather than those that employed their parents) and some are unemployed or not in the labor force. They generally occupy somewhat better positions than their parents did at the equivalent life stage, but this is only to be expected. In the United States, they do better than comparable members of disadvantaged native minority groups. To return to the basic questions posed at the outset, however, the central tendency across cities on both continents is that children from disadvantaged immigrant minority backgrounds are experiencing gradual upward mobility compared with their parents and are entering into lower middle-class skilled positions. They are not forming an alienated underclass or parallel society.

The markedly successful subgroups—defined as those with college or postgraduate degrees who are entering the professions—vary considerably in size across the U.S. and western European cities. Second-generation Turks in the Austrian and German cities are the negative outliers. The highly stratified German-speaking school system systematically sorts many of the youngsters into poor jobs or dead-end labor market prospects and does not allow for many second chances. Those who got their schooling in the comprehensive systems of the United States (both cities) and Europe (France and Sweden) all have similar and higher shares of successful young people. Comprehensive (less tracked) school systems seem to allow many children of disadvantaged immigrant backgrounds to enter colleges and universities and to find second-chance routes when the main ones are not open for them. Indeed, the French and Swedish second-generation respondents do somewhat better in this respect than their counterparts in New York or Los Angeles, because the supposedly equivalent public schools in these cities actually can be quite dysfunctional and cost remains a barrier for entry into better public and private university systems.

In every city, a substantial group is stuck in unstable and low-skilled jobs. This should not come as a surprise, given that they are growing up in the most deprived neighborhoods with parents who are in the worst labor market position in cities where this type of work is growing as a share of all jobs. The Turkish second generation in the German and Austrian cities once more has the worst outcomes. The high share of second-generation Turkish women not participating in the labor market is especially striking. Unemployment is also high for Turkish men. The European cases are thus characterized by relatively high levels of unemployment and inactivity as opposed to employment in jobs that barely lift one out of poverty, as is more frequent in the United States. Although the European welfare systems are under heavy attack, social provision offsets the consequences of unemployment and prevents even the worst-off immigrant families from becoming a permanent underclass by providing social housing, investment in neighborhood amenities, and minimum incomes.

In the U.S. cities, by contrast, the high degree of labor market participation among both the male and the female children of immigrants is the main integrative factor, but they receive relatively few of the welfare state benefits like social housing and income support that play such an important role in the western European cities. The high commitment to work often comes at the cost of holding precarious, low-paying jobs, however. Indeed, many Dominican and Mexican young people can now be counted among the working near-poor. This restricts them to living in relatively low quality and sometimes crime-ridden neighborhoods, a worrying starting situation for the third generation. Growing up, many faced a higher daily risk of violence than other residents of their cities.

On both sides of the ocean, the middle group often is unobserved. They have clearly moved up with respect to their parents, can afford certain luxuries, and will offer their children a significantly better future. This mobility may appear to be more substantial in the more unequal cities of the United States than is possible in the more egalitarian western European cities, where the distance between the lower class and the lower middle class is smaller.

The different patterns of racial and ethnic and class segregation also make it difficult to evaluate the domain of social relationships across the Atlantic. Residential segregation by race and immigrant origin is far higher in U.S. cities than European ones, but the European cities are far more likely to interpret immigrant ethnic concentrations as problematic for integration. European cities may be less segregated, but the dominant population more strongly frowns on any signs of ethnic concentration—and they remain socially, if not always spatially, distant from immigrant communities. Indeed, the social distance between the Muslim and non-Muslim population in Europe grows by the day.

Notwithstanding the negative framing of undocumented Mexican immigrants in the United States, the American mainstream sees Latino immigrants as hard working, and popular discourse (so far) lacks the poisonous elements of the Islam debate in Europe. The negative tenor of the European debate has not been moderated by the fact that Turkish Europeans overwhelmingly reject an activist Islam and are not particularly active Muslims. In the United States, the Latino second-generation groups are actually more religious and more committed to church participation than the Turkish second generation in Europe. The U.S. mainstream, however, sees this as a pathway to assimilation, not a barrier to it.

In sum, most members of the most deprived second-generation groups in western European cities are achieving real, if limited, social mobility and certainly enjoy a level of social protection not available in the United States. Most Dominican Americans and Mexican Americans are also achieving upward social mobility in New York and Los Angeles, but those who fail to do so may end up in worse material conditions and greater insecurity than their European counterparts. As groups, however, they seem to have a greater sense of belonging, greater identification with the host society, and more social relationships with native-born groups than second-generation Turks do, especially given the negative debate about how Islam hinders social integration.

In other words, while each group deserves a great deal of credit for striving to get good educations and jobs, their progress toward integration strongly reflects the broader socioeconomic conditions prevailing in the cities in which they have grown up. As the following detailed results suggest, the western European commitment to the welfare state and the U.S. commitment to competition in open labor markets define these broad patterns.

SOCIOECONOMIC POSITION

Of all outcomes discussed in this volume, educational attainment varies most strongly across city and nation. Here, we focus briefly on early school leavers (dropouts) and high achievers (those studying for or receiving a BA or MA). The size of the latter group is a key indicator of intergenerational mobility and an important clue to better contexts of integration. Although the BA or MA may have a slightly different social meaning in the United States than in Europe, comparing them is nonetheless relatively straightforward. It is more difficult to compare early school leavers, because children are expected to get their high school diploma at age eighteen in the United States, but children may normally finish school in Europe by age fifteen or sixteen. In Germany, Austria, and the Netherlands, pupils in a vocational track leave school at this early age to do an apprenticeship, which is considered postsecondary education. In Sweden and France, many second-generation Turks attend upper secondary vocational programs that have no direct counterpart in the United States.

See tables 10.1 and 10.2 for the percentages for those who leave school with no more than a lower secondary or upper secondary (high school) diploma. In Europe, the second category includes those who only have an upper secondary diploma or dropped out of postsecondary education without a diploma; in the United States, it includes those with a high school diploma only and those who attended a two-year college but did not get a degree. The first row of the tables thus represents those who have failed to achieve the socially expected minimum and the second those who have achieved the social minimum but no more. Four of the European cities have substantially worse outcomes than in the United

TABLE 10.1   Outcomes for Second-Generation Turks in Six European Cities

	Amsterdam	Berlin	Brussels	Paris	Stockholm	Vienna
Educational attainment						
Lower secondary diploma at the most	23.7%	32.4%	15.2%	10.0%	9.2%	29.8%
Upper secondary diploma at the most	0.4	5.4	41.8	19.6	47.0	15.5
Enrolled in higher education or received BA or MA	30.0	6.7	28.8	51.5	33.4	14.3
Labor market position						
Marginal	36.0	59.9	46.5	33.7	31.8	50.0
Professional jobs	25.2	13.5	23.8	30.3	31.3	14.8
Neighborhood has a lot of crime						
Agree	18.0	18.2	NA	19.3	NA	11.1
Very much agree	7.8	2.4	NA	5.8	NA	2.4
Acculturation						
Spouse (if any) is coethnic	91.5	86.7	94.8	68.2	71.9	90.1
Raised in Turkish	91.3	90.1	98.3	92.7	n.a.	97.6
Has a religion	84.1	64.4	75.7	82.7	74.5	88.9
Attends mosque more than once a month	21.6	36.8	11.5	16.4	11.6	48.8

Source: Authors' compilation of data from TIES survey 2007, 2008 (data not yet publicly available).

NA = not applicable, because the question wasn't asked; BA = bachelor's degree; MA = master's degree.

Note: The TIES survey comprises eight separate national data sets, collected by Institute for Studies on Migrations (IEM), Comillas Pontifical University, Spain; Swiss Forum for Migration and Population Studies (SFM), Neuchâtel, Switzerland; Netherlands Interdisciplinary Demographic Institute (NIDI), The Hague, Netherlands; Austrian Academy of Sciences (ÖAW), Vienna, Austria; the European Research Centre on Migration and Ethnic Relations (ERCOMER), Katholieke Universiteit Leuven, Belgium; National Institute for Demographic Studies (INED), Paris, France; Institute for Migration Research and Intercultural Studies (IMIS), University of Osnabrück, Germany; Centre for Research in International Migration and Ethnic Relations (CEIFO), Stockholm University, Sweden. The TIES national surveys will be made publicly available by the national TIES partners individually, but were not yet available at the time of publication.

TABLE 10.2   Outcomes for Second-Generation Dominicans and Mexicans in New York and Los Angeles

	New York	Los Angeles
Educational attainment		
No high school diploma	9.7%	12.7%
High school diploma at the most	30.7	35.4
Enrolled in higher education or received BA or MA	29.3	23.0
Labor market position		
Marginal	46.1	44.9
Professional jobs	29.3	25.1
Neighborhood crime		
Big problem	21.1	20.3
Somewhat of a problem	45.3	31.5
Acculturation		
Spouse (if any) is coethnic	44.8	62.8
Raised in Spanish	56.8	60.8
Has a religion	82.3	91.7
Attends church more than once a month	30.6	56.6

Source: Authors' compilation of data from ISGMNY (Mollenkopf, Kasinitz, and Waters 1999) and IIMMLA (Rumbaut et al. 2004) surveys.
BA = bachelor's degree; MA = master's degree.

States, with only Paris and Stockholm achieving results comparable to New York and Los Angeles. On the second row, the results vary widely in Europe: Amsterdam, Berlin, and Vienna have the smallest share (primarily because so many dropped out earlier), the U.S. cities the middle share, and Brussels and Stockholm the highest share of those who have only a high school diploma.

Berlin and Vienna have the largest group of dropouts. In most cases, respondents left lower secondary school at age fifteen or sixteen, some with only nine years of formal training. As chapter 2 details, the six European cities pose different challenges for lower-class children of immigrants. The countries differ in the availability of preschool, the starting age of primary school, the number of contact hours each day, and the age of selection for secondary school tracks. In Berlin, most second-generation Turkish children did not go to preschool and their parents could not help them to acquire German language skills. As a result, many entered primary school with a huge language deficit.

Because children mostly go to primary school only for half days in Germany, they again had to rely on their parents for help in learning to read and write German, but most Turkish parents could not provide this support. Finally, the German system sorts children into different school tracks at age ten or twelve. In such a compressed framework, it is no surprise that so many Turkish children are tracked into Hauptschule, the lowest secondary school track. Hauptschule pupils are supposed to transition into an apprenticeship at fifteen or sixteen, but this turns out to be highly problematic for second-generation Turkish pupils, about half of whom fail to secure apprenticeships. Although children from Realschule (middle level of schooling) usually have better access to such positions, even Hauptschule pupils with native parents are twice as likely to find an apprenticeship. As a result, many second-generation Turks in Berlin end up without an upper secondary (or high school) diploma, which is granted only on completion of an apprenticeship.

In France, Belgium, and Sweden, the vocational and academic tracks both potentially give access to higher education. In Brussels and Stockholm, however, many students following a vocational program stopped after upper secondary school, but many more in France continued into higher vocational institutions that grant a BA.

The U.S. results are hard to compare with those of Europe. Although a U.S. high school diploma can be considered equivalent to an upper secondary school diploma in Europe, high schools vary tremendously in quality, even within New York or Los Angeles. Although all European upper secondary school diplomas formally allow access to university education, the informal tracking within and between U.S. high schools shunts some graduates into two-year colleges (comparable to Europe's four-year apprenticeship tracks), at best leading to an associate's degree at around age twenty. Those who attended better high schools in New York or Los Angeles can and do enter four-year colleges or universities.

Unfortunately, we do not know whether the Dominican or Mexican second generation attended preschool or kindergarten. Based on the literature, however, it seems probable that many did not, only entering primary school at age six. Although they attended school all day, the U.S. school year is shorter than in many European countries. Although relatively few dropped out before completing high school, many got no more education than that. Another large group continued into a community (two-year) college but did not get a degree. (Many young people from immigrant and native backgrounds go to these institutions to make up for the poor quality of their high schools.) Their educational fate is decided in these institutions, and most leave without the associate's degree that might counteract their weak high school diploma. Thus, stratified and comprehensive school systems both create big groups at the bottom, though of different kinds. The stratified systems produce the biggest group at the absolute bottom.

Turning to the higher end of the educational pyramid, we find that many second-generation young people do get a college or university education. The two tables also show how many already have a BA or more as well as how many are still studying. Considering the low socioeconomic status of their parents, the large share of college goers in all cities except for Berlin and Vienna is a huge step forward. Moreover, the share of second-generation Dominican and Mexican college students is on a par with that of Turkish students in Amsterdam and Brussels.

Chapter 4 shows that the U.S. second generation took two routes into college. The larger group entered directly after high school, having followed an AP program or taken honors classes. Others, perhaps deterred by tuition costs or family situations, went to community colleges instead. Some eventually switched into a four-year college, often working part time or full time to pay for their educations. The increasing cost of attending public universities in the United States in the face of declining or stagnant financial aid has become a real burden for low-income students, and the deeper financial aid from prestigious private colleges and universities reaches only a few.

Second-generation Turks in Paris and Berlin have starkly different experiences.[1] The former are eight times more likely to reach higher education than the latter. Given that the Turkish guest-worker community in Paris shares many characteristics with that in Berlin, the key difference clearly lies in the dynamics of the educational systems, not in the groups' characteristics. Second-generation Turkish TIES respondents in Paris entered preschool at age two or three and began to learn French in an environment and at an age when children easily pick up a second language. Because Turkish parents in Paris were much less responsible for teaching their children French, the children started primary school with a much smaller language deficit than in Berlin. They also attended primary school for a full day and did not face selection until age fifteen, after more than ten years of schooling. They thus had far more time to close the gap with native parentage pupils than in Berlin. Most thus made an easy transition to upper secondary school at fifteen and a large majority entered an academic track, providing them access to higher education.

The comprehensive French and Swedish school systems provide direct access to higher education through lycées and gymnasia. University educations are free in Sweden and France. Together, these factors enable more children from poor immigrant families to enter a university than in New York or Los Angeles. The more highly tracked system in the Netherlands, in contrast, prevents most from reaching higher education directly, but a big group ultimately reaches that destination by taking a long route through institutions resembling U.S. community colleges.

Despite the varied quality of U.S. high school diplomas and the higher cost of college educations, the United States achieves results comparable to most European settings and far better than Germany and Austria, suggesting that comprehensive educational systems have advantages over those that are highly tracked. The comprehensive school systems of Europe show less variation in quality and lower costs of access, perhaps accounting for the positive results in Paris and Stockholm.

Viewed more broadly, results at the bottom clearly mirror those at the top. Where school dropouts are highest, college- and university-going is the lowest. At the same time, some cases are more polar than others, and the two ends of the distribution outnumber those in the middle, which is more likely to be the case in the United States than western Europe, particularly Sweden or France.

Although educational attainment is the most important outcome, educational advancement does not always produce good labor market results. Chapter 5 shows that the NEET rate (those not in education, employment, or training) is a good measure of present and future marginalization and that it generally reflects either men who are unemployed or women who are not in the labor force, either because they left it after having children or because they never entered it in the first place. We next look specifically at being unemployed; not participating in the labor market; or holding low-skilled, low-wage jobs.[2] For obvious reasons, we restrict the comparison to those who already finished full-time studies. This presents a somewhat pessimistic or premature picture, because many respondents are still in school and will improve the results when they graduate, particularly second-generation Turks in Paris, Amsterdam, and Stockholm. Berlin, Vienna, and Brussels have the largest share of marginalized second-generation Turkish young people, driven by low female labor force participation rates in Berlin and Vienna and high unemployment in Brussels. Some 65 percent of the second-generation Turkish women who did not go to university in Berlin and Vienna are out of the labor force and another 10 to 20 percent are unemployed. As chapter 5 shows in detail, many second-generation Turkish women in western Europe never even enter the labor market.

This low labor force participation is often attributed to Turkish attitudes about the traditional role of women in families. Indeed, a considerable group of Turkish second-generation men and women in the TIES survey feel that women should not work when they have young children.

However, these traditional attitudes clearly interact with local welfare arrangements around work and care. Chapter 6 shows that the conservative German and Austrian welfare regimes make it difficult for women to combine paid work and care work. Half-day primary schooling in particular makes it hard for them to work. Preschool and after-school facilities are also less available. As mentioned, second-generation Turkish women in Vienna and Berlin also tend to leave school earlier than in other countries. Leaving school at this young age makes girls more vulnerable to pressure to follow traditional gender patterns than when they leave school at later ages. In Stockholm and Paris, Turkish women are older when they leave school and are more likely to enter the labor market before they get married. And given the more elaborate preschool and after-school facilities in these cities, many more second-generation Turkish women in these cities remain in the labor force even after having children because they can combine paid work with care work.

In Berlin, Vienna, and Brussels, 25 percent of Turkish second-generation men who leave school early are unemployed, a highly worrisome outcome. Given how apprenticeship systems regulate access to decent jobs, which has worked far less well for them than for young men of native parentage, they are in an extremely vulnerable position.

Rates of labor market marginality for Dominicans in New York and Mexicans in Los Angeles are similar to those of members of the disadvantaged second generation in western Europe but for a different reason: far fewer are unemployed or not in the labor force, but far more have low-wage jobs. As chapter 6 highlights, Dominican and Mexican young women also work far more often than their Turkish counterparts in western Europe. Second-generation Dominican and Mexican women do not stay home to look after the children any more than do women of native parentage. In the United States, low-income or single parents must work to survive, even when that means juggling care work and paid work. Being employed in low-skilled jobs or being unemployed are the main reasons that Dominican and Mexican second-generation people end up holding marginal labor market positions, whereas being outside the labor force and relying on social assistance are the main reasons in Europe.

The United States therefore has a strikingly higher share of working poor or near-poor. More than 30 percent of the second-generation Dominicans in New York and 40 percent of the second-generation Mexicans in Los Angeles earn less than $16,000 a year. In Berlin, the European city with the largest group at the bottom, only 27 percent of those with jobs earn less than $16,000 a year (though fewer are working).

Conversely, the welfare-dependent poor are far more numerous in Berlin. In the sink-or-swim environments of New York and Los Angeles, you can sink deeply if you do not get the educational credentials that provide an avenue to skilled work. School failure thus has more dramatic financial consequences in the United States than in Europe. The highly tracked school systems in Germany and Austria come close to producing similar results, although the system of social housing and social benefits in these two countries cushion the group at the bottom.

Although Berlin, Vienna, New York, and Los Angeles have all produced substantial groups in marginal labor market positions, it would be wrong to classify the second-generation groups in these four cities as wholly downwardly mobile. An equally large number in New York and Los Angeles have gotten university degrees and hold middle or higher level jobs or are still studying in tracks that might lead them there. And most, even without university degrees, are earning more than these minimums. Indeed, a surprisingly large proportion have made an exceptional step into professional jobs in all the cities except for Berlin and Vienna (see tables 10.1 and 10.2). With respect to their unskilled worker parents, this is a major achievement. These big cities are enabling many members of poor immigrant families to form a new middle class.

Once more, Berlin and Vienna are the negative outliers for second-generation Turkish professionals. The pattern follows that of higher education, though second-generation Turks have found a surprising number of professional jobs in Berlin given how few make it through universities. A closer look shows that half of them have "only" finished apprenticeships. Apparently some Turkish-Berliners do find apprenticeships that allow them to move into managerial professions. Problems accessing these good apprenticeships compound the low rates of university education for second-generation Turks in Berlin. The Paris figure for professional employment seems low given the high percentage with higher education, but many Turkish-Parisian respondents are still in university and not yet pursuing careers.

Many children of disadvantaged immigrants are thus cashing in their educational achievements at work, demonstrating once more the crucial role of the way school systems sort educational attainment. Many have clearly advanced substantially beyond their parents' occupational positions. The successful group in Stockholm and New York is double the size of those in Berlin and Vienna, though these cities are also advanced service economies with many professional jobs. Here again, it seems that egalitarian educational contexts enable more children from the disadvantaged backgrounds to move into professional employment and that stratified school systems most reproduce the class position of the parents.

This positive conclusion does not negate the reality that many children of disadvantaged immigrants remain at the bottom of the labor market or out of it entirely. As Rubén Rumbaut (2008) argues, incarceration is an important indicator of downward assimilation. High percentages of second-generation Dominican and Mexican boys (relative to Europe) have been arrested or incarcerated, a circumstance strongly related to dropping out of school. In Los Angeles, 42 percent of the second-generation Mexican males who had no more than a high school diploma also reported that they had been arrested, and more than 25 percent had been incarcerated. Approximately 30 percent of male Dominican New Yorkers with no more than a high school diploma had been arrested and 14 percent incarcerated. By contrast, only 10 percent of the Mexican male college graduates reported arrests and 7 percent incarceration. Similarly, only 13 percent of Dominican male college graduates in New York had been arrested and none incarcerated.

The strong association between involvement with the criminal justice system and dropping out of school among the Mexican and Dominican respondents reflects the higher levels of crime in the neighborhoods where they grew up. Chapter 7 shows that 29 percent of the male early school leavers in New York say crime is a big problem and 47 percent somewhat of a problem in their neighborhoods. More than 50 percent of the early school-leaving males also say that drug-dealing and gangs are somewhat of a problem or a big problem. The TIES survey unfortunately did not ask about arrests or incarceration, but it did ask about crime in their neighborhoods. Although the questions are somewhat different, it is clear that the American second generation grew up in much more dangerous neighborhoods. Even in Berlin, where the Turkish neighborhoods are thought to be some of the most marginal in Europe, respondents did not think there was much more crime than in other neighborhoods. The huge neighborhood differences in poverty and crime in the cities of the United States provide a potentially much more negative context for the second generation compared to the smaller variations in European cities.

Social Relationships

The western European debate around immigrant integration increasingly revolves around belonging and social cohesion. Voices in the German debate fear that immigrants are forming parallel societies that live

TABLE 10.3   Coethnic Friendship Among Second-Generation
Turkish Youth in Six European Cities

	Amsterdam	Berlin	Brussels	Paris	Stockholm	Vienna
Three best friends are coethnics	28.7%	46.2%	NA	17.3%	10.8%	42.9%

Source: Authors' compilation based on TIES survey 2007, 2008.
NA = not applicable, because the question wasn't asked.

separately from people of native parentage (Crul and Schneider 2010). They associate the strong social cohesion of Turkish communities with such negative outcomes as school dropouts and low female labor force participation. Mainstream public opinion often interprets the strongly Turkish identification of Euro-Turks, their language retention, and their maintenance of their culture and religion as a reluctance to integrate into Europe, which in turn is alleged to constitute a potential threat to the social fabric.

Numerous studies have documented the strong social cohesion within Turkish communities (the 2003 *International Migration Review* special issue on the second generation in Europe provides an overview) and the TIES finding that second-generation Turks choose coethnic spouses supports this conclusion. In most cities, nine out of ten marry someone of Turkish descent, a far higher rate of in-marriage than among Dominican New Yorkers or Mexican American Angelinos.

Because of this concern about parallel societies, TIES researchers asked numerous questions about the ethnic composition of social networks, including the ethnic background of one's three best friends. Table 10.3 shows how many report only having Turkish friends.

Once more, Stockholm shows the most diverse friendship patterns and Berlin shows the least. Turkish Swedes report a more mixed friendship group partly because their community is more diverse than Turkish groups in other cities. (Approximately 25 percent of the Swedish sample of Turks are Kurdish or Christian.) Yet all second-generation respondents who are doing well socioeconomically move into more mixed circles. Stockholm respondents of native parentage are also likely to mix more, yielding the most blurred ethnic boundaries of any of the European cities (Alba 2009). In Paris and Amsterdam, socioeconomically disadvantaged respondents who live in immigrant neighborhoods are more likely to have only Turkish friends. Berlin and Vienna show an especially strong negative relationship between living in Turkish neighborhoods and having diverse friendship networks. About 50 percent of second-generation Turks in Berlin and 30 percent in Vienna live in such segregated neighborhoods.

The social network patterns of second-generation Turks thus vary considerably across European cities. Where members of the Turkish second generation mainly grow up with Turkish peers (Berlin and Vienna), they have more ethnically homogeneous networks, but where they grow up in more mixed neighborhoods (Paris) or indeed have many peers of native parentage (Stockholm), they have far more mixed friendship networks. The U.S. debate about immigrant integration is much less concerned with how ethnic concentrations affect social relationships. The United States seems much more comfortable with the idea that immigrant ethnic groups will congregate in distinct neighborhoods and engage coethnics in their social lives. Indeed, acutely high levels of racial segregation are a far greater concern; within this pattern, immigrant groups, particularly Latino immigrant groups, tend to live between blacks and whites, often near Asian immigrant neighborhoods, but at much lower levels of segregation than blacks. Although many grow up in poor and dangerous areas, they have often successfully avoided the poorest and most violent native minority ghettos. In this context, their concentration is interpreted as a sign of neighborhood solidarity that can be potentially helpful, not a threat to the larger social fabric.

The American debate seems much more strongly centered around language, the native white majority fearing that a Spanish-speaking population will overwhelm the English-speaking population. The deep divide in California around bilingual education has brought this into the open. In fact, however, as the third-to-last rows of tables 10.1 and 10.2 make clear, the European Turkish second generation is far more likely to be raised in the Turkish language than second-generation U.S. Latinos are to be raised in Spanish.

It is striking that the European debate never comments on Turkish as a serious threat to national languages, most likely because the number of Turkish-speaking people is simply not large enough. These disparate findings underline the fact that differences in individual behavior (such as speaking Spanish or Turkish or having coethnic friends) are not as important as how the larger public debate frames these differences. As chapter 9 argues, second-generation Latinos thoroughly and quickly assimilate into the English language and the majority prefer to speak English in their own homes, even when they partner with coethnics. Those who move up the socioeconomic ladder and marry someone outside their group prefer English even more strongly. So Spanish hardly seems to be a threat to the hegemony of English.

ISLAM

Is Islam in Europe like Spanish in the United States (Zolberg and Woon 1999)? Islam is certainly central to European debates about immigrant integration. And most Latino and Turkish members of the second generation on each side of the Atlantic say they are religious adherents. Second-generation Mexicans in Los Angeles are the most religious, followed by the second-generation Turks in Vienna and Berlin. But the social contexts for this religiosity are completely different.

Because most Mexican and Dominican Americans practice Catholicism or evangelical Protestantism, which are considered part of the American mainstream, the majority population does not see immigrant religiosity as a threatening development. Moreover, the majority population in the United States is far more religious than that of Europe. Indeed, between 65 percent and 75 percent of native-parentage European youth in the TIES survey claim they have no religion, and the majority of second-generation Turkish youth report that religion is important or very important to them. The Netherlands has the largest gap between native-parentage and second-generation young people (71 percentage points).

In terms of worshiping, second-generation Mexican Angelinos go to church most often, and the second-generation Turks of Vienna and Berlin go to the mosque much more than those in the other European cities. At the same time, 30 percent or more of those who call themselves Muslims in Paris, Stockholm, and Brussels never even pray daily, though some will take part in Ramadan festivities (see last rows of tables 10.1 and 10.2).

These findings show that the majority of second-generation Turkish Muslims do not actively practice their religion, a fact that evidently eludes European public opinion. Instead, the European media focus on the cultural clash around issues such as gender equality and sexual morality. And indeed, the TIES survey shows that second-generation Turkish Europeans have a more traditional stand on these issues, especially sexuality and virginity. At the same time, many agree that women should be allowed to have sex before marriage, and almost all espouse gender equality in education and the labor market. The European debate misses these nuances.

The TIES survey also tells us that, among the Turkish European second generation, relatively few agree or strongly agree that religion should be the ultimate political authority, and most agree that religion is a private matter and favor a strict separation of state and religion. Only in Berlin is there even a modicum of support for the conservative viewpoint. In every case, advocates of a modern Islam far outweigh those favoring a political Islam (see table 10.4).

TABLE 10.4   Islamic Leanings of Second-Generation Turkish Youth in Six European Cities

	Political Islam	Modern Islam
Amsterdam	10.1%	46.8%
Berlin	27.3	42.7
Brussels	8.6	56.1
Paris	7.7	80.8
Stockholm	4.4	85.3
Vienna	11.5	44.4

Source: Authors' compilation of data from TIES survey 2007, 2008.

With a push from populist parties and media hyping, the European debate has thus misconstrued the actual state of affairs. Its image that a large majority of Muslim youth are strongly religious and hold radical Islamic views does not resemble reality. Instead, this attitude pushes them out of society even as they advocate a modern Islam or even do not identify with or practice Islam. Islamic beliefs and practices among the Turkish European second generation are no more of a threat to the fabric of European culture than speaking Spanish is to that of the United States.

In each city, educational attainment is positively related to advocating for a modern form of Islam. Contrary to the public image that highly educated second-generation youth have become involved in radical Islamic thinking, such thinking—rare everywhere—is most common among poorly educated second-generation youth. In Berlin, where 27 percent of the respondents favored a political Islam, this view was most pronounced (43 percent) among school dropouts but was espoused by only 6 percent of those with higher education. In Vienna, the comparable figures are 18 percent among early school leavers and 3 percent among those with higher education. The most effective way to reduce radical religious views among second-generation Turkish Europeans would be to provide greater educational opportunities for them.

All over Europe, populist parties have heightened fear of Islamization, claiming that multicultural societies are making themselves vulnerable to an activist, fundamentalist Islam in which religious beliefs lead young Muslims to cultivate loyalty only to their ethnic group, not to the nation. Yet Germany, which has the least developed multicultural policies and the fewest state provisions for mosques and religious education, has created the most advocates for a political Islam. (This of course should not be equated with Islamic radicalism or Jihadism, which, while a real phenomenon, is restricted to a small subset of those advocating a political Islam.) Sweden, perhaps the most multiculturalist country, has produced the fewest. Political Islam evidently does not thrive in more tolerant environments and may be a group-based reaction to the least tolerant or most discriminatory.

HOW DISADVANTAGED SECOND-GENERATION GROUPS ARE INTEGRATING

Is the overall position of second-generation Turks in Europe and second-generation Dominicans and Mexicans in the United States a glass half empty or half full? The data reviewed here could provide evidence for either position. Some have failed to progress much beyond the vulnerable position occupied by their parents, and the mass media and anti-immigrant political figures often highlight this fact. But our evidence shows that between 50 percent and 65 percent of the second generation in each of the cities have risen to occupy at least a lower middle-class position that is better than that of their parents, and some have gone much further. The media and politicians pay much less attention to the half- to two-thirds-full part of the picture.

The successful group in our comparison is particularly interesting because it highlights practices and institutions that worked. For this reason, we need to pay attention to how they came to be successful, who helped them, and what institutional arrangements gave them the best opportunities. Our cross-city, cross-national, and transatlantic comparison of similarly disadvantaged groups demonstrates that the shape of the glass clearly has important consequences for how it is filled. Some cities are systematically better than others at maximizing the incorporation of the second generation into mainstream institutions and minimizing their marginalization at the bottom of society.

Although many institutional arrangements influence why some cities do better than others, their educational systems play a fundamental role. An early start in school, full-day attendance in primary school, a comprehensive rather than highly tracked approach, late selection for university admission, and the availability of second-chance mechanisms all contribute significantly to school success. An inclusive apprenticeship system smooths the way to work. Providing alternative or long routes through the vocational or community college system allows many second-generation Turks ultimately to reach universities even when direct access through the Gymnasium or lycée is cut off. At the same time, comprehensive school systems do not keep all second-generation youngsters on an academic track. For them, better apprenticeship programs that connect with real labor market opportunities would be helpful.

Labor market institutions also shape work life outcomes. Measures that enable men and women to combine paid work with family life, such as child care and pre- and after-school programs, are particularly important in increasing labor force participation.

The relative generosity of the western European welfare states explains a number of the essential differences in outcomes between western Europe and the United States. The large share of social housing in western European cities stops many immigrant neighborhoods from becoming like the urban ghettos of the United States. Extra investments in schools in immigrant neighborhoods and low tuitions for public higher education make schooling more affordable for the children of immigrants in Europe. Unemployment benefits and national health-care schemes keep families in marginal labor market positions from falling into destitution.

At the same time, the relative openness of the U.S. labor market, combined with the lack of social supports for young people to opt out of work or to live decently in the absence of earnings, pushes far more immigrant parents and their children into the labor force. As a result, they are more likely to be deemed productive and less likely to be negatively stereotyped as dependent on social provision.

The institutional "shape of the glass" thus has as a profound impact on the hopes, fears, strategies, aspirations, and opportunities of the second generation. No city has managed to combine all the positive aspects of the European and U.S. settings. Each city presents a distinct package of opportunities and barriers. Among the European cities, Berlin features a school system that yields the most early school leavers, a Turkish second generation that feels least accepted and most tied to its ethnic identity, and the most advocates of a political Islam. The Stockholm and Paris settings, in different ways, seem to promote far better outcomes.

Comparing the European and U.S. cities, we find that the latter do certain things comparatively well—for example, promoting a minority of high achievers through AP courses and honors programs. Many of the Dominican second generation in New York and the Mexican second generation in Los Angeles have made tremendous educational and professional strides, considering their parents' low levels of education and poorly paid jobs. However, many also attended low quality elementary and high schools in high crime neighborhoods where they were exposed to more violence than is generally true in western Europe. Although European welfare state arrangements prevent extreme deprivation among the most disadvantaged members of the second generation, they also limit access to the labor market and foster negative stereotyping. The more open U.S. labor market and weaker income supports compel disadvantaged immigrant groups and their children to sustain themselves and seek upward mobility through work, but they leave little to fall back on when labor market volatility or family misfortunes strike. As a result, members of the disadvantaged second generation in New York and Los Angeles are more exposed to risk than their counterparts in Europe. But this is also true of those with native-born parents.

Unlike the United States, western European nations do not see themselves as immigration countries. Even though the opening chapter of this volume shows that they all have long histories of immigration, chapter 2 shows that they tend to ignore that history. It is far easier for newcomers to feel American in the United States, or at least to become New Yorkers or Angelinos, than it is for newcomers to become German or French.

Our conclusions may be both surprising and dismaying to those who expect the United States, as the premier nation of immigrants, to have done a uniformly better job of integrating or assimilating disadvantaged second-generation groups. A longer and more intense history of immigration has indeed equipped large American cities with more engines of integration than their European peers. But the larger urban inequalities of the United States give these engines greater heights to climb. Although the U.S. urban settings have much to teach European cities, they also have much to learn. For example, some European countries give schools with high concentrations of immigrants twice as much funding per pupil to compensate for the challenges they face. The local public schools in many immigrant neighborhoods of the United States receive much less funding per pupil than those in more affluent suburban jurisdictions nearby. New York and Los Angeles may provide more paths of upward mobility, but these paths must scale greater heights and they wind through deeper valleys of inequality.

New and Segmented Assimilation and the Context of Integration Revisited

The introduction to this volume sketched out the historical development and contemporary operation of the most important theories of immigrant integration on the two sides of the Atlantic. By comparing similar groups across different national and urban settings, it shows that the local context of reception has just as much influence on the outcomes as the characteristics of the groups being received. Although highly attuned to the context of reception, segmented assimilation theory in the United

States also strongly emphasizes the role of ethnic differences (Portes and Rumbaut 1996, 2001, 2005; Stepick and Stepick 2010). Its three strands of assimilation are closely connected to the trajectories of three large immigrant ethnic groups (Mexicans, Cubans, and Chinese). Although new assimilation theory expects all immigrant ethnic groups ultimately to assimilate, it also expects that immigrant ethnic groups facing blurred rather than bright boundaries will assimilate faster (Alba and Nee 2003). In this sense, both theoretical approaches to assimilation in the United States place a major analytic focus on how different types of groups fit into a given context of reception rather than focusing on the variation in those contexts across places.

This volume has taken a different tack: it looks at how basically similar second-generation groups fit into substantially different contexts of reception. In particular, the huge range of outcomes for the Turkish second generation across European urban settings shows that we must be careful not to put too much emphasis on the intrinsic characteristics of ethnic groups and should pay more attention to how the institutional contours of school systems, labor markets, and welfare systems shape prospects for all disadvantaged immigrant ethnic groups. The German and Austrian debates about integration almost take it for granted that Turks tend to self-segregate, but comparable second-generation Turks in Sweden are more socially mobile and more likely to mix with people from other ethnic groups. The strong social cohesion of Stockholm's Turkish communities does not result in social isolation. It is hard to reach any conclusion except that the isolation of Turks in Germany is mainly a product of the organization of German society, not a characteristic of the Turkish community.

The transatlantic comparison also helps us see more clearly just what is distinctive about American contexts for integration or assimilation and why. The United States seems to have far more variation in school quality than European systems, the "black schools" of Europe notwithstanding. The children of immigrants who go to the worst schools in the most poverty stricken and violent neighborhoods in New York or Los Angeles face challenges at least as large as those in the most difficult European cases, and perhaps even larger. However, the comprehensive and relatively less tracked and open nature of the New York and Los Angeles school systems, combined with honors and AP classes, provides many opportunities for gifted children of immigrants to go far, even when the parents do not have great financial resources.

Put differently, the U.S. system for schooling the children of immigrants for entry into the labor market is basically one of swim or sink.

The new assimilation theory emphasizes the positive outcomes displayed by those whom various mechanisms teach to swim, whereas segmented assimilation theory highlights how the huge inequalities of life in urban America thwart many children of immigrants and cause them to tread water, if not sink. The transatlantic comparison teaches us that both may be characteristic of the American system of assimilating children in poor, minority communities, though we also conclude that the children of immigrants generally fare better than their native minority peers and their parents.

Segmented assimilation theory also posits that immigrant social cohesion, ethnic retention, and resistance to Americanization can have a positive impact on immigrant group trajectories. The new assimilation theory takes a contrary view. The European results do not fit neatly into either of the two frameworks. Segmented assimilation theory would suggest that the strong social cohesion and resistance to Europeanization in the Turkish community would have beneficial results, but second-generation outcomes are the poorest in those places, particularly Germany and Austria, where these traits are most pronounced. But where second-generation Turks do relatively better, they also do not marry outside their ethnic group or lose their home language or feel less Turkish. Although it may be reasonable to expect that the descendants of immigrants will become culturally similar to the mainstream majority in ethnically pluralistic countries like the United States or Canada, it will probably take a lot more time, or may even be impossible, for this to occur in national settings that stress ethnic homogeneity and are in denial about immigration. Indeed, in this context, the strong ethnic solidarity of the Turkish second generation may protect individual well-being against an increasingly hostile environment, regardless of its relation to economic mobility.

This transatlantic comparison has thus made us more aware of how the historic and contextual differences between the United States and western Europe and the variations among their leading cities both shape immigrant group trajectories. It also highlights how the distinctive features of each side of the Atlantic have both positive and negative influences. This drastically complicates the simplistic notion that the United States, with its long history of immigration, more open institutional arrangements, and birthright citizenship will always yield better outcomes than the more closed, regulated, and structured European urban settings. At the same time, it also sets the stage for new thinking about how each can learn from the strengths of the other.

NOTES

1. The share of college graduates in Paris may be high because it includes more respondents who are still studying and may not finish degrees. The figure also includes a few who are studying for professions that can be accessed with an associate's degree in other countries. Even if we restrict our French sample to the top end of the age distribution, however, Paris still ranks highly.
2. We exclude respondents from this marginal category if they have higher educations.

References

Abadan-Unat, Nermin. 2011. *Turks in Europe: From Guest Worker to Transnational Citizen.* New York: Berghahn Books.

Acevit, Ayǒegül, and Birand Bingöl, eds. 2005. *Was Lebst Du? Jung, Deutsch, Türkisch—Geschichten aus Almanya.* Munich: Knaur.

Achermann, Alberto, Christin Achermann, Gianni D'Amato, Martina Kamm, and Barbara Von Rütte. 2010. *Country Report: Switzerland.* San Domenico Di Fiesole, Italy: EUDO Citizenship Observatory, Florence European University Institute and Robert Schuman Centre for Advanced Studies.

Acuña, Rodolfo F. 1996. *Anything but Mexican.* New York: Verso.

Alba, Richard. 2004. *Language Assimilation Today: Bilingualism Persists More Than in the Past, But English Still Dominates.* Albany: Lewis Mumford Center.

———. 2005. "Bright vs. Blurred Boundaries: Second Generation Assimilation and Exclusion in France, Germany, and the United States." *Ethnic and Racial Studies* 28(1): 20–49.

———. 2009. *Blurring the Color Line: The New Chance for a More Integrated America.* Cambridge, Mass.: Harvard University Press.

Alba, Richard, and Nancy Denton. 2004. "Old and New Landscapes of Diversity: The Residential Patterns of Immigrant Minorities." In *Not Just Black and White: Historical and Contemporary Perspectives on Immigration, Race, and Ethnicity in the United States,* edited by Nancy Foner and George Fredrickson. New York: Russell Sage Foundation.

Alba, Richard, Nancy Foner, Philip Kasinitz, Peter Kivisto, John Mollenkopf, Ruben Rumbaut, and Mary Waters. 2010. "Review Symposium: Generational Succession in the Big Apple." *Ethnic and Racial Studies* 33(2): 336–57.

Alba, Richard, Philip Kasinitz, and Mary Waters. 2011. "The Kids Are (Mostly) Alright: Second Generation Assimilation." *Social Forces* 89(3): 763–73.

Alba, Richard, and John Logan. 1993. "Minority Proximity to Whites in Suburbs: An Individual-Level Analysis of Segregation." *American Journal of Sociology* 98(6): 1388–1427.

Alba, Richard, and Victor Nee. 2003. *Remaking the American Mainstream: Assimilation and Contemporary Immigration.* Cambridge, Mass.: Harvard University Press.

Alba, Richard, Albert Raboteau, and Josh DeWind, eds. 2008. *Immigration and Religion in America: Comparative and Historical Perspectives.* New York: New York University Press.

Aleinikoff, Thomas Alexander, and Douglas Klusmeyer. 2000. *From Migrants to Citizens: Membership in a Changing World.* Washington, D.C.: Carnegie Endowment for International Peace.

Alesina, Alberto, and Edward L. Glaeser. 2004. *Fighting Poverty in the U.S. and in Europe: A World of Difference.* Oxford: Oxford University Press.

Anderson, Elijah. 1990. *Streetwise: Race, Class, and Change in an Urban Community.* Chicago: University of Chicago Press.

————. 1999. *Code of the Street: Decency, Violence, and the Moral Life of the Inner City.* New York: W.W. Norton.

————. 2008. *Against the Wall: Poor, Young, Black, and Male.* Philadelphia: University of Pennsylvania Press.

Anderson, Elijah, and Douglas S. Massey, eds. 2001. *Problem of the Century: Racial Stratification in the United States.* New York: Russell Sage Foundation.

Andersson, Gunnar, and Kirk Scott. 2005. "Labour-Market Status and First-Time Parenthood: The Experience of Immigrant Women in Sweden, 1981–97." *Population Studies* 59(1): 21–38.

Arin, Cihan. 1991. "The Housing Market and Housing Policies for the Migrant Labor Population in West Berlin." In *Urban Housing Segregation of Minorities in Western Europe and the United States*, edited by Elizabeth D. Huttman, Wim Blauw, and Juliet Saltman. Durham, N.C.: Duke University Press.

Attewell, Paul, Philip Kasinitz, and Kathleen Dunn. 2010. "Black Canadians and Black Americans: Racial Income Inequality in Comparative Perspective." *Ethnic and Racial Studies* 33(3): 473–95.

Bade, Klaus J. 1983. *Vom Auswanderungsland zum Einwanderungsland? Deutschland 1880 bis 1980.* Berlin: Colloquium.

Bade, Klaus, Pieter Emmer, Leo Lucassen, and Jochen Oltmer, eds. 2007. *Enzyklopädie Migration in Europa vom 17. Jahrhundert bis zur Gegenwart.* Munich: Wilhelm Fink Verlag/Ferdinand-Schöningh-Verlag.

————. 2011. *Encyclopedia of Migration and Minorities in Europe.* New York: Cambridge University Press.

Bade, Klaus J., and Jochen Oltmer, eds. 1999. *Aussiedler: Deutsche Einwanderer aus Osteuropa.* Osnabrück, Germany: Rasch.

Bail, Christopher A. 2008. "The Configuration of Symbolic Boundaries Against Immigrants in Europe." *American Sociological Review* 73(1): 37–59.

Balibar, Etiénne, and Immanuel Wallerstein. 1991. *Race, Nation, Class: Ambiguous Identities.* London: Verso.

Bambra, Clare. 2007. "Defamilisation and Welfare State Regimes: A Cluster Analysis." *Journal of Social Welfare* 16(4): 326–38.

Barrett, James, and David Roediger. 1997. "In Between Peoples: Race, Nationality, and the New Immigrant Working Class." *Journal of American Ethnic History* 16(1): 3–44.

Barth, Fredrik. 1969. "Introduction." In *Ethnic Groups and Boundaries: The Social Organization of Culture Difference*, edited by Fredrik Barth. Oslo: Universitetsforlaget.

Basch, Linda, Nina Glick Schiller, and Cristina Szanton Blanc. 1994. *Nations Unbound: Transnational Projects, Postcolonial Predicaments, and Deterritorialized Nation-States*. Amsterdam: Gordon and Breach.

Bashi-Bobb, Vilna, and Averil Clarke. 2001. "Experiencing Success: Structuring the Perception of Opportunities for West Indians." In *Islands in the City: West Indian Migration to New York*, edited by Nancy Foner. Berkeley: University of California Press.

Bauböck, Rainer, ed. 2006. *Migration and Citizenship: Legal Status, Rights and Political Participation*. IMISCOE Series. Amsterdam: Amsterdam University Press.

Bean, Frank D., Mark A. Leach, Susan K. Brown, James Bachmeier, and John Hipp. 2010. "Axes of Early Political Incorporation: Parental Legalization and Naturalization Pathways and Their Influence on Children's Educational Attainment." Center for Research on Immigration, Population and Public Policy working paper. Irvine: University of California.

Bean, Frank D., and Gillian Stevens. 2003. *America's Newcomers and the Dynamics of Diversity*. New York: Russell Sage Foundation.

Bean, Frank D., Gillian Stevens, and Jennifer Van Hook. 2003. "Immigrant Welfare Receipt: Implications for Policy." In *America's Newcomers and the Dynamics of Diversity*, edited by Frank D. Bean and Gillian Stevens. New York: Russell Sage Foundation.

Behtoui, Alireza. 2008. "Informal Recruitment Methods and Disadvantages of Immigrants in the Swedish Labour Market." *Journal of Ethnic and Migration Studies* 34(3): 411–30.

Beriss, David. 2004. *Black Skins, French Voices: Caribbean Ethnicity and Activism in Urban France*. Boulder, Colo.: Westview Press.

Berry, John W. 1980. "Acculturation as Varieties of Adaptation." In *Acculturation: Theory, Models and Some New Findings*, edited by Amado M. Padilla. Boulder, Colo.: Westview Press.

———. 1997. "Immigration, Acculturation, and Adaptation." *Applied Psychology* 46: 5–68.

Berry, John W., Jean S. Phinney, David L. Sam, and Paul Vedder, eds. 2006. *Immigrant Youth in Cultural Transition: Acculturation, Identity, and Adaptation Across National Contexts*. London: Lawrence Erlbaum Associates.

Bevelander, Pieter. 1999. "The Employment Integration of Immigrants in Sweden." *Journal of Ethnic and Migration Studies* 25(3): 445–68.

Bevelander, Pieter, and Don J. DeVoretz. 2008. *The Economics of Citizenship*. Malmö, Sweden: Malmö Institute for Studies of Migration, Diversity and Welfare.

Bloemraad, Irene. 2006. *Becoming a Citizen: Incorporating Immigrants and Refugees in the United States and Canada*. Berkeley: University of California Press.

———. 2007. "Unity in Diversity? Bridging Models of Multiculturalism and Immigrant Integration." *Dubois Review: Social Science Research on Race* 4(2): 317–36.

Bommes, Michael. 2003. "Der Mythos des Transnationalen Raumes. Oder: Worin Besteht die Herausforderung des Transnationalismus für die Migrationsforschung?" In *Migration im Spannungsfeld von Globalisierung und Nationalstaat*, edited by Dietrich Traenhardt and Uwe Hunger. Wiesbaden: Westdeutscher Verlag.

Borjas, George J. 1999. *Heaven's Door.* Princeton, N.J.: Princeton University Press.

Borneman, John. 1992. *Belonging in the Two Berlins: Kin, State, Nation.* Cambridge: Cambridge University Press.

Borrel, Catherine, and Bertrand Lhommeau. 2010. "Être né en France d'un parent immigré." *INSEE Première* 1287(March).

Branger, Katja. 2009. "Modèles d'activité dans les couples, partage des tâches et garde des enfants: Quelques éléments de la conciliation entre vie familiale et vie professionnelle: La Suisse en comparaison internationale." *Actualités OFS: Situation économique et sociale de la population.* Bern: Bundesamt für Statistik.

Bratsberg, Bernt, James F. Ragan, and Zafar Mueen Nasir. 2002. "The Effect of Naturalization on Wage Growth: A Panel Study of Young Male Immigrants." *Journal of Labor Economics* 20(3): 568–97.

Breton, Raymond, Wsevolod W. Isajiw, Warren E. Kalbach, and Jeffrey G. Reitz, eds. 1990. "Introduction" and "Conclusion." In *Ethnic Identity and Equality: Varieties of Experience in a Canadian City.* Toronto: University of Toronto Press.

Brown, Susan K. 2007. "Delayed Spatial Assimilation: Multi-Generational Incorporation of the Mexican-Origin Population in Los Angeles." *City & Community* 6(1): 193–209.

Brubaker, Rogers, ed. 1989. *Immigration and the Politics of Citizenship in Europe and North America.* Lanham, Md.: The German Marshall Fund of the United States and the University Press of America.

———. 1992. *Citizenship and Nationhood in France and Germany.* Cambridge, Mass.: Harvard University Press.

Burri Sharani, Barbara, Denise Efionayi-Mäder, Stephan Hammer, Marco Pecoraro, Bernhard Soland, Astrit Tsaka, and Chantal Wyssmüller. 2010. *Die Kosovarische Bevölkerung in Der Schweiz.* Bern: Bundesamt für Migration.

Butterfield, Sherri-Ann. 2004. " 'We're Just Black': The Racial and Ethnic Identities of Second Generation West Indians in New York." In *Becoming New Yorkers*, edited by Philip Kasinitz, John Mollenkopf, and Mary C. Waters. New York: Russell Sage Foundation.

Çağlar, Ayőe. 1997. "Hyphenated Identities and the Limits of 'Culture.'" In *The Politics of Multiculturalism in the New Europe*, edited by Tariq Modood and Pnina Werbner. London: Zed Books.

Callan, Patrick M., and Joni E. Finney. 2003. *Multiple Pathways and State Policy: Toward Education and Training Beyond High School.* Boston: Jobs for the Future.

Castles, Stephen, and Mark J. Miller. 1993. *The Age of Migration: International Population Movements in the Modern World.* Basingstoke, UK: Macmillan.

Chai Kim, Karen. 2004. "Chinatown or Uptown? Second-Generation Chinese American Protestants in New York City." In *Becoming New Yorkers: Ethnographies of the New Second Generation,* edited by Philip Kasinitz, John H. Mollenkopf, and Mary C. Waters. New York: Russell Sage Foundation.

Chávez, Leo R. 1991. "Outside the Imagined Community: Undocumented Settlers and Experiences of Incorporation." *American Ethnologist* 18(2): 257–78.

———. 2006. "Culture Change and Cultural Reproduction: Lessons from Research on Transnational Migration." In *Globalization and Change in Fifteen Cultures: Born in One World and Living in Another,* edited by J. Stockard and George Spindler. Belmont, Calif.: Thomson-Wadsworth.

———. 2008. *The Latino Threat: Constructing Immigrants, Citizens and the Nation.* Palo Alto, Calif.: Stanford University Press.

Chiswick, Barry R. 1978. "The Effects of Americanization on the Earnings of Foreign-Born Men." *Journal of Political Economy* 86(5): 897–921.

Çil, Nevim. 2010. "Eine allzu deutsche Geschichte? Perspektiven türkischstämmiger Jugendlicher auf Mauerfall und Wiedervereinigung." *Nah & Fern* 44(May): 17–24.

Çinar, Dilek. 2010. *Country Report: Austria.* San Domenico Di Fiesole: EUDO Citizenship Observatory, Florence European University Institute and Robert Schuman Centre for Advanced Studies.

Coleman, James S. 1988. "Social Capital in the Creation of Human Capital." *American Journal of Sociology* 94(suppl): S95–S120.

Crowder, Kyle D. 1999. "Residential Segregation of West Indians in the New York/New Jersey Metropolitan Area: The Roles of Race and Ethnicity." *International Migration Review* 33(1): 79–113.

Crowder, Kyle, and Scott J. South. 2008. "Spatial Dynamics of White Flight: The Effects of Local and Extralocal Racial Conditions on Neighborhood Out-Migration." *American Sociological Review* 73(5): 792–812.

Crowder, Kyle, Scott J. South, and Erick Chavez. 2006. "Wealth, Race, and Inter-Neighborhood Migration." *American Sociological Review* 71(1): 72–94.

Crul, Maurice. 1994. "Springen over je eigen schaduw: De onderwijsprestaties van Marokkanen en Turken van de tweede generatie." *Migrantenstudies* 10(3): 168–86.

———. 2000a. *De sleutel tot succes: Over hulp, keuzes en kansen in de schoolloopbanen van Turkse en Marokkaanse jongeren van de tweede generatie.* Amsterdam: Het Spinhuis.

———. 2000b. "Breaking the Chain of Disadvantage: Social Mobility of Second Generation Moroccans and Turks in the Netherlands." In *Immigrants, Schooling and Social Mobility. Does Culture Make a Difference?* edited by Hans Vermeulen and Joel Perlmann. London: Macmillan.

Crul, Maurice, and Jeroen Doomernik. 2003. "The Second Generation in the Netherlands: Divergent Trends Between and Polarization Within the Two Groups." *International Migration Review* 37(4): 1039–64.

Crul, Maurice, and Liesbeth Heering. 2008. *The Position of the Turkish and Moroccan Second Generation in Amsterdam and Rotterdam.* Amsterdam: Amsterdam University Press.

Crul, Maurice, and Jennifer Holdaway. 2009. "Children of Immigrants in Schools in New York and Amsterdam: The Factors Shaping Attainment." *Teachers College Record* 111(6): 1476–507.

Crul, Maurice, and Jens Schneider. 2009. "Children of Turkish Immigrants in Germany and the Netherlands: The Impact of Differences in Vocational and Academic Tracking Systems." *Teachers College Record* 111(6): 1508–27.

———. 2010. "Comparative Integration Context Theory: Participation and Belonging in New Diverse European Cities." *Ethnic and Racial Studies* 33(7): 1249–68.

Crul, Maurice, Jens Schneider, and Frans Lelie, eds. 2012. *The European Second Generation Compared: Does the Integration Context Matter?* Chicago and Amsterdam: University of Chicago Press/Amsterdam University Press.

Crul, Maurice, and Hans Vermeulen, eds. 2003a. "The Future of the Second Generation: The Integration of Migrant Youth in Six European Countries." *International Migration Review* 37(4): 962–1144.

———. 2003b. "The Second Generation in Europe." *International Migration Review* 37(4): 965–86.

———. 2006. "Immigration, Education, and the Turkish Second Generation in Five European Nations: A Comparative Study." In *Immigration and the Transformation of Europe*, edited by Craig A. Parsons and Timothy M. Smeeding. Cambridge: Cambridge University Press.

Daniel, Cletus E. 1981. *Bitter Harvest: A History of California Farmworkers, 1870–1941*. Ithaca, N.Y.: Cornell University Press.

DeSipio, Louis. 1987. "Social Science Literature and the Naturalization Process." *International Migration Review* 21(2): 390–405.

———. 2001. "Building America, One Person at a Time: Naturalization and Political Behavior of the Naturalized in Contemporary U.S. Politics." In *E Pluribus Unum? Immigrant, Civic Life and Political Incorporation*, edited by John Mollenkopf and Gary Gerstle. New York: Russell Sage Foundation.

DeSipio, Louis, and Carole Jean Uhlaner. 2007. "Immigrant and Native: Mexican American 2004 Presidential Vote Choice Across Immigrant Generations." *American Politics Research* 35(2): 176–201.

Devereux, George. 1978. *Ethnopsychoanalysis: Psychoanalysis and Anthropology as Complementary Frames of Reference*. Berkeley: University of California Press.

DeVoretz, Don J. 2008. "The Economics of Citizenship: A Common Intellectual Ground for Social Scientists?" *Journal of Ethnic and Migration Studies* 34(4): 679–93.

Dietz, Barbara. 2006. "Aussiedler in Germany: From Smooth Adaption to Tough Integration." In *Paths of Integration: Migrants in Western Europe (1880–2004)*, edited by Leo Lucassen, David Feldman, and Jochen Oltmer. Amsterdam: Amsterdam University Press.

Dohan, Daniel. 2003. *The Price of Poverty: Money, Work, and Culture in the Mexican American Barrio*. Berkeley: University of California Press.

Dolton, Peter, Rita Asplund, and Erling Barth. 2009. *Education and Inequality Across Europe.* Northampton, Mass.: Edward Elgar.

Doomernik, Jeroen 1998. *The Effectiveness of Integration Policies Towards Immigrants and Their Descendants in France, Germany and the Netherlands.* Geneva: International Labour Organisation.

Drever, Anita I. 2004. "Separate Spaces, Separate Outcomes? Neighbourhood Impacts on Minorities in Germany." *Urban Studies* 41(8): 1423–39.

Drever, Anita I., and W. A. V. Clark. 2002. "Gaining Access to Housing in Germany: The Foreign-Minority Experience." *Urban Studies* 39(13): 2439–53.

Durand, Jorge, Nolan J. Malone, and Douglas S. Massey. 2003. *Beyond Smoke and Mirrors: Mexican Immigration in an Era of Economic Integration.* New York: Russell Sage Foundation.

Eldering, Lotty, and Jo Kloprogge. 1989. *Different Cultures Same School: Ethnic Minority Children in Europe.* Amsterdam: Swets and Zeitl.

Engelke, Jane, and Gertrude Astrom. 1992. "Equality, Difference, and State Welfare: Labor Market and Family Policies in Sweden." *Feminist Studies* 18(1): 59–87.

Erikson, Robert, and John H. Goldthorpe. 1992. *The Constant Flux: A Study of Class Mobility in Industrial Societies.* Oxford: Oxford University Press.

Ersanilli, Evelyn. 2010. "Comparing Integration: Host Culture Adoption and Ethnic Retention Among Turkish Immigrants and Their Descendants in France, Germany, and the Netherlands." Ph.D. diss. VU University, Amsterdam.

Ersanilli, Evelyn, and Ruud Koopmans. 2009. *Ethnic Retention and Host Culture Adoption Among Turking Immigrants in Germany, France, and the Netherlands: A Controlled Comparison.* Berlin: WZB.

Esping-Andersen, Gøsta. 1990. *The Three Worlds of Welfare Capitalism.* Cambridge: Polity Press.

Estevez-Abe, Margarita, Torben Iversen, and David Soskice. 2001. "Social Protection and the Formation of Skill: A Reinterpretation of the Welfare State." In *Varieties of Capitalism: The Institutional Foundations of Comparative Advantage,* edited by P. A. Hall and D. W. Soskice. New York: Oxford University Press.

Eurostat. 2010. *Key Indicators for Core Cities.* Available at: http://appsso.eurostat.ec. europa.eu/nui/submitviewtableaction.do?dvsc=5.http://epp.eurostat.ec.europa. eu/statistics_explained/index.php/european_cities (accessed March 15, 2011).

Faist, Thomas. 1995. *Social Citizenship for Whom? Young Turks in Germany and Mexican-Americans in the United States.* Aldershot, UK: Avebury.

———. 2007. *Dual Citizenship in Europe: From Nationhood to Societal Integration.* Burlington, Vt.: Ashgate.

Farley, Reynolds, and Richard Alba. 2002. "The New Second Generation in the United States." *International Migration Review* 36(3): 669–701.

Fase, Willem. 1994. *Ethnic Divisions in Western European Education.* New York: Waxmann.

Favell, Adrian. 1998. *Philosophies of Integration: Immigration and the Idea of Citizenship in France and Britain.* Basingstoke, UK: Palgrave Macmillan.

————. 2005. "Integration Nations: The Nation-State and Research on Immigrants in Western Europe." In *International Migration Research: Constructions, Omissions and the Promises of Interdisciplinarity*, edited by Bommes Michael and Ewa Morawska. Aldershot, UK: Ashgate.

Fibbi, Rosita. 2011. "Naturalisation." In *Les marges de manœuvre au sein du fédéralisme: la politique de migration dans les cantons*, edited by Nicole Wichmann, Michael Hermann, Gianni D'Amato, Denise Efionayi-Mäder, Rosita Fibbi, Joanna Menet, and Didier Ruedins. Berne, Switzerland: Commission fédérale pour les questions de migration.

Fibbi, Rosita, Mathias Lerch, and Philippe Wanner. 2007. "Naturalisation and Socio-Economic Characteristics of Youth of Immigrant Descent in Switzerland." *Journal of Ethnic and Migration Studies* 33(7): 1121–44.

Foner, Nancy. 2000. *From Ellis Island to JFK: New York's Two Great Waves of Immigration*. New Haven, Conn.: Yale University Press.

————. 2001. *Islands in the City: West Indian Migration to New York*. Berkeley: University of California Press.

————. 2005. *In a New Land: A Comparative View of Immigration*. New York: New York University Press.

————. 2010. "Black Identities and the Second Generation: Afro-Caribbeans in Britain and the United States." In *The Next Generation: Immigrant Youth in a Comparative Perspective*, edited by Richard Alba and Mary Waters. New York: New York University Press.

Foner, Nancy, and Richard Alba. 2006. "The Second Generation from the Last Great Wave of Immigration: Setting the Record Straight." *Migration Information Source* (October). Available at: http://www.migrationinformation.org/Feature/display.cfm?ID=439 (accessed January 30, 2012).

————. 2008. "Immigrant Religion in the U.S. and Western Europe: Bridge or Barrier to Inclusion?" *International Migration Review* 42(2): 360–92.

————. 2010. "Immigration and Legacies of the Past: The Impact of Slavery and the Holocaust on Contemporary Immigrants in the United States and Western Europe." *Comparative Studies in Society and History* 52(4): 798–819.

Foner, Nancy, and George Fredrickson, eds. 2004. *Not Just Black and White: Historical and Contemporary Perspectives on Immigration, Race, and Ethnicity in the United States*. New York: Russell Sage Foundation.

Fortuny, Carina, Randy Capps, and Jeffrey Passel. 2007. *The Characteristics of Unauthorized Immigrants in California, Los Angeles County, and the United States*. Washington, D.C.: The Urban Institute.

Fougère, Denis, and Mirna Safi. 2008. "Naturalization and Employment of Immigrants in France. (1968–1999)." *CEPR* discussion paper 7092. London: Centre for Economic Policy Research.

Fraser, Nancy, and Axel Honneth. 2003. *Redistribution or Recognition? A Political-Philosophical Exchange*. London. New York: Verso.

Freeman, Gary. 1986. "Migration and the Political Economy of the Welfare State." In *From Foreign Workers to Settlers? Transnational Migration and the Emergence of New Minorities,* edited by Martin O. Heiseler and Barbara Schmitter Heisler. Beverly Hills, Calif.: Sage Publications.

Friedrichs, Jürgen, and Hannes Alpheis. 1991. "Housing Segregation of Immigrants in West Germany." In *Urban Housing Segregation of Minorities in Western Europe and the United States,* edited by Elizabeth D. Huttman, Wim Blauw, and Juliet Saltman. Durham, N.C.: Duke University Press.

Furstenberg, Frank F. 2008. "The Intersections of Social Class and the Transition to Adulthood." *New Directions for Child & Adolescent Development* 2008(119): 1–10.

Furstenberg, Frank F., and Mary Elizabeth Hughes. 1997. "The Influence of Neighborhoods on Children's Development: A Theoretical Perspective and a Research Agenda." In *Indicators of Children's Well-Being,* edited by Robert M. Hauser, Brett V. Brown, and William R. Prosser. New York: Russell Sage Foundation.

Gans, Herbert 1992. "Second-Generation Decline: Scenarios for the Economic and Ethnic Futures of the Post-1965 American Immigrants." *Ethnic and Racial Studies* 15(2): 173–92.

Ganzeboom, Harry B. G., and Donald J. Treiman. 1996. "Internationally Comparable Measures of Occupational Status for the 1988 International Standard Classification of Occupations." *Social Science Research* 25(1996): 201–39.

GeoLytics. 2003. CensusCD Neighborhood Change Database, 1970–2000 Tract Data. New Brunswick, N.J.: GeoLytics.

Gerstle, Gary. 2001. *American Crucible: Race and Nation in the Twentieth Century.* Princeton, N.J.: Princeton University Press.

Gerstle, Gary, and John Mollenkopf, eds. 2001. *E Pluribus Unum? Contemporary and Historical Perspectives on Immigrant Political Incorporation.* New York: Russell Sage Foundation.

Girard, Alain, and Jean Stoetzel. 1953. *Francais et immigrés: L'attitude francaise, l'adaption des italiens et des polonais.* Paris: Cahier de l'INED no. 19: Presses Universitaires de France.

Gordon, Milton. 1964. *Assimilation in American Life: The Role of Race, Religion, and National Origin.* New York: Oxford University Press.

Gornick, Janet C., Marcia K. Meyers, and Katherin E. Ross. 1998. "Public Policies and the Employment of Mothers: A Cross-National Study." *Social Science Quarterly* 79(1): 35–54.

Granovetter, Mark S. 1973. "The Strength of Weak Ties." *American Journal of Sociology* 78(6): 1360–80.

Green, Nancy L. 1986. *The Pletzl of Paris: Jewish Immigrant Workers in the "Belle Époque."* New York: Holmes and Meier.

———. 2002. "Religion et Ethnicité. De la comparaison spatiale et temporelle." *Annales, Histoire, Sciences Sociales* 57(1): 127–44.

Greve, Martin, and Kalbiye Nur Orhan. 2008. *Berlin Deutsch-Türkisch: Einblicke in Die Neue Vielfalt.* Berlin: Der Beauftragte des Senats für Integration und Migration.

Guglielmo, Thomas. 2003. *White on Arrival: Race, Color, and Power in Chicago, 1890–1945*. New York: Oxford University Press.

Haab, Katharina, Claudio Bolzman, Andrea Kugler, and Ozcan Yilmaz, eds. 2010. *Diaspora Und Migrantengemeinschaften Aus Der Türkei in Der Schweiz*. Bern: Bundesamt für Migration.

Haller, William, Alejandro Portes, and Scott Lynch. 2011. "Dreams Fulfilled, Dreams Shattered: The Determinants of Segmented Assimilation in the Second Generation." *Social Forces* 89(3): 733–62.

Hamilton, Kimberly, and Patrick Simon. 2004. "The Challenge of French Diversity." Washington, D.C.: Migration Information Source. Available at: http://www.migrationinformation.org/Profiles/display.cfm?id=266 (accessed February 16, 2012).

Hammar, Tomas. 2004. "Research and Politics in Swedish Immigration Management, 1965–1984." In *Towards A Multilateral Migration Regime. Special Anniversary Edition dedicated to Jonas Widgren*, edited by Michael Jandl and Irene Stacher. Vienna, Austria: International Centre for Migration Policy Development.

Hansen, R. 2000. *Citizenship and Immigration in Post-War Britain: The Institutional Origins of a Multicultural Nation*. Oxford: Oxford University Press.

Harding, David J. 2010. *Living the Drama: Community, Conflict, and Culture Among Inner-City Boys*. Chicago: University of Chicago Press.

Harding, David J., Lisa Gennetian, Christopher Winship, Lisa Sanbonmatsu, and Jeffrey Kling. 2010. "Unpacking Neighborhood Influences on Education Outcomes: Setting the Stage for Future Research." In *Social Inequality and Educational Disadvantage*, edited by Greg Duncan and Richard Murnane. New York: Russell Sage Foundation.

Häussermann, Hartmut. 2007. "Behindert Ethnische Segregation die Integration?" *Archiv für Wissenschaft und Praxis der sozialen Arbeit* 38(3): 46–56.

Häussermann, Hartmut, and Andreas Kapphan. 2005. "Berlin: From Divided to Fragmented City." In *Transformation of Cities in Central and Eastern Europe: Towards Globalization*, edited by F. E. Ian Hamilton, Kaliopa Dimitrovska Andrews, and Natasa Pichler-Milanovic. Tokyo: United Nations University Press.

Heath, Anthony, and Sin Yi Cheung, eds. 2007. *Unequal Chances: Ethnic Minorities in Western Labor Markets*. Oxford: Oxford University Press.

Heath, Anthony F., Catherine Rothon, and Elina Kilpi. 2008. "The Second Generation in Western Europe: Education, Unemployment, and Occupational Attainment." *Annual Review of Sociology* 34(2008): 211–35.

Heckmann, Friedrich, H. Lederer, and Susanne Worbs. 2001. "Effectiveness of National Integration Strategies Towards Second Generation Migrant Youth in a Comparative European Perspective." *Final Report to the European Commission*. Bamberg, Germany: European Forum for Migration Studies.

Heckmann, Friedrich, and Dominique Schnapper, eds. 2003. *The Integration of Immigrants in European Societies. National Differences and Trends of Convergence*. Stuttgart: Lucius and Lucius.

Herzfeld, Michael. 1997. *Cultural Intimacy in the Nation State*. London: Routledge.

Herzog-Punzenberger, Barbara. 2003. "Ethnic Segmentation in School and Labor: 40-Year Legacy of Austrian Guest Worker Policy." *International Migration Review* 37(4): 1120–44.

———. 2007. "Gibt Es Einen Staatsbürgerschafts Bonus? Unterschiede in der Bildung und auf dem Arbeitsmarkt Anhand der Österreichischen Volkszählungsdaten 2001—Ergebnisse für die zweite Generation der Anwerbegruppen." In *Österreichischer Migrations- Und Integrationsbericht, 2001–2006*, edited by Heinz Fassmann. Vienna, Austria: Verlag Drava.

Hipp, John R. 2009. "Specifying the Determinants of Neighborhood Satisfaction: A Robust Assessment in 24 Metropolitan Areas." *Social Forces* 88(1): 395–424.

———. 2010. "Resident Perceptions of Crime and Disorder: How Much Is 'Bias', and How Much Is Social Environment Differences?" *Criminology* 48(2): 475–508.

Hochschild, Jennifer, and John Mollenkopf, eds. 2009. *Bringing Outsiders in: Transatlantic Perspectives on Immigrant Political Incorporation*. Ithaca, N.Y.: Cornell University Press.

Holmes, C., ed. 1978. *Immigrants and Minorities in British Society*. London: George Allen & Unwin.

Holzner, Lutz. 1982. "The Myth of Turkish Ghettos: A Geographic Case Study of West German Responses Towards a Foreign Minority." *Journal of Ethnic Studies* 9(4): 65–85.

Honohan, Iseult. 2010. *The Theory and Politics of Ius Soli*. San Domenico di Fiesole: EUDO Citizenship Observatory, Florence European University Institute and Robert Schuman Centre for Advanced Studies.

Hout, Michael. 2004. "Getting the Most Out of the GSS Income Measures." *GSS Methodological Report 101*. Chicago: National Opinion Research Center. Available at: http://publicdata.norc.org:41000/gss/DOCUMENTS/REPORTS/Methodological_Reports/MR101.pdf (accessed May 12, 2011).

Huddleston, Thomas, and Jan Niessen. 2011. "Migrant Integration Policy Index III," co-edited by Eadaoin Ni Chaoimh and Emilie White. Brussels: British Council and Migration Policy Group. Available at: http://www.mipex.eu (accessed January 15, 2012).

Huntington, Samuel P. 2004. *Who Are We?* New York: Simon & Schuster.

Iceland, John. 2004. "Beyond Black and White: Metropolitan Residential Segregation in Multi-Ethnic America." *Social Science Research* 33(2): 248–71.

———. 2007. "Beyond Segregation: Multiracial and Multiethnic Neighborhoods in the United States." *Social Forces* 85(3): 1444–46.

———. 2009. *Where We Live Now: Immigration and Race in the United States*. Berkeley: University of California Press.

Iceland, John, and Kyle A. Nelson. 2008. "Hispanic Segregation in Metropolitan America: Exploring the Multiple Forms of Spatial Assimilation." *American Sociological Review* 73(5): 761–65.

Ireland, Patrick. 1994. *The Policy Challenge of Ethnic Diversity: Immigrant Politics in France and Switzerland.* Cambridge, Mass.: Harvard University Press.

Jacobson, Matthew Frye. 1998. *Whiteness of a Different Color: European Immigrants and the Alchemy of Race.* Cambridge, Mass.: Harvard University Press.

Jargowsky, Paul. 1997. *Poverty and Place: Ghettos, Barrios and the American City.* New York: Russell Sage Foundation.

———. 2009. "Immigrants and Neighborhoods of Concentrated Poverty: Assimilation or Stagnation." *Journal of Ethnic and Migration Studies* 35(7): 1129–51.

Jonsson, Jan O. 2007. "The Farther They Come, the Harder They Fall? First- and Second Generation Immigrants in the Swedish Labour Market." In *Unequal Chances: Ethnic Minorities in Western Labour Markets,* edited by Anthony Heath, and Sin Yi Cheung. New York: Oxford University Press.

Joppke, Christian. 2007. "Transformation of Immigrant Integration: Civic Integration and Antidiscrimination in the Netherlands, France, and Germany." *World Politics* 59(2): 243–73.

Joppke, Christian, and Ewa Morawska. 2003. *Toward Assimilation and Citizenship: Immigrants in Liberal Nation-States.* New York: Palgrave Macmillan.

Jordan, Jason. 2006. "Mothers, Wives, and Workers: Explaining Gendered Dimensions of the Welfare State." *Comparative Political Studies* 39(9): 1109–32.

Kalter, Frank, and Nadia Granato. 2007. "Educational Hurdles on the Way to Structural Assimilation in Germany." In *Unequal Chances: Ethnic Minorities in Western Labour Markets,* edited by Anthony Heath, and Sin Yi Cheung. New York: Oxford University Press.

Kasinitz, Philip. 2001. "Invisible No More? West Indian Americans in the Social Scientific Imagination." In *Islands in the City: West Indian Migration to New York,* edited by Nancy Foner. Berkeley: University of California Press.

Kasinitz, Philip, Juan Battle, and Ines Miyares. 2001. "Fade to Black? The Children of West Indian Immigrants in Southern Florida." In *Ethnicities,* edited by Rubén Rumbaut and Alejandro Portes. Berkeley: University of California Press.

Kasinitz, Philip, Noriko Matsumoto, and Aviva Zeltzer-Zubida. 2011. " 'I Will *Never* Deliver Chinese Food': The Children of Immigrants in the New York Metropolitan Labor Force." In *The New Second Generation,* edited by Mary C. Waters and Richard Alba. New York: New York University Press.

Kasinitz, Philip, John Mollenkopf, and Mary C. Waters. 2004. *Becoming New Yorkers: Ethnographies of the New Second Generation.* New York: Russell Sage Foundation.

Kasinitz, Philip, John Mollenkopf, Mary C. Waters, and Jennifer Holdaway. 2008. *Inheriting the City: The Children of Immigrants Come of Age.* Cambridge, Mass.: Harvard University Press.

Kasinitz, Philip, and Jan Rosenberg. 1996. "Missing the Connection? Social Isolation and Employment on the Brooklyn Waterfront." *Social Problems* 41(2): 501–19.

Kazepov, Yuri. 2010. "Rescaling Social Policies Toward Multilevel Governance in Europe: Some Reflections on Processes at Stake and Actors Involved." In *Rescaling Social Policies: Toward Multilevel Governance in Europe*, edited by Yuri Kazepov. Farnham, Surrey: Ashgate.

Kemper, Franz-Josef. 1998. "Restructuring of Housing and Ethnic Segregation: Recent Developments in Berlin." *Urban Studies* 35(10): 1765–89.

Kim, Ann H., and Michael J. White. 2010. "Panethnicity, Ethnic Diversity, and Residential Segregation." *American Journal of Sociology* 115(5): 1558–96.

Kloosterman, Robert, and Jan Rath. 2001. "Immigrant Entrepreneurs in Advanced Economies: Mixed Embeddedness Further Explored." *Journal of Ethnic and Migration Studies* 27(2): 189–202.

Kogan, Irena. 2003. "Ex-Yugoslavs in the Austrian and Swedish Labour Markets: The Significance of the Period of Migration and the Effect of Citizenship Acquisition." *Journal of Ethnic and Migration Studies* 29(4): 595–622.

———. 2006. "Labor Markets and Economic Incorporation Among Recent Immigrants in Europe." *Social Forces* 85(2): 697–721.

Kogan, Irena, and Walter Müller, eds. 2003. *School-to-Work Transitions in Europe: Analyses of the EU LFS 2000 Ad Hoc Module*. Mannheim, Ger.: MZES.

Koopmans, Ruud. 2010. "Trade-Offs Between Equality and Difference: Immigrant Integration, Multiculturalism and the Welfare State in Cross-National Perspective." *Journal of Ethnic and Migration Studies* 36(1): 1–26.

Koopmans, Ruud, Paul Statham, Marco Giugni, and Florence Passy. 2005. *Contested Citizenship: Immigration and Cultural Diversity in Europe*. Minneapolis: University of Minnesota Press.

Korpi, Walter. 2000. "Faces of Inequality: Gender, Class and Patterns of Inequalities in Different Types of Welfare States." *Social Politics: International Studies in Gender, State & Society* 7(2): 127–91.

Kraler, Albert. 2006. "The Legal Status of Immigrants and Their Access to Nationality." In *Migration and Citizenship. Legal Status, Rights and Political Participation*, edited by Rainer Bauböck. Amsterdam: Amsterdam University Press.

Krivo, Lauren J., Ruth D. Peterson, and Danielle C. Kuhl. 2009. "Segregation, Racial Structure, and Neighborhood Violent Crime." *American Journal of Sociology* 114(6): 1765–802.

Kroneberg, Clemens. 2008. "Ethnic Communities and School Performance Among the New Second Generation in the United States: Testing the Theory of Segmented Assimilation." *Annals of the American Academy of Political and Social Science* 620(1): 138–60.

Kymlicka, Will. 1996. *Multicultural Citizenship: A Liberal Theory of Minority Rights*. Oxford: Oxford University Press.

Lamont, Michele, and Virag Molnar. 2002. "The Study of Boundaries in the Social Sciences." *Annual Review of Sociology* 28(2002): 167–95.

Le Bras, Hervé. 1998. *Le démon des origines: Démographie et extrême droite*. Latour d'Aigues: Editions de l'Aube.

Lee, Jennifer. 2002. *Civility in the City: Blacks, Jews, and Koreans in Urban America.* Cambridge, Mass.: Harvard University Press.

Lee, Jennifer, and Frank Bean. 2010. *The Diversity Paradox: Immigration and the Color Line in Twenty-First Century America.* New York: Russell Sage Foundation.

Lesthaeghe, Ron. 1996. *Diversiteit in Sociale Verandering—Turkse En Marokkaanse Vrouwen in België.* Brussel: VUB Press.

Levitt, Peggy, and Nina Glick Schiller. 2004. "Conceptualizing Simultaneity: A Transnational Social Field Perspective on Society." *International Migration Review* 38(3): 1002–39.

Levitt, Peggy, and Mary C. Waters, eds. 2006. *The Changing Face of Home: The Transnational Lives of the Second Generation.* New York: Russell Sage Foundation.

Lewis, Jane. 1992. "Gender and the Development of Welfare Regimes." *Journal of European Social Policy* 2(3): 159–73.

———. 2001. "The Decline of the Male Breadwinner Model: Implication for Work and Care." *Social Politics* 8(2): 152–69.

Logan, John R., Richard D. Alba, and Wenquan Zhang. 2002. "Immigrant Enclaves and Ethnic Communities in New York and Los Angeles." *American Sociological Review* 67(2): 299–322.

Logan, John R., Brian J. Stults, and Reynolds Farley. 2004. "Segregation of Minorities in the Metropolis: Two Decades of Change." *Demography* 41(1): 1–22.

Logan, John R., and Charles Zhang. 2010. "Global Neighborhoods: New Pathways to Diversity and Separation." *American Journal of Sociology* 115(4): 1069–109.

Lokrantz Bernitz, Hedvig. 2010. *Country Report: Sweden.* San Domenico Di Fiesole: EUDO Citizenship Observatory, Florence European University Institute and Robert Schuman Centre for Advanced Studies.

Lucassen, Jan, and Leo Lucassen, eds. 1997. *Migration, Migration History, History: Old Paradigms and New Perspectives.* Bern: Peter Lang.

———. 2009. "The Mobility Transition Revisited, 1500–1900: What the Case of Europe Can Offer to Global History." *Journal of Global History* 4(4): 347–77.

———. 2011. *Winnaars en verliezers: Een nuchtere balans van vijf eeuwen immigratie.* Amsterdam: Bert Bakker.

Lucassen, Jan, and Rinus Penninx.1985. *Newcomers: Immigrants and Their Descendants in the Netherlands, 1550–1985.* Amsterdam: Spinhuis.

Lucassen, Leo. 2002. "Old and New Migrants in the Twentieth Century: A European Perspective." *Journal of American Ethnic History* 21(4): 85–101.

———. 2005. *The Immigrant Threat: The Integration of Old and New Migrants in Western Europe Since 1850.* Urbana: University of Illinois Press.

———. 2010. "A Brave New World: The Left, Social Engineering and Eugenics in Twentieth-Century Europe." *International Review of Social History* 55(2): 265–96.

Lucassen, Leo, David Feldman, and Jochen Oltmer, eds. 2006. *Paths of Integration. Migrants in Western Europe (1880–2004).* Amsterdam: Amsterdam University Press.

Lucassen, Leo, and C. Laarman. 2009. "Immigration, Intermarriage and the Changing Face of Europe in the Post War Period." *The History of the Family* 14(1): 52–68.

Mahler, Sarah. 2001. "Transnational Relationships: The Struggle to Communicate Across Borders." *Identities: Global Studies in Culture and Power* 7(4): 583–619.

Mahnig, Hans. 1998. *Integrationspolitik in Grossbritannien, Frankreich, Deutschland Und Den Niederlanden: Ein vergleichende analyse.* Neuchâtel: Swiss Forum for Migration and Population Studies.

Maly, Michael T. 2005. *Beyond Segregation: Multiracial and Multiethnic Neighborhoods in the United States.* Philadelphia: Temple University Press.

Marshall, Gordon. 1998. "Goldthorpe Class Scheme." In *A Dictionary of Sociology,* edited by John Scott and Gordon Marshall. Oxford: Oxford University Press.

Marshall, Thomas H. 1950. *Citizenship and Social Class and Other Essays.* Cambridge: Cambridge University Press.

Martiniello, Marco. 2005. "Political Participation, Mobilisation and Representation of Immigrants and Their Offspring in Europe." *Willy Brandt* working paper 1/05. Malmö: School of International Migration and Ethnic Relations, Malmö University.

Massey, Douglas S. 1986. "The Social Organization of Mexican Migration to the United States." *Annals of the American Academy of Political and Social Science* 487(1): 102–13.

Massey, Douglas S., and Nancy Denton. 1985. "Spatial Assimilation as a Socioeconomic Outcome." *American Sociological Review* 50: 94–106.

———. 1989. "Hypersegregation in U.S. Metropolitan Areas: Black and Hispanic Segregation Along Five Dimensions." *Demography* 26(3): 373–93.

———. 1993. *Segregation and the Making of the Underclass.* Cambridge, Mass.: Harvard University Press.

Massey, Douglas S., and Kristin E. Espinosa. 1997. "What's Driving Mexico–U.S. Migration? A Theoretical, Empirical, and Policy Analysis." *American Journal of Sociology* 102(4): 939–99.

Massey, Douglas, Margarita Mooney, Kimberly Torres, and Camille Charles. 2007. "Black Immigrants and Black Natives Attending Selective Colleges and Universities in the United States." *American Journal of Education* 113: 243–71.

Menjivar, Cecilia. 1997. "Immigrant Kinship Networks: Vietnamese, Salvadoreans and Mexicans in Comparative Perspective." *Journal of Comparative Family Studies* 28(1): 1–24.

Merrien, Xavier, and Giuliano Bonoli. 2000. "Implementing Major Welfare State Reform: A Comparison of France and Switzerland." In *Survival of the European Welfare State,* edited by Stein Kuhnl. London: Routledge.

Moch, Leslie P. 1983. *Paths to the City: Regional Migration in Nineteenth-Century France.* Beverly Hills, Calif.: Sage Publications.

———. 2003. "Networks Among Bretons? The Evidence for Paris, 1875–1925." *Continuity and Change* 18(3): 431–56.

Modood, Tariq, and Pnina Werbner, eds. 1997. *The Politics of Multiculturalism in the New Europe.* London: Zed.

Mollenkopf, John Hull. 2000. "Assimilating Immigrants in Amsterdam: A Perspective from New York." *Netherlands Journal of Social Science* 36(1): 126–45.

Mollenkopf, John H., and Jennifer Hochschild. 2010. "Immigrant Political Incorporation: Comparing Success in the United States and Western Europe." *Ethnic and Racial Studies* 33(1): 19–38.

Mollenkopf, John H., Philip Kasinitz, and Mary C. Waters. 1999. "Immigrant Second Generation in Metropolitan New York" (ISGMNY). Ann Arbor, Mich.: Inter-University Consortium for Political and Social Research. Available at: http://dx.doi.org/10.3886/ICPSR30302.v1 (accessed February 16, 2012).

Monroy, Douglas. 1999. *Rebirth, Mexican Los Angeles from the Great Migration to the Great Depression.* Berkeley: University of California Press.

Morawska, Ewa. 1990. "The Sociology and Historiography of Immigration." In *Immigration Reconsidered. History, Sociology and Politics,* edited by Virginia Yans-Mclaughlin. New York: Oxford University Press.

———. 1997. "Moving Europeans in the Globalizing World: Contemporary Migrations in Historical-Comparative Perspective (1955–1994 v. 1870–1914)." In *Global History and Migrations,* edited by Wang Gungwu. Boulder, Colo.: Westview Press.

———. 2001. "Immigrants, Transnationalism, and Ethnicization: A Comparison of This Great Wave and the Last." In *E Pluribus Unum? Contemporary and Historical Perspectives on Immigrant Political Incorporation,* edited by Gary Gerstle and John Mollenkopf. New York: Russell Sage Foundation.

Mouw, Ted. 2003. "Social Capital and Finding a Job: Do Contacts Matter?" *American Sociological Review* 68(6): 868–98.

Müller, Walter, and Markus Gangl, eds. 2003. *Transitions from Education to Work in Europe: The Integration of Youth into EU Labour Markets.* Oxford: Oxford University Press.

Münz, Rainer, Wolfgang Seifer, and Ralf E. Ulrich. 1997. *Zuwanderung nach Deutschland. Strukturen, Wirkungen, Perspektiven.* Frankfurt-am-Main: Campus Verlag.

Mushaben, Joyce. 2009. "Up the Down Staircase: Redefining Gender Identities Through Migration and Ethnic Employment in Germany." *Journal of Ethnic and Migration Studies* 35(8): 1249–74.

Musterd, Sako, and Mariëlle De Winter. 1998. "Conditions for Spatial Segregation: Some European Perspectives." *International Journal of Urban and Regional Research* 22(4): 665–73.

Myers, Dowell. 2008. *Immigrants and Boomers: Forging a New Contract for the Future of America.* New York: Russell Sage Foundation.

Niessen, Jan, Thomas Huddleston, and Laura Citron, with Andrew Geddes and Dirk Jacobs. 2007. *Migration Policy Index.* Brussels: British Council and Migration Policy Group.

Noiriel, Gerard. 1984. *Longwy: Immigrés et prolétaires, 1880–1980*. Paris: Presses Universitaires de France.

———. 1988. *Le creuset français: Histoire de l'immigration, XIXe–XXe siècles*. Paris: Seuil.

O'Connor, Julia S. 1993. "Gender, Class and Citizenship in the Comparative Analysis of Welfare State Regimes: Theoretical and Methodological Issues" *British Journal of Sociology* 44(3): 501–18.

———. 1996. "From Women in the Welfare State to Gendering Welfare State Regimes." *Current Sociology* 44 (2): 1–130.

Oesch, Daniel. 2008. "Stratifying Welfare States: Class Differences in Pension Coverage in Britain, Germany, Sweden and Switzerland." *Swiss Journal of Sociology* 34(3): 533–54.

Oltmer, Jochen. 2006. "To Live as Germans Among Germans: Immigration and Integration of 'Ethnic Germans' in the German Empire and the Weimar Republic." In *Paths of Integration. Migrants in Western Europe (1880–2004)*, edited by Leo Lucassen, David Feldman, and Jochen Oltmer. Amsterdam: Amsterdam University Press.

Østergaard-Nielsen, Eva. 2009. "The End of Closet Transnationalism? The Role of Homeland Politics in the Political Incorporation of Turks and Kurds in Europe." In *The Future of Immigrant Political Incorporation: A Transatlantic Comparison*, edited by Jennifer Hochschild and John Mollenkopf. Ithaca, N.Y.: Cornell University Press.

Özüekren, Ôule, and Ebru Ergoz-Karahan. 2010. "Housing Experiences of Turkish (Im)Migrants in Berlin and Istanbul: Internal Differentiation and Segregation." *Journal of Ethnic and Migration Studies* 36(2): 355–72.

Padilla, Amado M., and Rosemary Gonzalez. 2001. "Academic Performance of Immigrant and U.S.-Born Mexican Heritage Students: Effects of Schooling in Mexico and Bilingual/English Language Instruction." *American Educational Research Journal* 38(3): 727–42.

Pais, Jeremy, Scott J. South, and Kyle Crowder. 2009. "White Flight Revisited: A Multiethnic Perspective on Neighborhood Out-Migration." *Population Research and Policy Review* 28(3): 321–46.

Parekh, Bhikhu. 2000. *Rethinking Multiculturalism: Cultural Diversity and Political Theory*. Basingstoke, UK: Palgrave.

Penn, Roger, and Paul Lambert. 2009. *Children of International Migrants in Europe: Comparative Perspectives*. New York: Palgrave Macmillan.

Perlmann, Joel. 1988. *Ethnic Differences: Schooling and Social Structure Among the Irish, Italians, Jews, and Blacks in an American City, 1880–1935*. Cambridge: Cambridge University Press.

———. 2005. *Italians Then, Mexicans Now: Immigrant Origins and Second-Generation Progress, 1890–2000*. New York: Russell Sage Foundation.

Perlmann, Joel, and Mary C. Waters. 2007. "Intermarriage and Multiple Identities." In *The New Americans*, edited by Mary C. Waters and Reed Ueda. Cambridge, Mass.: Harvard University Press.

Pettit, Becky, and Jennifer L. Hook. 2005. "The Structure of Women's Employment in Comparative Perspective." *Social Forces* 84(2): 779–801.

———. 2009. *Gendered Tradeoffs: Family, Social Policy, and Economic Inequality in Twenty-One Century.* New York: Russell Sage Foundation.

Phalet, Karen. 2007 "Down and Out: The Children of Migrant Workers in the Belgian Labour Market." In *Unequal Chances: Ethnic Minorities in Western Labour Markets,* edited by Anthony Heath, and Sin Yi Cheung. Proceedings of the British Academy No. 137. New York: Oxford University Press.

Pong, Suet-Ling, and Lingxin Hao. 2007. "Neighborhood and School Factors in the School Performance of Immigrants' Children." *International Migration Review* 41(1): 206–41.

Portes, Alejandro. 2010. *Economic Sociology: A Systematic Inquiry.* Princeton, N.J.: Princeton University Press.

Portes, Alejandro, Rosa Aparicio, William Haller, and E. Vickstrom. 2010. "Moving Ahead in Madrid: Aspirations and Expectations in the Spanish Second Generation." *Center for Migration and Development* working paper 10–2. Princeton, N.J.: Princeton University.

Portes, Alejandro, and John W. Curtis. 1987. "Changing Flags: Naturalization and Its Determinants Among Mexican Immigrants." *International Migration Review* 21(2): 352–71.

Portes, Alejandro, and Patricia Fernandez-Kelly. 2008. "No Margin of Error: Educational and Occupational Achievement Among Disadvantaged Children of Immigrants." *Annals of the American Academy of Political and Social Science* 620(2008): 12–36.

Portes, Alejandro, Patricia Fernandez-Kelly, and William Haller. 2005. "Segmented Assimilation on the Ground: The New Second Generation in Early Adulthood." *Ethnic & Racial Studies* 28(6): 1000–40.

———. 2009. "The Adaptation of the Immigrant Second Generation in America: A Theoretical Overview and Recent Evidence." *Journal of Ethnic and Migration Studies* 35(7): 1077–104.

Portes, Alejandro, and Rubén G. Rumbaut. 1996. *Immigrant America: A Portrait.* Berkeley: University of California Press.

———. 2001. *Legacies: The Story of the Immigrant Second Generation.* Berkeley and New York: University of California Press and Russell Sage Foundation.

———. 2005. "Introduction: The Second Generation and the Children of Immigrants Longitudinal Study" *Ethnic and Racial Studies* 28(6): 983–99.

———. 2006. *Immigrant America: A Portrait,* 3rd ed. Berkeley: University of California Press.

Portes, Alejandro, and Min Zhou. 1993. "The New Second Generation: Seg *Annals of the American Academy of Political and Social Science* 530(1993): 74–98.

Praag, Carlo Van, and Jeannette Schoorl. 2008. "Housing and Segregation." In *The Position of the Turkish and Moroccan Second Generation in Amsterdam and Rotterdam: The TIES Study in the Netherlands,* edited by Maurice Crul and Liesbeth Heering. Amsterdam: Amsterdam University Press.

Qian, Z.-C., and Daniel T. Lichter. 2007. "Social Boundaries and Marital Assimilation: Evaluating Trends in Racial and Ethnic Intermarriage." *American Sociological Review* 72(1): 68–94.

Quillian, Lincoln, and Devah Pager. 2001. "Black Neighbors, Higher Crime? The Role of Racial Stereotypes in Evaluations of Neighborhood Crime." *American Journal of Sociology* 107(3): 717–67.

Quintini, Glenda, and Sebastien Martin. 2006. "Starting Well or Losing Their Way? The Position of Youth in the Labour Market in OECD Countries." *Social Employment and Migration* working paper 39. Paris: Organisation for Economic Co-operation and Development.

Ramakrishnan, S. Karthick. 2005. *Democracy in Immigrant America: Changing Demographics and Political Participation.* Palo Alto, Calif.: Stanford University Press.

Read, Jen'nan Ghazal. 2004. "Cultural Influences on Immigrant Women's Labor Force Participation: The Arab-American Case." *International Migration Review* 38(1): 52–77.

Reed-Danahay, Deborah, and Caroline B. Brettell. 2008. *Citizenship, Political Engagement, and Belonging: Immigrants in Europe and the United States.* New Brunswick, N.J.: Rutgers University Press.

Robson, Karen. 2008. "Becoming NEET in Europe: A Comparison of Predictors and Later-Life Outcomes." Paper presented at the Global Network on Inequality Mini-Conference. New York (February 22, 2008). Available at: http://www.addmecop.eu/home/european/RobsonK_Neet_paper_gni.pdf (accessed April 20, 2011).

Rosenbaum, Emily, and Samantha Friedman. 2007. *The Housing Divide: How Generations of Immigrants Fare in New York's Housing Market.* New York: New York University Press.

Rountree, Pamela Wilcox, and Kenneth C. Land. 1996. "Perceived Risk Versus Fear of Crime: Empirical Evidence of Conceptually Distinct Relations in Survey Data." *Social Forces* 74(4): 1353–76.

Rumbaut, Rubén. 2005. "Turning Points in the Transition to Adulthood: Determinants of Educational Attainment, Incarceration, and Early Childbearing Among Children of Immigrants." *Ethnic and Racial Studies* 28(6): 1041–86.

———. 2008. "The Coming of the Second Generation: Immigration and Ethnic Mobility in Southern California." *Annals of the American Academy of Political and Social Science* 620(2008): 96–236.

Rumbaut, Rubén G., Frank D. Bean, Leo Chavez, Jennifer Lee, Susan Brown, Louis DeSipio, and Min Zhou. 2004. "Immigration and Intergenerational Mobility in Metropolitan Los Angeles (IIMMLA)." Ann Arbor, Mich.: Inter-University Consortium for Political and Social Research. Available at: http://dx.doi.org/10.3886/ICPSR22627.v1 (accessed February 16, 2012).

Salentin, Kurt, and Frank Wilkening. 2003. "Ausländer, Eingebürgerte und das Problem einer Realistischen Zuwanderer-integrationsbilanz." *Kölner Zeitschrift für Soziologie und Sozialpsychologie* 55(3): 278–98.

Sampson, Robert J. 2008. "Moving to Inequality: Neighborhood Effects and Experiments Meet Structure." *American Journal of Sociology* 114(1): 189–231.

———. 2009. "Disparity and Diversity in the Contemporary City: Social (Dis) Order Revisited." *British Journal of Sociology* 60(1): 1–31.

Sampson, Robert J., Jeffrey D. Morenoff, and Felton Earls. 1999. "Beyond Social Capital: Spatial Dynamics of Collective Efficacy for Children." *American Sociological Review* 64(5): 633–60.

Sampson, Robert J., Jeffrey D. Morenoff, and Thomas Gannon-Rowley. 2002. "Assessing 'Neighborhood Effects': Social Processes and New Directions in Research." *Annual Review of Sociology* 28(1): 443–78.

Sampson, Robert J., and Stephen W. Raudenbush. 1999. "Systematic Social Observation of Public Spaces: A New Look at Disorder in Urban Neighborhoods." *American Journal of Sociology* 105(3): 603–51.

———. 2004. "Seeing Disorder: Neighborhood Stigma and the Social Construction of Broken Windows." *Social Psychology Quarterly* 67(4): 319–32.

Sampson, Robert J., and Patrick Sharkey. 2008. "Neighborhood Selection and the Social Reproduction of Concentrated Racial Inequality." *Demography* 45(1): 1–29.

Sampson, Robert J., Patrick Sharkey, and Stephen W. Raudenbush. 2008. "Durable Effects of Concentrated Disadvantage on Verbal Ability Among African-American Children." *Proceedings of the National Academy of Sciences* 105(3): 845–52.

Sánchez, George J. 1993. *Becoming Mexican American: Ethnicity, Culture, and Identity in Chicano Los Angeles, 1900–1945.* New York: Oxford University Press.

Schinkel, Willem. 2007. *Denken in een Tijd van Sociale Hypochondrie: Aanzet Tot een Theorie Voorbij de Maatschappij.* Kampen: Klement.

Schneider, Jens. 2002. "Discourses of Exclusion: Dominant Self-Definitions and 'the Other' in German Society." *Journal of the Society for the Anthropology of Europe* 3(3): 13–21.

———. 2009. "Second-Generation Turks in German Culture and Politics." *International Journal on Multicultural Societies* 11(2): 219–40.

Schneider, Jens, and Maurice Crul. 2010. "New Insights into Assimilation and Integration Theory." *Ethnic and Racial Studies* 33(7): 1143–48.

Scholten, Peter. 2011. *Framing Immigrant Integration: Dutch Research-Policy Dialogues in Comparative Perspective.* Amsterdam: Amsterdam University Press.

Schönwälder, Karen. 2007. "Residential Concentrations and Integration: Preliminary. Conclusions." In *Residential Segregation and the Integration of Immigrants: Britain, the Netherlands and Sweden,* edited by Karen Schönwälder. Berlin: Social Science Research Center.

Schönwälder, Karen, and Janina Sohn. 2009. "Immigrant Settlement Structures in Germany: General Patterns and Urban Levels of Concentration of Major Groups." *Urban Studies* 46(7): 1439–60.

Schurer, Stefanie. 2008. "Labour Market Outcomes of Second-Generation Immigrants: How Heterogeneous Are They Really?" *Ruhr Economic Paper* 57. Essen: Rheinisch-Westfälisches Institut für Wirtschaftsforshung.

Scott, James. 1998. *Seeing Like a State: How Certain Schemes to Improve the Human Condition Have Failed.* New Haven, Conn.: Yale University Press.

SFS. 2001. *Utlänningslag* [The Swedish Citizenship Act]. Stockholm: Svensk författningssamling.

Sharkey, Patrick. 2006. "Navigating Dangerous Streets: The Sources and Consequences of Street Efficacy." *American Sociological Review* 71(5): 826–46.

———. 2008. "The Intergenerational Transmission of Context." *American Journal of Sociology* 113(4): 931–69.

———. forthcoming. *Stuck in Place.* Chicago: University of Chicago Press.

Shavit, Yossi, and Walter Müller, eds. 1998. *From School to Work: A Comparative Study of Educational Qualifications and Occupational Destinations.* Oxford: Clarendon Press.

Shaw, Clifford R., and Henry McKay. 1942. *Juvenile Delinquency and Urban Areas.* Chicago: University of Chicago Press.

Shearer, Darlene L., Beverly A. Mulvihill, Lorraine V. Klerman, Jan L. Wallander, Mary E. Hovinga, and David T. Redden. 2002. "Association of Early Childbearing and Low Cognitive Ability." *Perspectives on Sexual and Reproductive Health* 34(5): 236–43.

Silberman, Roxanne, Richard Alba, and Irène Fournier. 2007. "Segmented Assimilation in France? Discrimination in the Labor Market Against the Second Generation." *Ethnic and Racial Studies* 30(1): 1–27.

Silverstein, Paul A. 2004. *Algeria in France: Transpolitics, Race and Nation.* Bloomington: Indiana University Press.

Simon, Patrick. 2003. "France and the Unknown Second Generation: Preliminary Results on Social Mobility." *International Migration Review* 37(4): 1091–19.

Simon, Patrick, and Valérie Sala Pala. 2009. " 'We're Not All Multiculturalist Yet': France Swings Between Hard Integration and Soft Antidiscrimination." In *The Multiculturalism Backlash: European Discourses, Practices and Policies*, edited by Steve Vertovec and Susanne Wessendorf. London: Routledge.

Small, Mario L. 2004. *Villa Victoria: The Transformation of Social Capital in a Boston Barrio.* Chicago: University of Chicago Press.

Smith, Andrea L., ed. 2003. *Europe's Invisible Migrants.* Amsterdam: Amsterdam University Press.

Smith, Robert C. 2008. "Horatio Alger Lives in Brooklyn: Extra-Family Support, Intra-Family Dynamics, and Socially Neutral Operating Identities in Exceptional Mobility Among Children of Mexican Immigrants." *The Annals of the American Academy of Political and Social Science* 62(1): 270–90.

Social Exclusion Unit. 1999. *Bridging the Gap: New Opportunities for 16–18 Year-Olds Not in Education, Employment or Training.* Cm 4405. London: The Stationery Office.

South, Scott J., Kyle Crowder, and Erick Chavez. 2005a. "Exiting and Entering High-Poverty Neighborhoods: Latinos, Blacks and Anglos Compared." *Social Forces* 84(2): 873–900.

————. 2005b. "Geographic Mobility and Spatial Assimilation Among U.S. Latino Immigrants." *International Migration Review* 39(3): 577–607.

————. 2005c. "Migration and Spatial Assimilation Among U.S. Latinos: Classical Versus Segmented Trajectories." *Demography* 42(3): 497–521.

South, Scott J., Kyle Crowder, and Jeremy Pais. 2008. "Inter-Neighborhood Migration and Spatial Assimilation in a Multi-Ethnic World: Comparing Latinos, Blacks and Anglos." *Social Forces* 87(1): 415–43.

Staff, Jeremy, and Jeylan Mortimer. 2008. "Social Class Background and the School-to-Work Transition." *New Directions for Child & Adolescent Development* 119(1): 55–69.

Statistik Austria. 2010. *Migration + Integration: Zahlen, Daten, Indikatoren 2010.* Vienna: Statistik Austria.

Statistisches Bundesamt. 2007. *Bevölkerung und Erwerbstätigkeit: Bevölkerung mit Migrationshintergrund, Ergebnisse des Mikrozensus 2005* (Fachserie 1, Reihe 2.2). Wiesbaden: Statistisches Bundesamt.

————. 2011. *Bevölkerung und Erwerbstätigkeit: Bevölkerung mit Migrationshintergrund, Ergebnisse des Mikrozensus 2010* (Fachserie 1, Reihe 2.2). Wiesbaden: Statistisches Bundesamt. Available at: http://www.destatis.de (accessed February 15, 2012).

Statistisches Jahrbuch der Stadt Wien. 2011. *Statistisches Jahrbuch der Stadt Wien.* Vienna: Magistrat der Stadt Wien. Available at: https://www.wien.gv.at/statistik/publikationen/jahrbuch-2011.html (accessed February 16, 2012).

Steinhardt, Max Friedrich, Thomas Straubhaar, and Jan Wedemeier. 2010. *Studie zur Einbürgerung und Integration in der Schweiz,* edited by Sibille Duss. Hamberg: Hamburgisches Weltwirtschaftsinstitut.

Stepick, Alex, and Carol Dutton Stepick. 2010. "The Complexities and Confusions of Segmented Assimilation." *Ethnic and Racial Studies* 33(7): 1149–67.

St. John de Crevécoeur, J. Hector. 1912[1792]. *Letters from an American Farmer.* London: J.M. Dent & Sons/New York: E.P. Dutton & Co. Inc. (courtesy of Jeffrey Reitz).

Suárez-Orozco, Carola, Marcelo Suárez-Orozco, and Irina Todorova. 2008. *Learning a New Land: Immigrant Students in American Society.* Cambridge, Mass.: Harvard University Press.

Sundström, Eva. 1999. "Should Mothers Work? Age and Attitudes in Germany, Italy and Sweden." *International Journal of Social Welfare* 1999(8): 193–205.

Suttles, Gerard D. 1968. *The Social Order of the Slum: Ethnicity and Territory in the Inner City.* Chicago: University of Chicago Press.

Szelényi, Katalin, and June C. Chang. 2010. "Educational Aspirations in an Urban Community College: Differences Between Immigrant and Native Student Groups." *Community College Review* 37(3): 209–42.

Tam Cho, Wendy. 1999. "Naturalization, Socialization, Participation: Immigrants and (Non-) Voting." *Journal of Politics* 61(4): 1140–55.

Tamas, Kristof. 2004. "Internationalising Migration Control: Swedish Migration Policy from 1985 to 2004." In *Towards a Multilateral Migration Regime.*

Special Anniversary Edition Dedicated to Jonas Widgren, edited by Michael Jandl and Irene Stacher. Vienna, Austria: International Centre for Migration Policy Development.

Taylor, Charles. 1994. "The Politics of Recognition." In *Multiculturalism: Examining the Politics of Recognition*, edited by A. Gutmann. Princeton, N.J.: Princeton University Press.

Telles, Edward, and Vilma Ortiz. 2008. *Generations of Exclusion: Mexican Americans, Assimilation, and Race*. New York: Russell Sage Foundation.

Thomson, Mark, and Maurice Crul. 2007. "The Second Generation in Europe and the United States: How Is the Transatlantic Debate Relevant for Further Research on the European Second Generation?" *Journal of Ethnic and Migration Studies* 33(7): 1025–41.

Tienda, Marta. 1991. "Poor People and Poor Places: Deciphering Neighborhood Effects on Poverty Outcomes." In *Macro-Micro Links in Sociology*, edited by Joan Huber. Newbury Park, Calif.: Sage Publications.

Tienda, Marta, and Faith Mitchell. 2006. *Multiple Origins, Uncertain Destinies: Hispanics and the American Future*. Washington, D.C.: National Academies Press.

Tilly, Chris, and Charles Tilly. 1994. "Capitalist Work and Labor Markets." In *The Handbook of Economic Sociology*, edited by Neil Smelser and Richard Swedberg. New York and Princeton, N.J.: Russell Sage Foundation/Princeton University Press.

Timberlake, Jeffrey M., and John Iceland. 2007. "Change in Racial and Ethnic Residential Inequality in American Cities, 1970–2000." *City & Community* 6(4): 335–65.

Titmuss, Richard. 1958. *Essays on the Welfare State*. London: Allen and Unwin.

Tran, Van C. 2011. "How Neighborhoods Matter, and for Whom: Disadvantaged Context, Ethnic Cultural Repertoires and Second Generation Socioeconomic Mobility in Young Adulthood." Ph.D. diss., Harvard University, Department of Sociology.

Tribalat, Michèle. 1995. *Faire France: Une enquête sur les immigrés et leurs enfants*. Paris: La Découverte.

U.S. Census Bureau 2009. Current Population Survey, March Annual Demographic Supplement File. Washington: U.S. Census Bureau.

———. 2000. U.S. Census. 5-Percent Public Use Microdata Sample (PUMS) Files. Washington: U.S. Census Bureau.

Valencia, Richard R. 2002. "Mexican Americans Don't Value Education! On the Basis of the Myth, Mythmaking, and Debunking." *Journal of Latinos and Education* 1(2): 81–103.

van Kempen, Ronald, and A. Ôule Özüekren. 1998. "Ethnic Segregation in Cities: New Forms and Explanations in a Dynamic World." *Urban Studies* 35(10): 1631–56.

Veenman, Justus. 1996. *Keren de kansen? De tweede generatie allochtonen in Nederland*. Assen, the Netherlands: Van Gorcum.

Venkatesh, Sudhir A. 2000. *American Project: The Rise and Fall of a Modern Ghetto.* Cambridge, Mass.: Harvard University Press.

———. 2006. *Off the Books: The Underground Economy of the Urban Poor.* Cambridge, Mass.: Harvard University Press.

Verba, Sidney, and Norman Nie. 1972. *Participation in America: Political Democracy and Social Equality.* Chicago: University of Chicago Press.

Verba, Sidney, Kay Lehman Schlozman, and Henry Brady. 1995. *Voice and Equality: Civic Voluntarism in American Politics.* Cambridge, Mass.: Harvard University Press.

Vermeulen, Hans. 2010. "Segmented Assimilation and Cross-National Comparative Research on the Integration of Immigrants and Their Children." *Ethnic and Racial Studies* 33(7): 1214–30.

Vertovec, Steve. 2007. "Super-Diversity and Its Implications." *Ethnic and Racial Studies* 29(6): 1024–54.

Vertovec, Steve, and Susanne Wessendorf, eds. 2009. *The Multiculturalism Backlash: European Discourses, Practices and Policies.* London: Routledge.

Vickerman, Milton. 2001. "Tweaking a Monolith: The West Indian Immigrant Encounter With 'Blackness.'" In *Islands in the City: West Indian Migration to New York,* edited by Nancy Foner, Berkeley: University of California Press.

Vink, Maarten P., and Gerard-René deGroot. 2010. "Citizenship Attribution in Western Europe: International Framework and Domestic Trends." *Journal of Ethnic and Migration Studies* 36(5): 713–34.

Vogelgesang, Waldemar. 2008. *Jugendliche Aussiedler: Zwischen Entwurzelung, Ausgrenzung und Integration.* Weinheim, Germany: Juventa.

Wacquant, Loïc. 2008. *Urban Outcasts: A Comparative Sociology of Advanced Marginality.* Cambridge: Polity.

Waldinger, Roger. 1996. *Still the Promised City.* Berkeley: University of California Press.

———. 2007. "Did Manufacturing Matter? The Experience of Yesterday's Second Generation: A Reassessment." *International Migration Review* 41(1): 3–39.

Waldinger, Roger, and Cynthia Feliciano. 2004. "Will the New Second Generation Experience 'Downward Assimilation'? Segmented Assimilation Re-Assessed." *Ethnic and Racial Studies* 27(3): 376–402.

Waldinger, Roger, Nelson Lim, and D. Cort. 2007. "Bad Jobs, Good Jobs, No Jobs? The Employment Experience of the Mexican American Second Generation." *Journal of Ethnic and Migration Studies* 33(1): 1–35.

Waldinger, Roger, and Joel Perlmann. 1998. "Second Generations: Past, Present, Future." *Journal of Ethnic and Migration Studies* 24(1): 5–24.

Waldrauch, Harald, and Christoph Hofinger. 1997. "An Index to Measure the Legal Obstacles to the Integration of Migrants." *New Community* 23(2): 271–85.

Walzer, Michael. 1983. *Spheres of Justice: A Defense of Pluralism and Equality.* New York: Basic Books.

Warner, William Lloyd, and Leo Srole. 1945. *The Social Systems of American Ethnic Groups.* New Haven, Conn.: Yale University Press.

Waters, Mary C. 1994. "Ethnic and Racial Identities of Second Generation Black Immigrants in New York City." *International Migration Review* 28(4): 795–820.

———. 1999. *Black Identities: West Indian Immigrant Dreams and American Realities.* Cambridge, Mass.: Harvard University Press.

———. 2000. "The Sociological Roots and Multidisciplinary Future of Immigration Research." In *Immigration Research for a New Century,* edited by Nancy Foner, Ruben Rumbaut, and Steven Gold. New York: Russell Sage Foundation.

———. 2001. "Growing Up West Indian and African American: Gender and Class Differences in the Second Generation." In *Islands in the City: West Indian Migration to New York,* edited by Nancy Foner. Berkeley: University of California Press.

Waters, Mary C., and Tomás R. Jiménez. 2005. "Assessing Immigrant Assimilation: New Empirical and Theoretical Challenges." *Annual Review of Sociology* 31(1): 105–25.

Weil, Patrick, Alexis Spire, and Christophe Bertossi. 2010. *Country Report: France.* San Domenico Di Fiesole: EUDO Citizenship Observatory, Florence European University Institute and Robert Schuman Centre for Advanced Studies.

Wen, Ming, Diane S. Lauderdale, and Namratha R. Kandula. 2009. "Ethnic Neighborhoods in Multi-Ethnic America, 1990–2000: Resurgent Ethnicity in the Ethnoburbs?" *Social Forces* 88(1): 425–60.

Westin, Charles. 2003. "Young People of Migrant Origin in Sweden." *International Migration Review* 37(4): 987–1010.

White, Michael J., and Jennifer E. Glick. 2009. *Achieving Anew: How New Immigrants Do in American Schools, Jobs, and Neighborhoods.* New York: Russell Sage Foundation.

White, Michael J., and Sharon Sassler. 2000. "Judging Not Only by Color: Ethnicity, Nativity, and Neighborhood Attainment." *Social Science Quarterly* 81(4): 998–1013.

Whyte, William Foote. 1941. *Street Corner Society: The Social Structure of an Italian Slum.* Chicago: University of Chicago Press.

Wierling, Dorothee, ed. 2004. *Heimat Finden: Lebenswege von Deutschen, die aus Russland Kommen.* Hamburg: Körber-Stiftung.

Wilkes, Rima, and John Iceland. 2004. "Hypersegregation in the Twenty-First Century: An Update and Analysis." *Demography* 41(1): 23–36.

Willems, Wim. 2003. "No Sheltering Sky: Migrant Identities of Dutch Nationals from Indonesia." In *Europe's Invisible Migrants,* edited by A. L. Smith. Amsterdam: Amsterdam University Press.

Wilson, William Julius. 1987. *The Truly Disadvantaged: The Inner City, the Underclass, and Public Policy.* Chicago: University of Chicago Press.

———. 1996. *When Work Disappears.* Chicago: University of Chicago Press.

———. 2009. *More Than Just Race: Being Black and Poor in the Inner City.* New York: W. W. Norton.

Woortmann, Ellen Fensterseifer. 2001. "Lembranças e esquecimentos: Memórias de Teuto-Brasileiros." In *Devorando O Tempo. Brasil, O País Sem Memória,* edited by Annette Leibing and Sibylle Benninghoff-Lühl. São Paulo, Brazil: Mandarim.

Worbs, Susanne. 2003. "The Second Generation in Germany: Between School and Labour Market." *International Migration Review* 37(4): 1011–38.

Young, Iris Marion. 1990. *Justice and the Politics of Difference.* Princeton, N.J.: Princeton University Press.

Yuval-Davis, Nira. 2006. "Belonging and the Politics of Belonging." *Patterns of Prejudice* 40(3): 197–214.

Zhou, Min. 1997. "Growing Up American: The Challenge Confronting Immigrant Children and Children of Immigrants." *Annual Review of Sociology* 23(1): 63–95.

———. 2009. "How Neighborhoods Matter for Immigrant Children: The Formation of Educational Resources in Chinatown, Koreatown, and Pico Union, Los Angeles." *Journal of Ethnic and Migration Studies* 35(7): 1153–79.

Zhou, Min, and Carl L. Bankston III. 1998. *Growing Up American: How Vietnamese Children Adapt to Life in the United States.* New York: Russell Sage Foundation.

Zhou, Min, and Jennifer Lee. 2007. "Becoming Ethnic or Becoming American? Tracing the Mobility Trajectories of the New Second Generation in the United States." *Du Bois Review* 4(1): 1–17.

Zhou, Min, Jennifer Lee, Jody Agius Vallejo, Rosaura Tafoya-Estrada, and Yang Sao Xiong. 2008. "Success Attained, Deterred, and Denied: Divergent Pathways to Social Mobility Among the New Second Generation in Los Angeles." *Annals of the American Academy of Political and Social Science* 620 (November): 37–61.

Zhou, Min, and John Logan. 1991. "In and Out of Chinatown: Residential Mobility and Segregation of New York City's Chinese." *Social Forces* 70(2): 387–407.

Zolberg, Aristide, and Long Litt Woon. 1999. "Why Islam Is Like Spanish: Cultural Incorporation in Europe and the United States." *Politics & Society* 27(1): 5–38.

INDEX

Boldface numbers refer to figures and tables.

participation of women, 137–38,
140–43, 148, **150–51**, 152, 153;
labor market outcomes, 246–49;
naturalization, 184–85, 189, 194–
95, **197**; past immigration legacies,
28, 35–41; racial issues, 35, 38–41,
42; religion's importance in, 225,
252; residential segregation, 39,
102, 240, 251; second-generation
immigrants' outcomes vs. Europe,
238–41; spatial distribution of
ethnic groups, 159–60; welfare
state, 59, 131, 133. *See also* Los
Angeles; New York City; *specific
immigrant groups*
University of California College
Bound program, 81
University of Rotterdam, 32
upward mobility, 6, 16, 24, 35–41,
100, 214, 256
Urban Institute, 164
urban underclass, 127
U.S. Census, 70, 73, 158, 164

values, 55, 58
vandalism, **171**
Vedder, Paul, 209
Vermeulen, Hans, 14
Vienna, second-generation
immigrants in: apprenticeship
programs, 101; characteristics
of, 212–13; citizenship, **18,
19**; co-ethnic friendship, **250**;
community organization
participation, **201**; educational
attainment, **17, 242**, 243; family
background, **19**; identity and
belonging, 218; income, 121–26;
incorporation into labor force,
127; Islamic leanings, **253**;
language use, 219–20; NEET rates,
106–15, 110–11, **112**; population,
99; professional occupations,

115–21; religious identity,
222–23; socioeconomic status
outcomes, **242**; studies of, 15;
transnationalism, **226,** 227; voting
rates, **199**
Vietnamese immigrants: IIMMLA
survey, 14; labor force participation
of women, **142**
violence, 163
visibility of immigrant differences,
55–56
vocational education: in Austria, 241;
in France, 85, 95, 241, 244; in
Germany, 67, 241; in Netherlands,
67, 86, 91–92, 95, 241; in Sweden,
241, 244
voting, 198–200
Voting Rights Act (1965), 41

wages and earnings, 102. *See also*
income
Waldinger, Roger, 37, 103
Warner, William Lloyd, 36
Waters, Mary, 13, **17, 18,** 133, 206
welfare benefits, 98, 100, 101, 239–40
welfare state: in Europe, 9, 59, 255;
feminist critiques, 129, 130; and
labor force participation of women,
134–39, 152–54; and labor market
integration of immigrants, 132–33;
regimes, 129, 131–32; role in
integration, 126–27, 255; in U.S.,
131, 133
Westin, Charles, 14
West Indian immigrants: family
background, 135; in Great Britain,
27; income, **122**; labor force
participation of women, **142, 151**;
NEET rates, **110**; neighborhoods,
160; in NYC, 39–40, 103, 158;
professional occupations, **117**.
See also Dominican immigrants;
Puerto Rican immigrants